# Defiant Hope

ESSAYS ON LIFE, FAITH,
AND FREEDOM

Michael Gerson

Simon & Schuster

NEW YORK  LONDON  TORONTO  SYDNEY  NEW DELHI

1230 Avenue of the Americas
New York, NY 10020

First Simon & Schuster hardcover edition November 2024

SIMON & SCHUSTER and colophon are registered trademarks of Simon & Schuster, LLC

Simon & Schuster: Celebrating 100 Years of Publishing in 2024

For information about special discounts for bulk purchases,
please contact Simon & Schuster Special Sales
at 1-866-506-1949 or business@simonandschuster.com.

The Simon & Schuster Speakers Bureau can bring authors to your live event.
For more information or to book an event, contact the Simon & Schuster Speakers Bureau
at 1-866-248-3049 or visit our website at www.simonspeakers.com.

*Interior design by Ruth Lee-Mui*

Manufactured in the United States of America

1   3   5   7   9   10   8   6   4   2

Library of Congress Cataloging-in-Publication Data is available on file.

ISBN 978-1-6680-7026-0
ISBN 978-1-6680-7028-4 (ebook)

*For Bucky and Nicholas.*

*In loving memory of your father, who loved both of you so, so much.*

# Contents

# Introduction by David Brooks

IT IS NOT AN EXAGGERATION to say that Michael Gerson possessed one of the most important consciences of his generation. I first met him in the 1990s, when he was working as a Senate staffer, devising a package of proposals to help the poor and the marginalized. He then went on to become chief speechwriter for George W. Bush. In that role, he wrote the speeches that rallied and ennobled the nation after September 11. He helped design and champion Bush's PEPFAR program, which saved upwards of 20 million lives as HIV ravaged Africa. He then became one of the nation's most eloquent columnists. In that role, he was never content to do political horse race punditry, but devoted himself to the most essential causes of his time, pushing back on the authoritarian cruelty of Donald Trump, and pushing for the kind of compassionate conservatism that he spent his life helping to design, champion, and embody.

In short, he led a life of astonishing moral coherence and grace in a political world that bends toward cynicism and egomania. He became that rarest of creatures—an attractive moralist. We came to trust him to skillfully and authoritatively discern right from wrong, without becoming self-righteous, callously judgmental, or self-satisfied. He could be critical when criticism was merited, but deep down he loved humanity, he loved God, he loved his dog, he loved his boys and wrote touchingly about the sadness we all feel when we drop our own children off at college.

Some people are born good. They are openhearted from birth, blessed with an outgoing nature, a warm personality. They effortlessly and volubly share and express the emotions of others. I always got the sense that Mike wasn't born this way. Nature made him a bit of an introvert, a bit reserved; his personality had a hint of waspishness (disdain is a great quality in a newspaper columnist). But Mike rose above his nature and became a beacon of compassion, a man who saw the world with realistic but tender eyes.

How did he do it? Or perhaps more accurately, how was it done to him? My theory is that Mike's great act was an act of submission. The most obvious way to put it is that he submitted himself to the person and example of Jesus. The more complete way to put it is that, more than most American Protestants, he also submitted himself to the two thousand years of Christian social teaching. He studied and learned to emulate the great line of people who, down through the centuries, were inspired by the example of Jesus to repair the world and bring us closer to one in which suffering is eased and human dignity is honored. Mike didn't just possess faith, he became a participant in a great spiritual and intellectual tradition.

In this book you will get a sense of that tradition. You will read a few chapters from a book Mike never finished, about some of the men and women who formed this great procession of Christian Reformers—John Wesley, Jonathan Edwards, William Wilberforce, and Olaudah Equiano. You'll read about the great causes they devoted themselves to—the Great Awakenings, abolitionism, civil rights, service to the poor, and opposition to authoritarian tyranny around the world.

You'll also get to read some of Mike's newspaper columns. If you're like me, you'll savor being back in the company of Mike's voice. But more than that, you'll see how his own judgments and his whole sensibility flow from this inheritance—the accumulated wisdom of these centuries of Christian social teaching. He became strong with that tradition's strength, wise with that tradition's wisdom. He illustrated how submitting to a tradition can be both an act of humility and a source of quiet power.

So what are the features of this tradition and how did they form and inform Mike?

This tradition did not provide Mike with a preset political platform. He got something far deeper, an underlying worldview, a set of priorities, an order of loves. This worldview, and way of being, starts with the great inversions that Jesus embodies. "The whole Christmas story is pregnant with enigma and violated expectations," Mike wrote. "The Creator pulls on a garment of blood and bone. Almighty God is somehow present in a fragile newborn. The deliverer of humankind is delivered, slimy with vernix, in a place smelling of dung." The last shall be first. The meek shall inherit the earth. Proclaim good news to the poor, and liberty to those who are captive.

This tradition places great emphasis on the infinite dignity of each person, on the fact that each human is made in God's image. None of us, Mike continued, are mere skin and bones. "We are skin and bones and the life of God within us. Even lives that feel relentlessly ordinary or hopelessly broken are vessels of divine purpose. We are embraced, elevated, and dignified by God's astounding humility." One of my favorite Gerson observations is this one: There is no such thing as an insignificant human life.

A person who orients himself around this truth is going to have an egalitarian frame of mind. The ground is flat at the foot of the cross, and we see each other eye to eye. All human souls are equal before God and worthy of equal treatment and dignity.

Such a person is also going to have a quietly impassioned frame of mind. Those of us who live by tapping the keyboard have a tendency to grow emotionally detached and cerebral, but this social gospel tradition smashes the categories of reason and emotion, guiding us to seek to understand the world around us by using the empathetic eyes of the heart, to probe the spiritual and emotional mysteries using the rigor of the intellect.

A person with this frame of mind is also going to have a hyperactive conscience, making him acutely sensitive to the pains and injustices of the world, acutely aware of his own shortcomings. But such a person, like Mike, will also be propelled by a fundamental sense of hope, even amid hardship: "In enforced isolation and loneliness, God is with us. In chronic pain and degenerative disease, God is with us. In a shattered relationship or a cancer diagnosis, God is with us. In an intensive care unit or a mental ward, God is with us. In life and in death, God will not leave us or forsake us."

Those last few sentences of Mike's were autobiographical. It was as if the book of Job fell upon Michael in the final years of his life: He suffered from cancers, Parkinson's, depression, loneliness amid the pandemic, lingering heart ailments, even some dental woes thrown in for good measure. Bitterness, self-absorption, and self-pity would have been understandable responses to this cascade of pain. But Mike endured it with steadfastness, tenacity, and grace that all remarked upon. He was a man strengthened by what he'd read, experienced, and believed in, and his mind and soul were able to withstand the storms his body threw at them.

"It has been said that when you choose your community, you choose your character," Mike once wrote. Look at the people featured in this book and you'll see what Mike admired and whom he strove to become like:

- John Wesley, whose Methodism provided community, home, and salvation to the working classes in the most brutal years of the Industrial Revolution.
- Jonathan Edwards, a man, Mike writes, who was conservative in tone, temperament, and deportment, but who was also a force for progressive social disruption.
- Dorothy Day, who not only served the poor but lived a life of sacrificial service among them. "The mystery of the poor," she wrote, "is this: They are Jesus, and what you do for them you do for him."
- Chuck Colson, one of Mike's first bosses, who ministered to the incarcerated. "Chuck led a movement of volunteers attempting to love some of their least lovable neighbors."

• Pope Francis, who sees the church as a field hospital after a battle. First you sew up the suffering, and then we can talk about everything else.

These are all people who, like Mike, scramble political categories—conservative in their deference to tradition, progressive in their demands for change. These are people who experienced a spiritual transformation that eventually led them to social action. These are all people who looked at the Kingdom of God as revealed by Jesus and were shocked by how far our own worldly societies fall short. "The idea of the Kingdom," Mike writes, "is a mental instrument by which individual faith is transformed into social vision."

Mike did not believe that politics could ever be our ultimate concern, but he did believe in the nobility of politics. I used to hear Mike tell young people: If you don't care about politics it's because you are privileged to live in a nation in which it is possible to not care about politics. People who live in fear of the knock on the door in the middle of the night, or the gun put to the head, do not have that luxury.

Mike saw firsthand how much can be achieved through politics—those 20 million lives saved in Africa. He saw firsthand the difference between a politics of service, which is what American government provides at its best, and the politics of domination, which is what it provides at its worst. Mike thought hard about how to work within the morally corrosive environment of politics, without being spiritually corroded by it:

When we are caked with the mud of political struggle, and tired of Pyrrhic victories that seed new hatreds, and frightened by our own capacity for contempt, the way of life set out by Jesus comes like a clear bell that rings above our strife. It defies cynicism, apathy, despair, and all ideologies that dream of dominance. It promises that every day, if we choose, can be the first day of a new and noble manner of living. Its most difficult duties can feel much like purpose and joy. And even our halting, halfhearted attempts at faithfulness are counted by God as victories.

What a classically Gersonian passage—humble, self-effacing, tenacious, persevering, obedient, earnest, and inspired. You'll enjoy the
personal essays in this book, the ones about his dog, his kids, his public battle with depression, but what really lingers, at least to me, is the
tone of voice, the weight and substance of his prose, the moral convictions marked by graciousness more than piety—plus the various roles he
played: a prophet lamenting iniquity, a father and a friend capable of
great bursts of gratitude and appreciation, a Christian who is sometimes
buried under sadness and close to despair, but who never loses sight of
that distant illuminating beacon of hope.

# PART I

# America

# What a Strange People

AFTER A LIFE OF PERPETUAL MOTION—having traveled hundreds of thousands of miles on preaching tours, having delivered some forty thousand sermons, having written hundreds of pamphlets and eighty-seven volumes of published journal entries running to a million words—John Wesley was feeling his eighty-six years. With his white hair, his beak-like nose, his trim clothing, and his piercing gaze, Wesley still had a presence some described as "apostolic." But on New Year's Day, 1790, he wrote: "I am now an old man, decayed from head to foot." He was nearly blind in one eye and suffered from chronic dry mouth. His right hand shook, and he reported "a lingering fever almost every day."

In this condition, Wesley promptly embarked on preaching trips to the West County, the Midlands, Lancashire, Yorkshire, the Northeast, Scotland, Lincoln, Epworth, Bristol, South Wales, Bristol again, the Isle of Wight, Sussex, Kent, Essex, Suffolk, and Norfolk. His disabilities limited his activity to one sermon a day, rather than his accustomed three or four. In the pulpit, according to one account, "Two held him up, having their hands under his armpits. His feeble voice was barely audible; but his reverend countenance, especially his long white locks, formed a picture never to be forgotten."

By mid-February of 1791, Wesley's feverishness grew worse and he preached what proved to be his final sermon. He knew death was near. But still he managed to finish up the five-hundred-page autobiography of a slave called Olaudah Equiano. *The Interesting Narrative of the Life of*

*Olaudah Equiano, or Gustavus Vassa the African,* was a late eighteenth-century bestseller chronicling Equiano's restless adventures as a slave and freedman. He was, at various points, the personal slave of a British navy officer, a member of a naval press gang, a Royal Navy able seaman, a London house servant, a barber, a musician, an arctic explorer, an entrepreneur, an assistant to an English inventor, and an early abolition activist. But it is Equiano's firsthand accounts of slavery that stuck in the conscience of many readers. He described slaves who jumped off slave ships because they preferred drowning to servitude; slaves who were beaten until their bones broke; a ten-year-old black child raped by white sailors; and a slave who was castrated for associating with a white prostitute.

It could not have escaped Wesley's attention—as the founder of Methodism—that Equiano was a Christian, converted through the influence of Methodists in 1774 (the year that Wesley published his abolitionist tract, *Thoughts on Slavery*). Equiano described a spiritual journey that took him from Quakerism to Roman Catholicism to Judaism to Islam (he found Turks more consistently ethical than their Christian counterparts). Equiano then encountered a kindly Methodist ship captain and his wife who invited him to a Methodist chapel for a "love feast" (involving prayer, hymn singing, personal testimonies, and a meal). The enslaved man grew worried about the state of his soul. "I fretted, I mourned, and prayed," he wrote, "till I became a burden to others." But his despair, in typical Methodist fashion, gave way to an emotional experience of grace. "It was given to me at that time to know what it was to be born again," Equiano explains. "I was sensible of the invisible hand of God, which guided and protected me when in truth I knew it not: still the Lord pursued although I slighted and disregarded it; this mercy melted me down."

The spiritual melting Equiano described is the experience at the heart of Methodism and of evangelicalism more broadly. For more than fifty years, Wesley had taught the need for a personal experience of God's love and grace, rather than a dry ascent to religious dogma. Particularly early in his preaching career, Wesley saw conversions like Equiano's take place in an atmosphere of convulsive crying and cathartic shouts of joy that respectable clergy found disturbing and disreputable. Encouraging this "born again" experience was the central goal of the Great Awakening and of Wesley's career.

Yet Wesley's deathbed reaction to Equiano's book—rather than mentioning its conversion narrative—focused on the lack of basic English justice for black people in British colonies. Wesley described his shock that "a man who has a black skin, being wronged or outraged by a white man, can have no redress; it being a *law* in our Colonies that the *oath* of a black against a white goes for nothing. What villainy is this!"

With Wesley's death now imminent, slavery was much on his mind. After finishing Equiano's book, he sent off the final letter of his life to a thirty-year-old Tory member of Parliament named William Wilberforce, who was just beginning his lifelong legislative fight against slavery and the slave trade. Wesley strained to transfer his hyperactive sense of mission into a younger body. "Unless the divine power has raised you up to be as *Athanasius contra mundum*," wrote Wesley, "I see not how you can go through your glorious enterprise in opposing that execrable villainy, which is the scandal of religion, of England, and of human nature. Unless God has raised you up for this very thing, you will be worn out by the opposition of men and devils. But if God be for you, who can be against you? Are all of them stronger than God? O be not weary of well doing. Go on, in the name of God and in the power of his might, till even American slavery (the vilest that ever saw the sun) shall vanish away before it."

In his final hours Wesley asked for pen and ink but found he could no longer write. A close friend named Elizabeth Ritchie—the last in a series of earnest young women he enjoyed mentoring—offered, "Let me write for you, sir, tell me what you would say." To which Wesley replied, "Nothing, but that God is with us." Wesley then broke into a hymn—"I'll praise my maker while I have breath . . ."—before slipping into delirium and breathing his last.

At least from the perspective of our current political life, there is something wrong with this story. The greatest figure of evangelical revivalism,

John Wesley, and the model of the evangelical statesman, William Wilberforce, were both strong Tories—loyal to the right-wing, king-and-country party in late eighteenth-century politics. Yet both were also strong, even radical, critics of slavery, which, at that time, was supported by the king and generally seen as essential to the economy of the country. Slavery was the original social justice issue in Western politics—eventually the object of petitions, parliamentary investigations, sugar boycotts, and media campaigns. Why is it that politically conservative eighteenth- and nineteenth-century Christians—key progenitors of modern evangelicalism—should feel led by their faith to oppose the systematic oppression of black people?

The answer turns out to be complex. The Christian Bible (as many pro-slavery Christians in the American South would eventually point out) does not clearly or categorically forbid slavery. Until the rise of the Quaker movement in the seventeenth century, there was no organized resistance to slavery in the Christian world. The missionary arm of the Church of England, the Society for the Propagation of the Faith in Foreign Parts, actually owned the Codrington plantation in Barbados, where the word "Society" was branded into the chests of slaves. The hypocrisy of the English religious establishment was burned into human skin.

The role played by evangelical revivalism in shaking this settled social consensus involved a paradox. In one way, evangelicals were moral and religious reactionaries. Their stated intention was to return to the piety and emotional immediacy of the early Christian church. Any movement that calls for close fidelity to a literally interpreted Bible is bound to be conservative in morality. And Methodists (as we'll see) had a particularly rigorous concern for personal piety, condemning all swearing, drunkenness, idleness, and unseemly mirth.

Such moral conservatism is probably expected of evangelicalism. But there was also something subversive and unpredictable about this religious movement, buried deep within its theology. By placing the choosing individual at the center of the religious universe, it planted a revolutionary idea in human affairs. Early evangelicals viewed all people as equal in their need for God's grace and equal in their capacity for receiving grace. They taught (as the old Christian saying goes) that the ground is level at the foot of the cross. The radical equality of God's mercy challenged divisions of class, race, and gender at a deep level. It implied a theory of human rights and dignity—in theological terms, an "anthropology"—that helped turn many evangelicals into opponents of slavery and other forms of oppression. A movement of personal transformation became a force for political reform, almost against its will. And understanding why requires understanding Wesley.

The Great Awakening that Wesley helped to ignite was, above all, a reform movement. Its evangelical adherents had no intention of founding a church or any other religious institution—though the origins of many religious institutions can be traced to this period. Before evangelicals were the creators of institutions they were the disrupters of institutions. The converted faithful saw themselves not as the builders of sandcastles, but as a spiritual wave crashing upon them. Those who experienced a fresh outpouring of grace regarded institutional Christianity in England— particularly the Church of England—as spiritually dead, theologically compromised, and in sore need of overhaul. And their commitment to biblical moral norms brought evangelicals of all backgrounds into conflict with the moral complexity of the society around them.

For a moral reform movement, the eighteenth century offered much in need of reform. Pre-Victorian—really, pre-Wesley—England was not known for piety or propriety. By one estimate, as many as one in five women in eighteenth-century London were involved in prostitution, with many girls beginning the trade at thirteen or fourteen years old. Venereal disease in children was not uncommon. Executions were a popular form of public entertainment, routinely attended by children. Cock fighting, bear baiting, bull baiting, and other blood sports were gruesome and popular spectacles. At the Dog and Duck pub in London, the entertainment consisted of ducks with tied wings being placed in a pond. Dogs were then released to kill them in a fly of feathers. People gambled on almost any topic, including a case in which an Irishman devoured live fox cubs on a bet. During the "gin craze"—analogous to America's opioid epidemic—Londoners consumed an average rate of one quart per week per person. The 1751 Hogarth print *Gin Lane* depicts a busy pawnshop, a dead body being stripped of valuables, and a drunken mother dangling her child off a railing. In one infamous instance, a woman named Judith Dufour strangled her two-year-old child and sold his clothes for gin money.

The Church of England in the eighteenth century offered only sporadic resistance to the prevailing culture and, in many ways, reflected its corruption. In theory, it represented a tolerant, third-way alternative to revanchist Catholicism and rigid Puritanism—both of which had cursed British history with religious conflict for generations. In practice, the Church of England was dominated by the aristocracy, drained of moral and theological vigor, and sometimes barely recognizable as Christian. After English jurist William Blackstone toured a series of London's prominent churches, he observed: "Not one of the sermons contained more Christianity than the writings of Cicero." Plum clerical positions were often gained through political influence. To pad their income, some Church of England clerics were appointed to several parishes at once, which they rarely visited. As a group, ministers were known more for hunting and hard drinking rather than for holiness. Many simply purchased the texts of the tedious sermons they read aloud each week. And—significant for later developments—the Church of England roundly ignored the rising working class produced by the Industrial Revolution. By 1750, the industrial city of Manchester had a population of twenty thousand but only a single parish church.

One historian termed the eighteenth century "a religious ice age." Another diagnosed a "spiritless rationalism." It was a period in which members of the religious establishment derided religious emotion and earnestness as "enthusiasm." They were soon to be drowning in it.

John Wesley's family history paralleled the history of his time. Both his parents came from rigorously Puritan stock. Both abandoned Puritanism for the moderation and respectability of the Church of England. Each tradition—that of spiritual intensity and that of cold rationality—left a mark on John Wesley.

Wesley's father, Samuel, was a clergyman and amateur literary figure who seemed to excel at neither calling. His poetic oeuvre included such gems as "On a Supper of Stinking Ducks." His service as a minister—interrupted at one point by a stay in debtors' prison—involved the frequent expression of controversial political opinions. It is a measure of Samuel's popularity that some disgruntled parishioners eventually burned down the parish rectory, attempting to murder him and his family in their sleep. After most family members had escaped the flames, they discovered that five-year-old John remained in the burning building. Samuel knelt in prayer, commending his son's soul to God. A less pious but more practical neighbor pulled John out through a window. Thereafter, Wesley was known in family lore as "a brand plucked from the burning." It is the kind of experience that feeds a gnawing sense of destiny.

John's mother, Susanna, was a bright, opinionated, spiritually ambitious woman who eventually (before her husband intervened to stop it) led a prayer meeting regularly attended by hundreds. Susanna's childrearing methods were harsh. Children, she said, should be "taught to fear the rod and cry softly." In the Wesley household, no loud talking by children was allowed and playing of any kind was forbidden. But in conditions of excessive discipline, John thrived. He also gained an example of strong, outspoken womanhood that surely influenced his later acceptance of spiritual leadership by women within Methodism.

A contest of wills emerged between John's father and mother that spilled over into politics. At one point, Samuel noticed that his wife was silent during family prayers for England's new monarch King William of Orange. Susanna, it turned out, thought that James II—the monarch William had overthrown—was the rightful ruler. "If that be the case," said Samuel, "you and I must part; for if we have two kings, we must have two beds." So Samuel left his family for a time. Susanna summarized the standoff: "Since I'm willing to let him quietly enjoy his opinions, he ought not to deprive me of my little liberty of conscience." The rift was eventually healed, but the opinionated stubbornness proved to be hereditary.

After an Oxford education, John was elected to a prestigious fellowship, studied for his ordination, and ended up teaching at Oxford as an instructor in logic. It was a good fit for an orderly mind. (Samuel once complained of his son: "As for Jack, he will have a reason for everything he has to do. I suppose he will not even break wind, unless he had a reason for it.") John Wesley read deeply in the works of English Enlightenment figures such as John Locke. And he embarked on a program of rigorous, even ruthless, self-improvement, renouncing sloth and resolving to be "busy as long as I live." His regimen sought to exclude all frivolous things from his life, such as sleeping and eating. In the process, he became conspicuous around campus for his spiritual discipline and introspection.

Many are chosen for a historical role by their restless ambition. Few—in the company of Martin Luther—are selected for influence by a hyperactive conscience. Wesley's meticulous diary was, at the time, filled with self-condemnation for empty hours and impure thoughts—what many young men, then and now, have regarded as the goals of living. At one point, Wesley resolved to measure his progress on certain moral resolutions in his diary once every hour, giving himself a rating for religious devotion between one and nine. This obsessive spiritual pulse taking was accompanied by weekly communion, daily prayer, hours of daily Bible and devotional reading, fasting, and regular visits to comfort prisoners at a local prison. Wesley's updated, Protestant form of monasticism soon attracted a group of like-minded young men, whom Oxford students mocked as "Bible moths" and members of the "holy club" or "saint's club." The pejorative that stuck was "methodists."

The group that gathered around Wesley is one of history's best examples of how a small knot of committed, talented, and mutually supportive people can change the world. (Indeed, it has seldom been changed by anything else.) One member was George Whitefield, generally viewed as the greatest preacher of his age. Another was John's brother Charles, perhaps the most prolific and influential hymn writer in Christian history.

(Among his more than eight thousand hymns are "Hark the Herald Angels Sing" and "O for a Thousand Tongues to Sing.") And there was John Wesley, destined to become the most influential religious reformer since the Reformation. The spiritual intensity of this exceptional group, however, brought a reputation for fanaticism. One member, William Morgan, had a mental breakdown and committed suicide. (Morgan's father, for a time, blamed the group for his son's death.) The form of "enthusiasm" stirring at Oxford stirred controversy from the start.

The progress of Methodism almost ended before it fully began. Wesley, seized with missionary zeal, headed to the new English colony of Georgia to preach to settlers and Native Americans. He proceeded to alienate his congregants with impossible spiritual demands and to embark on a disastrous romance. As a pastor, Wesley recommended lifelong celibacy as the Christian ideal, and it might have been better for all concerned if he had practiced it. Instead, Wesley loved and sought the company of women, which led to considerable internal turmoil. In Georgia, he became infatuated with a woman named Sophy Hopkey and, as he put it, "groaned under the weight of an unholy desire." Yet he could not bring himself to propose marriage. Hopkey eventually married another man, but Wesley's attentions continued, leading to a messy lawsuit brought by Sophy's husband, alleging that Wesley had tarnished his wife's reputation. (Later in life, Wesley had a disastrous dalliance with a nurse that ended in recrimination, and an even more disastrous marriage to a woman who became insanely jealous of her husband's completely imaginary affairs and subjected him to mental and physical abuse.)

Wesley left Georgia pursued by the courts. But during this otherwise dismal period, he had a life-changing encounter with a group of German Christians called the Brethren or Moravians. On his initial crossing to Georgia, a particularly nasty storm arose that left Wesley fearing for his life. His Brethren fellow passengers, in contrast, sang hymns and waited calmly in the close company of death. Even the Brethren children exuded a preternatural peace. This practical demonstration of Christian confidence left Wesley deeply impressed. When he later asked its source, a Brethren leader responded with the question: "Do you know Jesus Christ?" Wesley answered, "I know he is Saviour of the world." "True," came the reply, "but do you know he has saved *you*?" The question would haunt Wesley through a long, dark night of soul searching.

The Brethren were German pietists—a sect of Lutherans dedicated to the reform of a spiritually dormant Lutheranism in much the way Wesley sought a more rigorous sort of Anglicanism. The pietist distinctive was an overriding emphasis on an intense, personal, emotional encounter with Jesus Christ. While evangelicalism would develop in many theological directions over time, this type of pietism has remained definitional. All evangelicals would regard an affirmative answer to the question "Do you know Jesus Christ?" as the foundation of a life of true faith. In Georgia and back in England, Wesley believed he had seen such faith in the Moravians. He admired their cheerful busyness and spiritual single-mindedness. And he sensed they possessed an inner assurance of salvation that all his energetic self-improvement could not provide.

Wesley returned to England at a time—in the 1730s—when spiritual reform was bubbling to the surface across the Protestant world. In addition to pietism on the Continent, religious enthusiasm was sweeping across Wales and the New England colonies. Together with Methodism, these movements of spiritual renewal eventually became known as the Great Awakening—the first of many such revivals that were to shake and shape the English-speaking world. Historian Mark Noll defines revivals as "intense periods of unusual response to gospel preaching linked with unusual efforts at godly living." Wesley had the godly living part down cold. He was a Christian by any moral or intellectual measure. But the pietists had challenged his belief that moral and intellectual measures were sufficient. Real Christianity, in their view, involved a supernatural assurance of forgiveness and salvation—an experience so overwhelming that it could be compared to a second birth.

Wesley had been convinced by the Brethren that the assurance of God's saving grace was possible. But he was equally convinced, during years of spiritual struggle, that he lacked it. Wesley asked his Brethren mentor, Peter Böhler, if he should stop preaching, given his lack of a conversion experience. "Preach faith until you have it," responded Böhler, "and then because you have it, you will preach faith."

On May 24, 1738, Wesley went "very unwillingly" to a Christian meeting on Aldersgate Street where Martin Luther's *Preface to Romans*—a text highly valued by German pietists—was read aloud. "I felt my heart strangely warmed," Wesley recounted. "I felt I did trust in Christ, in Christ alone, for salvation; and an assurance was given to me that He had taken away my sins, even mine, and saved me from the law of sin and death." This is a prime example of what evangelicals mean by conversion. Theologian and preacher Jonathan Edwards described it as an "inward, sweet delight in God and divine things." For many, conversion involves a feeling of release, like giving up a burden or falling backwards into a pool. For most, it divides life into before and after.

If Wesley is any indication, that division is not always clean or neat. His diary records that during the night after his conversion he was "much buffeted by temptations." A few days later, with typically harsh self-judgment, he wondered why he didn't feel more joy. "If thou doest believe," he wrote, "why is there not more sensible change?" A few months later, he could still insist, "I am not a Christian. . . . I have not the fruits of the Spirit of Christ." The example of Wesley's journey to evangelical belief does little to encourage spiritual smugness; rather, it dignifies doubt. Even thirty years later, Wesley could write to his brother Charles, "I do not love God. . . . I am only an honest heathen." In Wesley's complex inner life, self-questioning came in recurring bouts.

Wesley's faith arrived with considerable birth pains. But his conversion quickly unleashed a talent for organization and a charism of leadership. After breaking with the Brethren over theological and personal matters, Wesley and his friends established a religious community in an abandoned ironworks they called The Foundry. From the start, Methodism was a movement of small groups or "bands," similar to what Wesley had experienced at Oxford. Joining a Methodist band did not require the affirmation of any creed or doctrine (since formal membership in the state church was assumed); it was sufficient to seek God and desire to be saved from sin. But remaining a Methodist in good standing involved a commitment to certain moral standards and practices. People were regularly excluded for swearing, habitual Sabbath-breaking, drunkenness, brawling, wife beating, lying, laziness, and "lightness and carelessness." Band meetings consisted mainly of prayer and confession, with each member expected to speak "as freely, plainly, and concisely as he can, the real state of his heart, with his several temptations and deliverances." To encourage complete openness, bands were sorted by sex. Such continual self-revelation might seem intrusive according to modern sensibilities, but mutual accountability was accompanied by mutual support. Such loving rigor proved more appealing than the cold permissiveness of Anglicanism. Who wants to sacrifice for a lackadaisical faith?

Initially, Wesley was not the most famous Methodist. That honor fell to his friend George Whitefield, who became a transatlantic phenomenon as the first great celebrity preacher. Whitefield was the son of a stableman who got into Oxford and discovered a gift for innovative communication. At a time when organized religion was largely confined to the dark interiors of sacred buildings, Whitefield spoke to vast crowds in the open air. At a time when sermons were generally dry and formal, Whitefield spoke with great passion and sometimes acted out the parts of biblical characters. The English actor David Garrick, with obvious envy, said that Whitefield could bring an audience to tears while delivering the word "Mesopotamia." At the tender age of twenty-five, Whitefield embarked on a preaching tour of America that covered seven colonies over the course of ten weeks. In some places, he was met by crowds of fifteen thousand people—gatherings that were larger than any in American colonial history to that point. By one estimate, Whitefield ended up speaking to about half the total population of the colonies he visited. Benjamin Franklin was a frequent attendee at Whitefield's sermons and observed that "every Accent, every Emphasis, every Modulation of Voice, was so perfectly well turned and well placed that without being interested in the subject, one could not help being pleased with the

Discourse, a Pleasure of much the same kind with that received from an excellent Piece of Music."

But perhaps the most influential of Whitefield's utterances turned out to be an invitation. Having returned to England, Whitefield was preaching in Bristol—a town surrounded by coal mines that fueled the Industrial Revolution. When Whitefield decided to move to another town, he invited Wesley to take his place. A traditionalist by temperament, Wesley was not a fan of open-air preaching. All his life, he wrote in his journal, he had been "so tenacious of every point related to decency and order that I should have thought the saving of souls almost a sin if it had not been done in a church." But Wesley—in one of his nearest approximations of humor—conceded that the Sermon on the Mount was "one pretty remarkable precedent of field preaching." And it was hard to argue with Whitefield's results. At one outdoor sermon in Bristol, Wesley watched his friend speak to thirty thousand people. When Wesley began preaching in fields and graveyards, his crowds averaged more like three thousand. But within a few months, he was speaking to audiences that ranged from twelve thousand to twenty thousand.

People attending such events were witnessing a new way of doing public religion. Anglican pews were generally filled (if filled at all) by landowners and their allies. Wesley preached to miners, tanners, and small manufacturers. His first sermon was normally at 5 a.m. so that workers could attend before their shifts started. Revival rhetoric was different from what most people had ever heard. Both Whitefield and Wesley spoke in a manner that was direct and emotional rather than florid and formal. "It was preaching," writes Noll, "aimed directly at popular affections, expecting life-changing results, emphasizing the message of divine grace." And the response of crowds was often electric. Some people, according to Wesley, "cried out with the utmost vehemence." Others were "seized with strong pain and constrained to roar for the disquietness of heart." Wesley's style of discourse was less overtly dramatic than Whitefield's. But he possessed the peculiar skill of a great preacher. "He told me my own heart," said one woman. "And when I look at him I thought he spake to me only." Soon the fire of evangelical revival was burning across the whole industrial south of England.

The image here is arresting for its incongruity. Wesley was not a populist by instinct. He dressed like a gentleman—in silk stockings, gloves, and shoes with silver buckles. And he expected the deference owed to his position as an Oxford-trained clergyman. Contrast this to the coal-smudged faces, work clothes, and raw emotions of his audience. How is it that a conservative Oxford don sparked such a spiritually rowdy, overwhelmingly working-class revival?

Both Wesley and his audience would certainly have given credit for this state of affairs to God. Just as Wesley attributed his own conversion to God's intervention, he saw mass conversion as collective evidence that a new work of the Holy Spirt was afoot. It is essential to the theory of evangelical revivalism that God—according to some unknowable plan—chooses certain moments and places to perform widespread miracles of grace and spiritual renewal. In some periods, the gospel seemed to spread slowly, adhering in small, sticky clumps. At other times, it seemed to flow freely, like "a rushing, mighty wind" (as Acts 2 puts it). In the mid-eighteenth century, that wind was blowing at gale force. The evangelical message spread, not just life by life, but town by town and region by region. And the participants in the Great Awakening did not believe their movement could be explained merely by historical or sociological causes.

But it does not detract from this ultimate explanation to observe that the Methodist revival also had discernible, proximate explanations. And the first was the founder of Methodism himself.

If any human being could conjure up a movement by sheer force of will it was Wesley. His conversion opened a period of preaching, argument, guidance, organization, and public commentary that reached across six decades and more than a quarter million miles of travel. He was the religious equivalent of Napoleon—tireless, fast moving, highly productive, and always in command. While riding on horseback (and, later in life, in a carriage specially equipped with bookshelves) he read voraciously in political philosophy, medicine, religion, and the natural sciences. He also produced hundreds of pamphlets in a rushing, endless stream. Many were reprints of sermons, extracts of his voluminous journal, and direct apologetic appeals: *A Word to a Street Walker*, *A Word to a Sabbath Breaker*, *A Word to a Drunkard*. Other works were designed as primers for his followers: *A Short Latin Grammar*, *A Short English Grammar*, *Directions Concerning Pronunciation and Gesture*. Others explicated the latest scientific theories: *Electricity Made Plain and Useful*, *A Compendium of Natural Philosophy* (which Wesley promised to be free from "all the Jargon of Mathematics, which is mere heathen Greek to common readers"). Others engaged the large political and social issues of Wesley's time: *A Calm Address to Our American Colonies*, *Thoughts on the Current Scarcity of Provisions* (which recommends both shutting down the distilleries and cutting taxes), *Thoughts Upon Slavery*. Others reflected the eccentric range of his enthusiasms: *A Letter to a Friend Concerning Tea* (which he regarded as unhealthy and expensive), *Serious Thoughts Concerning Godfathers and Godmothers*, *The Cause and Cure of Earthquakes*. Wesley was a polymath in the same sense that Thomas Jefferson was a polymath—combining universal curiosity with limited expertise. While Wesley's works generally do not reflect profound learning, they reveal a profound respect for learning. Educational uplift and self-improvement were essential to Methodism from the start.

The small accountability groups that defined early Methodism—as anyone involved in a therapy group or a 12-step program might tell you—provided a powerful sense of belonging. Wesley collected these decentralized cells into an enduring institution through rigid discipline. While he lived, little occurred among British Methodists without his approval. Local groups reported upward to a sort of synod called The Connexion, which reported to Wesley. He personally owned all property held by the movement and had to approve any public writing done by his followers. Such centralization served an important purpose. Pietism brimmed with a spiritual energy that could easily become spiritual excess, including claims of extra-biblical prophetic insight (as we'll see in America's profusion of millenarian and heretical sects). Wesley's hierarchical leadership acted much like the control rods inserted into a nuclear reactor—allowing the charismatic fission of the movement to be safely managed. And there are few social forces more powerful than well-regulated passion.

The contrast with Whitefield reveals Wesley's true genius. Whitefield preached through England and the American colonies like a holy hurricane. But his gains were not gathered into any lasting institution. Wesley combined his version of revivalism with a particular gift for organization—or at least a knack for recognizing and codifying the self-ordering that emerges from within a growing movement. Later in life, Whitefield admitted: "My brother Wesley acted wisely. The souls he awakened under his ministry he joined in class [organized groups] and thus preserved the fruit of his labours. This I neglected, and my people are a rope of sand." For this reason, more than any other, Wesley can be considered the founding father of evangelicalism.

A founder's influence is not always positive, and Wesley's life previewed some typical evangelical failures. Even though his heart had been "strangely warmed," he was not a particularly warmhearted man. To a woman whose children had all died before reaching adulthood, Wesley wrote: "I believe the death of your children is a great instance of the goodness of God toward you. Now that time is restored to you, and you have nothing to do but serve the Lord without distraction." Anyone who looks on the bright side of child mortality lacks a certain pastoral sensitivity. Wesley was also a prig. Upon making landfall in Georgia, Wesley confiscated and destroyed all the rum intended to celebrate his safe arrival, which presumably put a damper on the party. He was the author of an anti-masturbation pamphlet titled *Thoughts on the Sin of Onan*, warning Methodists how "self-pollution" by both sexes could result in "lethargies, epilepsies, madness, blindness, convulsions, dropsies, and the most painful of all gouts." Wesley's views on this topic were rooted in contemporary scientific opinion, but they also foreshadowed an evangelical obsession with sexual matters that has amounted to a destructive and losing battle

against human nature. And Wesley had the presumptuous tendency, mir-
rored by later evangelicals, to impute divine design to cruel and random
catastrophes. In his pamphlet *Thoughts on the Earthquake at Lisbon*, Wesley
discerned the "hand of God" in an event that took tens of thousands of
lives, contending that it was "designed either to wean us from what is not,
or to unite us to what is worthy of our affection." Such an explanation
would have offered little comfort to the families of the dead.

Yet Wesley can't be called a hypocrite. The requirements he placed
on himself were far harsher than the expectations he placed on others.
He was entirely uninterested in money and gave away all he touched, as
if British pounds were hot bricks. And he loved the poor, whom he considered his complete equal in the only thing that really mattered—their
capacity to receive God's grace. During decades of evangelistic travel,
Wesley went to the brickyards, mines, and foundries where the poor
worked, ate at their tables, and generally spent the night in their homes,
which sometimes meant sleeping in the cellar or sharing a bed with a
male family member. (His only requirement was that his lodging have a
"necessary house.") The true test of solidarity with the poor is not the offering of hospitality but the acceptance of their hospitality, which Wesley
did with grace. And Wesley not only loved the poor but defended them,
particularly from the charge of being lazy. After visiting some slums of
London, he said: "I found not one of them unemployed who was able to
crawl about the room. So wickedly, devilishly false is that common objection, they are poor only because they are idle." The primary reason that
Wesley's message resonated with members of the working class is that
Wesley addressed them as worthy and valued citizens of God's kingdom.

Systematic theologians and philosophers of religion have sometimes dismissed Wesley's belief system as a jumble of contradictions. But his eclec-
ticism was the basis for evangelicalism's enduring appeal. While calling
people to the rigorous application of an ancient set of beliefs, Wesley
was actually constituting a very different approach to faith. The religious contradictions inside his head became a powerful new synthesis.

There was Wesley's Puritan heritage, which affirmed a sincere and rigorous Protestantism as the basis for all of life. There was his High Church Anglicanism, emphasizing reason, balance, and tradition. There was his pietism, insisting on a direct, personal experience of saving grace. And there was the influence of the English Enlightenment, which has gotten less attention than it deserves.

Given later conflicts between religion and science, it is easy to assume that the Enlightenment and evangelicalism were in tension from the start. But these two streams of thought emerged side by side as the most influential movements of the eighteenth century. The Age of Reason was also the Age of Enthusiasm, and both were revolts against an ossified status quo. In the colonies, as we'll see, the rationalism of Jefferson and the pietism of the revivalists formed a natural alliance that helped propel the American Revolution. In England, there was no initial conflict between the new learning and the new religion. Wesley, of course, strongly disagreed with the religious skepticism of David Hume and the atheism of Voltaire. He was strongly influenced, however, by the icons of his time, Isaac Newton and John Locke (who were roughly his contemporaries). Far from being in revolt against modernity, evangelicalism grew so rapidly because it was a modern and modernizing force.

Wesley was an enthusiast for science as an instrument to better understand God's world. He urged Methodists to read Newton's *Opticks* and encouraged his lay preachers to be familiar with the latest scientific trends. He was fascinated by electricity and corresponded with Benjamin Franklin on the topic. Wesley's scientific passions did, on occasion, slip over into crank beliefs. His pamphlet on electricity, for example, recommended therapeutic shocks for a variety of ailments, including depression, stuttering, and migraines. Wesley facilitated such treatments by installing electrostatic generators at Methodist properties in London for use by the general public. (Most people, it seems, came away unharmed and highly satisfied.) Influenced by Wesley, the adherents of Methodism saw themselves as part of a revolt against dead and nominal religion, not a revolt against modern science.

This viewpoint was possible because of Wesley's position on the relationship between science and the Bible. Instead of assuming confrontation, he taught that each provided a different but valid perspective. Concerning the author of Genesis, Wesley argued: "The inspired penman in this history [wrote] for the Jews first and, calculating narratives for the infant state of the church, describes things by their outward sensible appearances, and leaves us, by further discoveries of the divine light, to be led into understanding of the mysteries couched under them." Where the Bible touched upon nature, in Wesley's view, its purpose was not to provide scientific information, which would have done ancient Hebrews and first-century Christians little good. Discovering the physical reality beneath biblical descriptions was left to scientists such as Newton, who were illuminating the work of God in a different way. If evangelicals of the late nineteenth and early twentieth centuries had accepted such an enlightened division of labor between revelation and science, a lot of pointless conflict might have been avoided.

Like many of his era, Wesley was heavily influenced by John Locke's theory of knowledge. Along with Locke—and influenced by Locke's *Essay Concerning Human Understanding*—Wesley believed that sensory experience was the proper basis for all understanding. This left Wesley with little respect for speculative theology, for church tradition, or for the formal authority of the Church of England. His spiritual views were informed by his practical experience of grace. He could not deny the reality of his own conversion, or the evidence of God's work in the extraordinary revival he led. This was the source of his certitude in dealing with critics. He held to the epistemology of the blind beggar: "One thing I know, that though I was blind, now I see." Going beyond Locke, Wesley postulated the existence of a "spiritual sense capable of immediate response to God's mediate revelation to man." Wesley had no use for any philosophy or theology that did not account for his defining experience. This put individuals and their perception of felt calling at the center of religious life.

It was a new and radical way to conceive religion. In the traditional Anglican approach, men and women were born into a geographic parish, which assigned a set of beliefs and communal expectations. People were baptized, raised, married, and buried according to the customs of a certain plot of ground. But a Methodist was responding to an individual experience of God and making the personal choice to join a voluntary organization (which actually, at the beginning, gave out membership cards). He was staking this claim when he insisted, "The world is my parish." He preached across parish lines, often in places where local clergy did not welcome him. What mattered was not the boundaries and habits of a place but the individual call-and-response of faith, creating a fellowship of equals. These emphases matched the new social and economic mobility of his age.

The priority of individual choice had unavoidably democratic implications, despite Wesley's own political convictions. In Locke's political philosophy, free individuals contract with each other to form a government. Legitimacy is based on the consent of the governed. As a died-in-the-wool royalist, Wesley had no patience for such subversive political views. But his application of these ideas in the context of religion was every bit as revolutionary. "Every man living, as a man," wrote Wesley, "has a right to this, as he is a rational creature. The Creator gave him this right when he endowed him with understanding. And every man must judge for himself to God. Consequently this is an indefeasible right; it is inseparable from humanity. And God did never give authority to any man, or number of men, to deprive any child of man thereof, under any color or pretense whatever." In describing the priority of religious conscience, Wesley could sound very much like some of the American rebels he criticized.

Methodism advanced so rapidly because of the skills and sympathies of its founder, and because it embodied a distinctly modern way of thinking, oriented toward individual choice and voluntary association. But there are limits to what biography and sociology can explain. Any description of the causes of the Methodist revival must take one fact into account: The religious revolution of pietism took root in precisely those places where the Industrial Revolution was taking strongest root. The geography of Methodist growth was also the geography of economic dislocation. The Holy Spirit, it turns out, was working in tandem with the invisible hand.

It does not require being an economic determinist to recognize that massive economic upheaval changes ways of living and thus ways of thinking. The region near Bristol where Whitefield and Wesley found their first success was experiencing the dark side of industrialization—squalor, hunger, drug abuse, and crime. Horrendous working conditions for miners had resulted in violent protests that the military had to put down. The year 1739—when the Methodist revival broke out—was a time of acute economic crisis, caused by a bad harvest and a bad winter. Wages were falling and grain prices were rising. Wesley's initial audiences gathered in an air of desperation.

From the start, Wesley regarded works of compassion as inseparable from the spread of real Christianity. Methodists helped organize relief efforts and made supportive visits to the poor and sick. In the early years of the revival, Wesley opened a weaving workshop to help the unemployed and created the first free dispensary of medicine in London. Wesley's concern for individual salvation did not translate into selfish individualism. He believed that the demands of the gospel were essentially communal. Though later evangelicals were to criticize the "social gospel" as liberal and heretical, Wesley embraced the concept. "The gospel of Christ knows of no religion but social," he said, "no holiness but social holiness."

Methodist influence, however, did not come primarily through acts of charity. It came by offering the working class a sense of belonging and purpose in the midst of economic and social turmoil. As work became more depersonalized, Methodism offered a personal relationship with God. In areas largely ignored by the Church of England, Methodists were a constant, insistent presence. In a society of increasing geographic mobility and attenuated family ties, Methodism offered a particularly intense form of community that amounted to a substitute family. All the hardest edges of a new economic era—isolation, destitution, loneliness, indignity, rootlessness—were softened by membership in a Methodist band. It is for this reason that the late nineteenth- and early twentieth-century French historian Élie Halévy—who wrote about Methodism with the same fresh insight that Alexis de Tocqueville brought to America—concluded: "The despair of the working class was the raw material to which Methodist doctrine and discipline gave shape."

Methodism was not only a movement that responded to human needs; it helped form a certain type of character. Men, women, and children were expected to adhere to a rigorous code, including temperance, diligence, honesty, thrift, and hard work. These eventually came to be known as the middle-class virtues for a reason. They were the human traits most likely to prevent extreme poverty and increase upward economic mobility. Economist and moral philosopher Adam Smith called this "the system of morality conducive to the welfare of the poor." Unfairly but inalterably, the wages of sin vary by economic category. A wealthy man might be able to manage an occasional drunken bender. For a poor man, such an episode could cost his job and ruin his life. For men and women of a certain class, large gambling debts might be sustainable. For the poor, they could lead to debtors' prison and ruin. "When the Industrial Revolution fully set in," according to historian Maldwyn Lloyd Edwards, "it found Methodism wholly prepared. Taught by Wesley the lessons of steadiness, sobriety, and industry, men were able to profit from the new order of things."

In this way, the virtues fostered by Methodism were not only useful in navigating the harsh working-class world; they were preparing the way for the stage in economic development beyond it. Wesley taught an ethic of self-improvement, bodily health, moral respectability, and community concern that eventually formed the basis for something entirely new: middle-class prosperity.

Wesley foresaw this development and feared it. He was concerned that Methodist virtues would produce wealth, and that wealth would result in luxury, and that luxury would feed materialism, and that materialism would undermine dependence on God and the Methodist virtues. Toward the end of his long ministry, Wesley began seeing something previously unimaginable—rich Methodists. The result, in his view, was an "increase in worldly-mindedness and conformity to the world." So Wesley took the radical position that, after paying for the "necessaries" of life, Christians should give all their remaining income away. "After providing those of thine own household things needful for life and godliness," he preached, "feed the hungry, clothe the naked, relieve the sick, the prisoner, the stranger, with all thou hast." Wesley was, in essence, recommending against the accumulation of surplus wealth. From the start there was tension between evangelicalism and capitalism. The restraint of self-destructive passions and an orientation toward the future—which evangelicalism helped supply—were the moral preconditions for a productive economy. In this way, religion was essential to the new economic order. But Wesley regarded the habits of mind fostered by that order—consumerism, avarice, haughty independence—as dangerous diversions from true faith. It is not the last time we will see this tension between God and mammon emerge.

Public officials in the eighteenth century naturally wondered about the implications of this evangelical way of thinking for British political life. And they not only wondered; they worried. The English establishment in both church and state was highly conscious of the destructive role played by religious fanatics in the previous hundred years or so. When the Puritans—another group of Protestant religious zealots—took power, they chopped off a king's head and established a military dictatorship. Catholics had caused no end of trouble in attempting to undo the English Reformation and return England to Catholic control. England's version of the culture war had played out as a bloody civil war. Both zealous Protestantism and zealous Catholicism had been destabilizing forces. So it was not unreasonable for English authorities to be wary of a new crop of enthusiasts who claimed to hear God's voice over their shoulders. At the same time, the establishment feared the growth of republican and egalitarian political ideas and movements—the sort of social forces that eventually produced the American and French revolutions.

In this environment, Methodism offered ample cause for suspicion. The movement was highly organized, displayed alarming enthusiasm, and was growing dramatically among the emerging working class in mines and factories. It encouraged the rabble to meet outdoors in large groups, often in open defiance of the established church. Its lay preachers moved from place to place, teaching that rich and poor were equal before God. In the early 1800s, the British home secretary, Lord Sidmouth, introduced a bill to protect the Church of England against Methodist competition by increasing the legal obstacles to evangelical lay preaching. During debate on the bill in Parliament, Sidmouth described Methodists as the "pious champions" of French revolutionary thought, who "decreed the subversion of all the established religions of the world." (Despite such warnings, the legislation failed.)

Conservative elements of the towns and villages where Methodists lived and preached often viewed them as a foreign and destabilizing force. Local clergy, justices of the peace, and landowners accused them of a variety of vivid, often contradictory crimes. They were supposedly allied with the Catholic pretender to the English throne, or conspiring with a planned Spanish invasion, or being used as pawns of French agitators. They were variously criticized, according to historian David Hempton, because they "encouraged sexual license, disrupted patterns of work, undermined participation in village sports and festivals, split families, induced madness and displays of paranormal behavior, extorted money for corrupt purposes, and transformed religion from an inclusive emphasis on community solidarity to an exclusive preserve of 'the saved.'"

In the early years, Wesley's open-air preaching was sometimes greeted by riots, jeering, and rock throwing. When the evangelist faced down hostile crowds, it was often raw charisma that saved him from serious injury. In one case, a local tough came at him with a cudgel. As the man was about to strike, he paused, changed his mind, and began stroking Wesley's head, saying, "What soft hair he has." Charles Wesley offered a more prosaic explanation for his brother's frequent deliverances: "Many blows he escaped through his lowness of stature." But a disturbing number of Wesley's followers did not escape violence. The homes of Methodist families were sometimes burned or looted, usually with complete impunity (until Wesley finally permitted the filing of lawsuits against the arsonists and looters). Some of the disruptions were clever, including the herding of cattle into the middle of Wesley's audience. Other persecutions were darkly horrible, including gang rape and a case where a pregnant mother was kicked to death.

Wesley's response to charges of sedition was a categorial and sincere assertion of loyalty to the king. He was a firm believer in benevolent monarchy and contemptuous of any political theory that put ultimate authority in the hands of the people. Wesley affirmed the patriotism of his growing movement in a series of public letters to the monarch and expressed a warm affection for George III. With the outbreak of the Seven Years' War, he offered to raise a company of militia. After some initial sympathy with the cause of the American colonists, Wesley turned hard against the revolutionaries, arguing in a widely distributed pamphlet that their resistance to taxes was illegal and their claims of servitude were specious. As Englishmen, in his view, they already enjoyed spacious protections under the unwritten British Constitution for their political and religious freedoms. "What more liberty could men want?" he wrote. "We have no chain on us, even as big as a knitting needle." At home, Wesley strongly discouraged his lay preachers from entering political debates, even as the Industrial Revolution was beginning to provoke strong (and sometimes violent) reactions from exploited laborers. He specifically argued against Locke's contract theory of political authority and taught a nearly unlimited obligation for Christians to respect and obey the lawful acts of a legitimate government.

Wesley took great pains to show that Methodists were a source of social stability and order. And some historians have argued that he succeeded in remarkable ways. For Halévy, it was "the miracle of modern England" that the roiling, economic revolution of the eighteenth and nineteenth centuries did not result (as it did in France and other places) in violent political turmoil. "If the materialist interpretation of history is to be trusted," he wrote, "if economic facts explain the course taken by the human race and its progress, the England of the nineteenth century was surely, above all countries, destined to revolution, both political and religious." But what distinguished Britain from France, in Halévy's view, was an evangelical revival that channeled revolutionary discontent into socially conservative forms. Revivalism, he argued, encouraged the creation of voluntary associations, which gave rise to a spirit of voluntary obedience. "A force capable of expending itself in displays of violence or popular upheavals, assumes, under the influence of a century and a half of Methodism, the form least capable of unsettling the social order." And so Halévy concluded: "Between, say, 1789 and 1815, England was spared the revolution toward which the contradictions in her polity and economy might otherwise have led her, through the stabilizing influence of evangelical religion, particularly of Methodism."

Halévy, on the whole, saw this as a positive development. Some Marxist historians shared Halévy's analysis, but not his appreciation. While admitting that Methodism had great appeal among the working class that emerged in the eighteenth and nineteenth centuries, E. P. Thompson saw its main social role as transforming laborers and artisans into "submissive industrial workers." This was accomplished by confiscating their emotional and spiritual energies and turning them, uselessly, to the service of the church. "The box-like, blackening chapels," he said, "stood in the industrial districts like great traps for the human spirit." Workers who should have been organizing marches and communes were turned toward a "ritualized form of psychic masturbation" in emotional meetings and hysterical revivalist campaigns. This made Methodism, in Thompson's view, a counter-revolutionary, repressive force in British history.

Whether positive or negative, constructive or reactionary, it is difficult to deny that Methodism helped shape a unique working-class ethos in Britain. Historian E. J. Hobsbawm offered an example from slightly

later in history. In 1855, the quarry workers of western France, looking
to protest against exploitative economic conditions, marched on the regional capital of Angers and proclaimed a revolutionary commune. Nine
years later, the British coal miners of southern Wales, facing similar hardship, marched out of their villages and met in the mountains. "Speeches
were made," recounted Hobsbawm, "tea was provided by the Ebbs Vale
lodge and the meeting ended with the singing of the Doxology."

What accounted for the difference between working-class radicalism
in France and working-class hymn singing in Wales? There are a thousand contingencies that historians have explored. But it can't be irrelevant that Welsh mines had been ground zero for the Great Awakening
in Britain. The difference, at least in part, was an intense, transformative
form of religious belief that pervaded working-class life and turned many
away from radical, secular ideologies of power. This helped cultivate a
national morality inconsistent with violent, radical fervor.

Even as Methodism helped prevent one type of revolution, it was in the
process of causing another. While the political philosophy of Wesley's
Methodism was conservative, its social ethic was unavoidably democratic. Revivalism is a form of religious faith in which authority is ultimately based on divine, charismatic blessing rather than institutional
approval. In a charismatic faith, leaders are determined by the evident
working of God through their ministry. In an institutional faith, such as
Anglicanism, leaders are elevated through education and advancement
in a hierarchical system. In a charismatic faith, the main emphasis is on
inspiration. In an institutional faith, it is legitimacy and good order that
take precedence.

The distinction between charismatic religion and institutional religion is fluid and sometimes cyclical. Religious traditions often have a
founder who appears chosen by God and uniquely blessed for some divinely appointed purpose. Christianity is an obvious example. Jesus of
Nazareth had no formal preparation for religious leadership. Rather,
it was his access to the miraculous and the inherent authority of his

teaching that set him apart. But movements of this type quickly become institutionalized, lest they splinter into endless sects and heresies. In the case of Christianity, divinely appointed apostles gave way to institutionally chosen bishops and church councils. Inspiration naturally gave way to systemization.

Over time, however, religious institutions can become ossified and hostile to inspiration, leading to a new round of reform. So, the spiritual compromises of the medieval church provoked St. Francis of Assisi's radical vision of love, poverty, and service. Clerical corruption and the accretion of unbiblical traditions led to Martin Luther's fiery reassertion of Christian essentials. A spiritually dormant Lutheranism, in turn, became the object of pietist reform. This dynamic can be seen in the whole history of Christianity. But Protestantism—by ensuring access to vernacular versions of the Bible and asserting the priesthood of all believers—went further than anything before it in making individuals the ultimate arbiter of religious truth. And Methodism was a particularly rigorous application of Protestantism.

The social implications of this approach to faith are considerable:

**Charismatic religion is ecumenical in spirit.** The revivalist fervor that Wesley and Whitefield unleashed did not respect denominational boundaries, at least among Protestants. "I saw regenerate souls," said Whitefield, "among the Baptists, among the Presbyterians, among the Independents, and among the Church [Anglican] folks—all children of God, and yet all born again in a different way of worship: and who can tell us which is the most evangelical?" Evangelicalism gained influence, in part, because it was not merely another religious sect, but rather a broad movement within a variety of Protestant sects. Theological controversies—particularly the argument between evangelicals (such as Whitefield) who believed that salvation was predestined and those (such as Wesley) who believed it could be freely chosen—did not go away. But revivalism encouraged a focus on the shared essentials of Christianity—later referred to as "mere Christianity"—rather than denominational distinctives. "It was best to preach the new birth," Whitefield concluded, "and the power of godliness, and not to insist so much on the form: for people would never be brought to one mind as to that; nor did Jesus Christ ever intend it."

**Charismatic religion encourages egalitarian habits of mind.** Methodists preached that a lord and a mill worker were equal before God, to the quiet delight of mill workers everywhere. At least in this one area of life, an absolute equality reigned. Some among the upper class correctly saw Methodism as a threat to the class system. "It is monstrous," said the Duchess of Buckingham, "to be told that you have a heart as sinful as the common wretches that crawl the earth. This is highly offensive and insulting and at variance with high rank and good breeding." The aristocracy's religious allies—Anglican clergymen—correctly saw Methodism as a threat to the hierarchy of the established church. Methodists were often harshly critical of Anglican coldness and deadness, and relied on traveling lay preachers who were chosen for their piety, talent, and sense of calling. Traditionalists correctly saw Methodism as a challenge to the patriarchal order. The movement encouraged women (a clear majority of its adherents) to engage in intense and purposeful religious activities outside the home and allowed women to assume some positions of spiritual leadership. Wesley even permitted women to preach if he felt confident in their conversion and calling (a practice discontinued by later Methodist leaders).

Methodism was also socially subversive when it came to race. Wesley preached to racially mixed audiences, baptized black believers and addressed blacks as spiritual equals. As we saw in the case of Equiano, many blacks found Methodist meetings to be places—perhaps the only places—where their hopes and desires were treated equally to the hopes and desires of whites. It was a Methodist journal that first published the work of Phillis Wheatley, an African-American poetess who had been born into slavery: "Take him, ye Africans, he longs for you, / Impartial savior is his title due: / Washed in the fountain of his redeeming blood, / You shall be sons, and kings, and priests to God."

**Above all, charismatic religion assumes and requires an exalted view of human dignity and destiny.** In theological terms, evangelical soteriology (its theory of salvation) dictated a distinctive anthropology (its conception of human nature and worth). In Wesley's view, human beings were created in God's image, fell into sin and rebellion, but remain universally capable of accepting God's offer of saving grace, revealed in the life, sacrifice, and resurrection of Jesus Christ. Every individual thus faces a decision of cosmic and eternal significance. "How can one not have a kind of superstitious awe for the human personality," observed Halévy, "when the individual is regarded as an impenetrable temple in whose bosom God chooses to work the miracle of grace?"

There is a Christian saying: "Call no man worthless for whom Christ died." For Wesley, this was not merely a private conviction, but an element of a public theology. Wesley taught that a life of Christian holiness should be characterized by love for God and neighbor. Such love is practically demonstrated in the pursuit of "justice, mercy, and truth." And all of those commitments brought Wesley into conflict with the theory and practice of slavery.

The height of Wesley's public influence coincided with the height of the British slave trade. While the practice of slavery was not deeply rooted in British soil, it was deeply rooted in the British economy. The king had granted an exclusive right to trade in slaves to the Royal African Company, which profited from supplying human cargo to markets in Spanish America. Slavery provided unpaid labor for plantations in the southern American colonies and for profitable British sugar plantations in the West Indies. Apart from Quakers (such as early American abolitionist Anthony Benezet) and a few malcontents (such as British reformer Granville Sharp), there was little organized opposition to slavery in the mid-eighteenth century. Some religious leaders, such as Whitefield (eventually a slave owner), advocated for the humane treatment of slaves rather than their emancipation. Many Enlightenment figures ignored or justified the practice. David Hume compared educated blacks to talking parrots and argued that blacks were "naturally inferior to whites." Thomas Jefferson agreed. Even John Locke, the great theorist of natural rights, defended slavery in the Fundamental Constitution of Carolina and was an investor in the Royal African Company.

Wesley, in contrast, became one of the first major figures in British history to openly call for the abolition of the slave trade. He read the eyewitness accounts of slavery collected by Benezet, corresponded with Sharp, and produced a pamphlet, *Thoughts on Slavery*, that was a remarkable preview of later abolitionist arguments. Wesley began by asserting that the traditional, African way of life disrupted and destroyed by slavery was peaceful, prosperous, and admirable. He regarded Africans as naturally intelligent and blamed slavery itself for racial differences in educational attainment. Promising to set the Bible "out of the question," Wesley makes his arguments generally in nonreligious terms that would appeal to British readers influenced by Enlightenment ideas. While Wesley was dismissive of natural law as the basis for democracy, he applied it boldly in relation to human rights. All human beings, in his view, have the right to make decisions about their life and spiritual destiny, and no human institution has the right to interfere. "If therefore you have any regard for justice (to say nothing of the mercy, nor the revealed law of God) render unto all their due," Wesley wrote. "Give liberty to whom liberty is due, that is to every child of man, to every partaker of human nature."

As important as what Wesley argued was how he argued it—in intense, emotion-laden language designed to encourage sympathy and tenderheartedness. Wesley both displayed and encouraged an emerging humanitarian impulse, which would come to literary fruition in books such as Harriet Beecher Stowe's *Uncle Tom's Cabin*. He addressed slave traders directly in one passage that remains moving across the centuries:

Are you a man? Then you should have a *human* heart. But have you indeed? What is your heart made of? Is there no such principle as Compassion there? Do you never *feel* another's pain? Have you no sympathy? No sense of human woe? No pity for the miserable? When you saw the flowing eyes, the heaving breasts, or the bleeding sides and tortured limbs of your fellow creatures, was you a stone, or a brute? . . . When you squeezed the agonizing creatures down in the ship, or when you threw their poor mangled remains into the sea, had you no relenting? Did not one tear drop from your eye, one sigh escape from your breast? Do you feel relenting now? If you do not, you must go on, till the measure of your iniquities is full. Then will the Great GOD deal with *You*, as you have dealt with *them,* and require all their blood at your hands.

Wesley's *Thoughts on Slavery* went through four editions in two years and became one of the most influential antislavery tracts of his era. The most unexpected element of the work was Wesley's willingness to follow his arguments to their radical conclusion. As a Tory, Wesley was a sworn enemy of social chaos. Yet as an advocate of universal human rights, he went so far as to justify slave uprisings, which he described as oppressed people "asserting their native liberty, which they have as much right to ask to the air they breathe." Addressing slave owners, Wesley asked, "What wonder they should cut your throat? And if they did, whom could you thank except yourself? You first acted the villain by making them slaves whether you stole them or bought them."

This is a dynamic we will see repeatedly in the early history of evangelicalism—a broad social and moral conservatism, paired with a radical anthropology. It was a combination that had unexpected, even explosive, consequences.

This was the dual mission that Wesley attempted to pass along in his deathbed letter to William Wilberforce, the young parliamentarian pursuing a legislative campaign against the slave trade. "God Almighty has set before me two great objects," Wilberforce said, "the suppression of the Slave Trade and the Reformation of Manners." Wilberforce and his circle of religious, antislavery crusaders were generally drawn from the upper and middle classes. Though they had a similar theology to the Methodists—along with the same earnestness and anthropology—they were known by the more general appellation "Evangelical." In a class-ridden society, the distinction mattered. Evangelicals had access to the halls of power while Methodists did not. As a youth, Wilberforce had been sent for a time to stay with a Methodist aunt, who began to exert considerable influence on his beliefs. Wilberforce's grandfather grew alarmed, promising, "If Billy turns Methodist he shall not get a sixpence of mine." Billy was quickly recalled home. "If I had stayed with my uncle," he later recalled, "I should probably have become a bigoted, despised Methodist."

But both pietist groups ended up playing essential, complementary roles in the fight against slavery. Evangelicals assumed political leadership, and Methodists, however despised, provided grassroots support. In Wilberforce's 1791 petition drive against the slave trade, it is estimated that Methodists provided 65 percent of the signatures. During the 1832-33 petition drive, Methodists were responsible for 79 percent of the signatures; an estimated 95 percent of all Methodists in Britain signed the petition. Together, Evangelicals and Methodists took on an entrenched economic interest and pioneered the practice of a modern advocacy movement.

Historical events generally lack a single or simple cause. But it seems undeniable that one of the most influential events of the eighteenth century took place in the tortured conscience of a single man. The Methodist branch of the Great Awakening began in a prayer group led by a teacher of logic at Oxford University, spread rapidly among miners, seamen, and weavers, leaped to the American colonies, became favored among both slaves (Frederick Douglass was converted to Christianity by a Methodist preacher) and slave owners (whom Douglass routinely mocked for hypocrisy), and was the largest denomination in America on the eve of the Civil War. Methodism helped bring civilization and compassion to the rough settlements of the American frontier, became the backbone of American reform and philanthropic movements, and shaped America as fundamentally as any social force of the nineteenth century. By 1909, there were around 35 million Methodist worshipers on six continents. An even more rigorous offshoot, the holiness tradition, took root in rural America, including in rural Kentucky, where my grandfather served as pastor to a circuit of holiness churches. Out of the holiness movement emerged the Pentecostal movement, which has transformed religion in vast regions of Africa and Latin America and now counts about half a billion adherents.

Methodism—and the Great Awakening more broadly—was an approach to religion particularly well suited to the modern world. This was religion based on individual choice rather than communal identity; religion that resulted from internal crisis and catharsis; religion organized into small, supportive groups of the like-minded; religion that stood up new institutions of civil society as traditional ones were failing; religion that encouraged both the moral habits rewarded by capitalism and the reforming zeal capable of challenging capitalist abuses.

This was not primarily a political phenomenon, which was a source of strength. Nothing is more quickly dated than a politicized faith; its holy book is yesterday's newspaper. But the Great Awakening did draw out the full implications of the Reformation by placing the choosing individual at the center of a cosmic struggle. And this led to the most enduring form of revolution: a revolution in self-conception. Beings who are capable of choosing God are not beasts to be ridden. This recognition had radical implications for human equality and human dignity. Without intending it, evangelicalism helped prepare the political groundwork for the English-speaking world to deal with systematic racism and industrial squalor.

This is a dynamic that Marxists and some traditionalists have never understood. Religion often justifies existing social arrangements—and is the main source of challenge to those arrangements. It encourages moral conventionality—as well as the most powerful and persistent sorts of reforming zeal. Vital Christianity offers a hope—the promise of an arriving kingdom of peace and justice—that unsettles the calculations of the violent and oppressive. "There is in the Gospels," said Halévy, "too pronounced a messianic element for the governing classes not to be truly alarmed whenever Christian sects advocate a return to primitive Christianity."

And at the center of it all is a warmed and transformed human heart. In a 1905 letter to his mother, Halévy—a skeptic with a Huguenot background—wrote of visiting a Sunday evening, open-air Methodist service in London. After prayers and hymn singing, the preacher began his sermon. "Not a word about hell," recounted Halévy, "not a word about death. But: 'You are not alone. You are never alone. Jesus is with you. Jesus is near you. Jesus has put his hand on your shoulder.' And, repeated several times, a phrase of a spiritual mesmerist: 'Believe me, whatever you may think, whatever you may do, Jesus is here. You could not leave here in the same spirit in which you have come. You are helpless to change this. You could not leave here in the same spirit in which you have come.'" Halévy concluded his account: "What a strange people."

No doubt, a strange people.

# First Great Awakening / Jonathan Edwards and George Whitefield: "Mysticism for the Masses"

THE QUALITY OF PORNOGRAPHY BEING POOR in 1740s Massachusetts, a group of young men had taken to handing around midwife manuals and other "informational" literature about sexual functions. One book, *The Midwife Rightly Instructed*, was found hidden up a chimney by a sister who informed on her brother. Another young man, in time-honored fashion, "had the Book and Kept it between his cot and the lining." According to the meticulous notes kept by the local pastor, Jonathan Edwards, the mother of one offender reported seeing "Pictures that seem'd to be these parts of a womans body."

In Puritan New England, such moral violations were handled by the minister. Edwards—a thin, sickly, cerebral man, not known for his people skills—launched his investigation of the matter with a blunder. The list of people he summoned to a meeting at his home included both witnesses and offenders without distinguishing between them. Gossips started speculating which was which. "The town," Edwards recounted, "was suddenly all in a blaze."

The accused were not, as you might suspect, randy teenagers. This was a time of late marriages, so there were a lot of unattached men and women in their twenties living at home. The offenders in this case were all between twenty and twenty-seven. And the knowledge they had acquired was not just put to private use. Some of the young men had taken to harassing young women in vulgar ways. One offender claimed to know that a woman was having her period by the blue circles around her eyes (a myth of the time). Another man boasted he knew more about female anatomy than the women themselves.

What Edwards uncovered in his questioning was somewhat more serious than it had first appeared. A witness said that some of the accused had "catch hold of the Girls and shook 'em." And the men quickly added insolence to their offenses. During one church meeting on the topic, a number conspicuously went off to the local tavern. Waiting to be questioned at another session, one man loudly stated that "We won't stay here all day." A particularly hard case dismissed his accusers—in what passed for Puritan profanity—"I don't care a Fart for any of them."

What was behind this youth revolt in Northampton? One answer might have been changing sexual norms in a colony that had begun racing toward modernity. You might also blame the woeful state of Puritan sex education, which turned human biology into a source of titillation for twenty-year-olds. Perhaps it reflected the natural reaction of a father with daughters (as Edwards had). Or just maybe it was due to a pastor who was overly focused on the frolicking of tavern culture. Offending a prig has its own rewards.

Edwards thought (as he almost invariably thought) that great principles were at stake. Wouldn't tolerance for such lasciviousness bring more of it and thus poison other impressionable minds? How could he serve the young men Communion without becoming complicit in their hypocrisy?

Some of the men eventually issued forced apologies for defying church authority (though not for harassing young women). But it was Edwards's reputation that had suffered most. Many in the town thought their pastor was trying to quench youthful urges that were unquenchable. Even leaders in the church thought the whole matter should have been handled more privately and skillfully. And all of this confirmed a general public impression that Edwards was stiff and censorious (which had more than a kernel of truth).

For Edwards, the whole squalid affair had the added bitterness of personal failure. Fifteen years before, he had led a revival that burned hot up and down the Connecticut River Valley, leaving no other topic of conversation. At his sermons, people had groaned under the weight of their sins, cried out in fear, and wept tears of release as they came to faith. Edwards had speculated that the awakening he was witnessing might be the beginning of a revival that would sweep the world, culminating in the promised arrival of Christ's kingdom.

Edwards's widely read description of the Northampton revival—*A Faithful Narrative of the Surprising Work of God*—had made him into something of a religious celebrity. In the book, he had taken particular pride in his church's youth. It was amongst this group that the first glimmers of religious renewal had begun to appear, including within a young woman known to Edwards as one of the "greatest company-keepers in the whole town." He had organized this growing youth piety into small prayer and mutual accountability groups. For Edwards, this change in youth attitudes was among the best evidence for the reality and durability of the Awakening.

Now he had to deal with *The Midwife Rightly Instructed* and young men acting like twelve-year-olds? This was a sign that the embers of revival in his part of the world were truly cold.

After a few years of escalating conflict with his own congregation—culminating in a serious argument over the strict standards he imposed for church membership—Edwards was dismissed from his post. His farewell sermon reminded his flock that on Judgment Day both he and they would need to account for how they treated each other. Edwards moved to Stockbridge in the further wilds of the colonial frontier to preach to the Indians and write thick books of theology.

Yet the surprising work had a life of its own. The example of Northampton had already inspired a generation of pietist reformers in Britain and on the European continent who were also frustrated by the sterility of their state churches. Years before Edwards's exile, in October 1738, on "a walk from London to Oxford," John Wesley had chanced upon

AMERICA                                            41

a recently published book. He began to read (as he put it in his journal) "the truly surprising narrative of the conversions lately wrought in
and about the town of North Hampton in New England." The account
struck him as important (he later published an abridged version of it,
along with other works by Edwards). *A Faithful Narrative* was also read by
Wesley's rhetorically gifted young friend, George Whitefield, whom we
have met before. Soon afterward, Whitefield would embark on his first
evangelistic mission to America, where he carried the message of revival
to a vast and rapt audience.

Whitefield was everything Edwards was not: charismatic, person-
able, extemporaneous, dramatic, self-promoting, and somewhat unstable
(he sometimes feared that turning any corner might bring him face-to-
face with Satan). But both men had mastered their natures with almost
cruel self-discipline, which made them productive beyond belief. Edwards created the model of mass conversion and provided a compelling
theological framing to justify intense religious experience. Whitefield
was America's first master of mass communication, who tied a transformational message to the egalitarian trends of his time. The marriage of
emotion and technique that Edwards and Whitefield pioneered would
destroy the shaky foundation of Puritan legitimacy, modify the social
fabric of colonial life, prepare Americans for revolution, encourage the
rapid democratization of the new nation, and dominate American religion and politics for 150 years and more. No ideological plan, no utopian
dream, no revolutionary manifesto has hit the world with more force or
consequence than America's Great Awakening.

America's story began with a revolution—but not our own.

Not long after the Massachusetts Bay Colony was founded in 1629, a
bloody civil war broke out back in England between Puritans and their
parliamentary allies on one side, and the nobility and the Anglican religious establishment on the other. The main Puritan aim was to finish the
work of Britain's accidental Reformation (inaugurated by King Henry
VIII's dynastic concerns and physical appetites). Purging the last vestiges

of Catholicism from the Church of England would be the first, necessary step toward building a new Christian society. No more extra-biblical ceremonies and sacraments. No more bowing and scraping to popes and bishops. Just earnest Protestantism in a stripped-down, purified form. (Thus the term "Puritan.")

The Puritan vision always had a utopian and revolutionary edge. Puritans possessed—and were possessed by—a total vision of life, faith, and politics. They sought to reform the Reformation, as well as themselves, in accordance with high ideals. Both proselytizing and the exercise of just power were inherent to their beliefs. This made Puritanism the first international movement of revolutionary purpose in the modern era. It was followed by more secular American, French, and Russian versions of revolutionary zeal.

The fortunes of the English Puritans and their parliamentary allies varied greatly over time. At one point, they took control of the British government, decapitated King Charles I, and helped establish a short-lived Commonwealth. At other points, Puritans were imprisoned, executed, and hounded out of the country. Fleeing Puritan refugees had the option of resettlement and sanctuary only in certain parts of Europe. The continent-wide conflict unleashed by the Reformation had left Lutheran lands ravaged by war and largely off-limits. But Puritan refugees were welcomed in Calvinist (also known as Reformed) locales such as Holland, France, and Switzerland. John Calvin's Geneva—the main testing ground for Reformed belief and discipline—threw open its arms. The ideals and inspiration that Puritans picked up in these places were carried across the Atlantic to their new Puritan homeland, making Calvinism the most influential international form of Protestantism.

All good Protestants—of both Calvinist and Lutheran varieties—affirmed the basic Reformation principles of justification by faith in Christ alone (not good works), the ultimate authority of the Bible (not the pope or church tradition), and the priesthood of all believers (rather than grace being mediated through a special priestly caste). Calvinists added an overriding emphasis on God's sovereign control over all things and humanity's complete inability to choose God or goodness without the enabling intervention of God himself. Otherwise, the theological differences between Calvinism and Lutheranism were relatively minor.

Yet when it came to the relationship between religion and politics, these two Reformation traditions had very different emphases. The Lutheran alternative drew a sharper distinction between two kingdoms— the Kingdom of God on one hand and the realm of human government on the other. Luther believed that, while Christian faith should shape political decision-making, this influence should come through the instrument of secular authorities. The church, as an institution, had no proper role in making human political systems embody some heavenly ideal.

The Lutheran approach ruled out one temptation: theocracy. But it created another—a tendency among Lutherans to err in the other direction and grant broad deference to oppressive rulers. During the Great Peasants' Revolt of the 1520s in Central Europe, for example, Luther sided with law, order, and the vengeful nobility. His typically temperate tract, *Against the Murderous, Thieving Hordes of Peasants*, urged secular authorities to "smite, slay, and stab" the rebels without mercy. "It is just as one must kill a mad dog," Luther explained, "if you do not strike him he will strike you." In the course of putting down the rebellion, the German nobility slaughtered some one hundred thousand peasants.

Followers of Calvin, in contrast, believed that every area of life, including public life, should be brought under God's authority. In their view, Christian belief was not just a matter of individual assent; it was also the calling of their community, bound to God by a solemn agreement. This idea of a "covenant" was central to the Puritan vision of a Christian society. Their precedent and inspiration was biblical Israel. In the Hebrew scriptures, God had established a covenant with the Jewish people. God's chosen—set apart by the potent symbol of circumcision— were corporately punished for their sins and corporately blessed for their obedience.

The Puritan leaders constructing a Christian commonwealth in the North American wilderness saw their community as the successor of this covenant—as a new Israel. If God's people—set apart by the potent symbol of infant baptism—remained faithful, He would bless their revolutionary experiment. If God's people were unfaithful to their calling, they could expect the opposite of blessing. "The Lord will surely break out in wrath against us," warned the Puritan lawyer John Winthrop, "[and] be avenged of such a perjured people and make us know the price of the breach of such a Covenant." In practice, this put limits on the conduct of earthly rulers, whose authority was conditioned on the pursuit of godly purposes. But it also gave public authorities a major role in cultivating a Christian society.

Back in Britain, the Puritan project ultimately failed—dissipating as an ecclesiastical and political force until it mainly became a source of moving devotional literature (such as *The Pilgrim's Progress*). The Church of England ended up with the uneasy but enduring compromise that Queen Elizabeth I had initially crafted: an English Church, with a Protestant theology and vernacular worship, paired with Catholic approaches to the sacraments and church hierarchy that had been expressly rejected by the Reformers. A considerable amount of theological diversity within Anglicanism was contained within a broad respect for the Book of Common Prayer, a work of theological and poetic genius and the greatest Christian liturgy written in English.

The Puritans who headed to the New World in the early seventeenth century had a distinct advantage over their British brethren. They did not need to fight an entrenched religious and political establishment. The New World was a blank religious and political canvas (apart, of course, from the natives, who were not consulted). While the colonial Puritans did not formally leave the Church of England, they hoped their example of purified Christianity would eventually inspire and transform the Church of England and England itself. That never happened. But the North American Puritans pursued their mission—their "errand into the wilderness"—with exceptional zeal and little interference (at least initially) from the mother country.

America's Puritan founders came to America in search of religious

freedom—but only their own. They did not embrace the dangerous un-
certainties of the New World in search of religious freedom as a goal in
itself. They wanted it in order to institute their vision of a better world,
their "further Reformation," which they defined as a fully Protestant
church, state, and society. Puritans were the elite guard of the Reformation. Their mission was to embody their own view of truth, not to provide legal protections for someone else's falsehood.

As a group, the Puritans have gotten bad historical press. The Salem
Witch Trials did their reputation no good (though New England engaged
in considerably less witch hunting than many parts of Europe). Nathaniel
Hawthorne's *The Scarlet Letter* has given generations of high school students a mental picture of Puritans as judgmental, hypocritical prudes.
Even more discrediting was the Puritans' occasional ruthlessness toward
Native Americans and religious minorities. In the mid-seventeenth century, Puritan authorities executed four Quakers by hanging in Boston.
Baptists were sometimes sentenced to public flogging. Dissenters who
trample on the rights of other dissenters are properly described as hypocrites.

But this is far from the whole Puritan story. Many of the early Puritan ministers had been trained back in England at Cambridge University, then a hotbed of Puritan theology and activism. These leaders
valued knowledge highly, both from ancient pagan sources and from contemporary science. (Puritan minister Cotton Mather was both a nagging
moralist and a promoter of science, who introduced smallpox inocula-
tions to Boston.) Since Puritans believed that everyone needed the ability
to read the Bible and understand the legal code, literacy was a priority.
Every town of one hundred or more families was required to build and
support a grammar school that could prepare children to attend Harvard
College. And Harvard, from its beginnings, maintained a broad, liberal
arts focus. Both piety and rationalism are authentic elements of the Puritan heritage.

It is true that punishments could be harsh against what the Puritans
deemed aberrant sexuality. But evidentiary requirements were strict, and

extreme punishments were rare and usually reserved for the openly defiant. Within marriage, Puritan ministers encouraged mutual respect and intimacy. Married sex was viewed as a positive good. Men could be disciplined by the church for refusing to engage in intercourse with their spouses. One James Mattock, for example, was excommunicated by his Boston congregation in 1640 for having "denied conjugal fellowship unto his wife for the space of two years together." Both sexes were expected to experience "delight" during intercourse, on the theory that fertilization could only happen if the female also reached orgasm. The inability to provide sexual satisfaction was actually grounds for divorce. In such cases, a man was viewed as a "pretended husband." (There is no record, however, of men being forced to wear a scarlet "E" for erectile dysfunction.)

At their best, the Puritans cultivated an intense desire to know God and experience His love. As strong Calvinists, they were convinced that fallen human beings could do nothing to earn God's grace. But once that grace was given, it was described as a source of intense joy. "Their hearts are engaged to him," wrote one Puritan pastor, "devoted to his praise, and so fixed in their love to him, that all the waters of affliction cannot extinguish it." While Puritan sermons did often warn of hellfire for unbelievers, they also raised the prospect of a personal, intense, emotional relationship with God that was nearly romantic in nature. Puritans could talk of being "ravished" by God and refer to the soul as a "womb" impregnated by Christ. "Perhaps the most remarkable aspect of Puritan sexuality," according to historian Richard Godbeer, "was not its spiritualization of the erotic but its eroticization of the spiritual." Puritans aspired to a level of intimacy with God that demanded description in sexual terms.

When it came to governance, Puritan New England was theocentric, but not, strictly speaking, theocratic. Church officials did not directly control the government. The state—though expected to acknowledge true religion—remained a separate entity and public officials had separate duties. As a rule, Puritan clergy interfered in secular affairs mainly through confrontational sermons (known as jeremiads), or when specifically invited by governing authorities (as in the witch trials). Yet both church and state shared the same ultimate goal: to build a righteous society based on biblical principles. Public officials were expected to play an active part in encouraging general godliness and orthodoxy. And this implied and required an established church—in this case, a system of independent Congregational churches, supported by general taxation. Only church members in good standing were allowed to vote. Public affairs were conducted by baptized males who could attest to a personal experience of God's saving grace. The political community was defined as the community of the faithful.

Puritanism was not, of course, the only religious tradition in early British America. The southern colonies—where the religious establishment was Anglican rather than Congregational—pursued a different path. But other regions of colonial America did not have anything close to New England's spiritual and intellectual standing. This region led the colonies in both literacy and publishing. Its vivid sense of divine mission eventually pervaded the colonies as a whole. For good and ill, Puritanism was the defining Anglo-American religious tradition—the initial carrier of American identity.

Even in the distant mirror of the seventeenth and early eighteenth centuries, it is possible to see some enduring American traits. Having fled from persecution by a powerful state church, the Puritans had a deep fear of concentrated ecclesiastical influence. So they decentralized authority to individual congregations, which were governed by a kind of rudimentary democracy. Congregationalist meetinghouses were the location of town meetings and the center of self-governing community life. The Puritan conception of the covenant—involving a tie between corporate faithfulness and divine blessing—was a type of social contract, created by a consenting community. When John Locke's more secular version arrived, it would find immediate resonance. The Puritan sense of millennial mission—the belief they had been chosen by God to inaugurate a new phase of his plan for humanity—was readily secularized into American exceptionalism. And because the Puritans had fled oppression,

they were highly sensitive to any hint of meddling by imperial bureaucra-
cies of state or church. Even small moves to rationalize the British imperial system were interpreted as assaults on their autonomy.

The Puritans were strong moral traditionalists. But they were not, at
the most fundamental level, political conservatives. Traditional conservatives (as we now know them) are content to build from existing social
materials. The Puritans were captured instead by a shining vision of the
good society, organized according to divine principles. The American
reform impulse—the whole idea of reordering society to conform to high
moral ideals—is a Puritan contribution, or a curse. From the start, their
goal was to blaze a new trail for humanity. And that hope endured far
beyond the era of Puritan religious dominance. There was a natural pro-
gression from the "City on a Hill" to the *Novus Ordo Seclorum*.

## PURITANISM UNDER PRESSURE

Almost from the beginning, the Puritans labored to overcome an internal
tension. On one hand, they wanted a church characterized by authentic,
intense, personal piety. On the other hand, they regarded the whole community as the new Israel, held to corporate account by God. But what
happens when, over time, significant portions of the community cease to
share the defining Puritan mission? How should a commonwealth called
to purity deal with growing religious diversity and declining religious
attachment and zeal?

By the third generation of New England Puritans, the commercial
success of the colonies had created an array of vivid consolations outside
the realm of religion. Boston had become a busy, successful port that
attracted merchants and seamen inspired by distinctly worldly goals.
Newly wealthy colonists imported both luxury goods and cosmopolitan
norms from London. Sailors found their comforts closer to home. It must
have shocked Puritan sensibilities when it was discovered that seamen
(and others) were frequenting a Boston brothel run by the widow Alice
Thomas.

In the early to mid-eighteenth century, the American colonies were undergoing something of a sexual revolution. When the Massachusetts General Court complained that fornication was "much increased among us," the concern was not imaginary. Premarital pregnancies were rising in both numbers and social acceptability. One study of the period found that the percentage of couples with a child born within eight and a half months of marriage was about 10 percent during the period from 1720 to 1740. By 1740 to 1760, the figure was nearer to half. One Church of England missionary who sought souls on the colonial frontier, Charles Woodmason, reported that 94 percent of women whose marriages he conducted were pregnant as brides. "Polygamy is very Common," he observed, "Bastardy, no Disrepute—Concubinage general."

Some of this rapid cultural change was the result of non-Puritan immigration to the colonies. But the main problem with any community organized to seek a vision of virtue is that children born into that community are not self-selecting. They may or may not share the disciplined idealism that defined their parents. Nearly every rising generation seems to their elders like a barbarian invasion. And the Puritans were more eager than most to blame youth culture for lowered moral standards.

A fast-day sermon preached by a solemn twenty-six-year-old Jonathan Edwards in 1729 was typical of Puritan anxiety. The community, he said, had grown "exceedingly corrupted and degenerated." Debauchery and licentiousness had come "like a flood." The rich flaunted "their buildings, apparel and way of living." Drunkenness was commonplace. Parents tolerated things that were "looked on as shameful and disgraceful in Canada, New York[, and] England." Here Edwards was referring (as all his listeners would have known) to the New England practice of "bundling," in which parents allowed young people to get better acquainted by spending the night together while clothed. "Such things are commonly winked at by parents here," said Edwards, "trusting in their children that they won't give way to temptation, would in almost any other country ruin a person's reputation."

American colonial society was growing more secular. There were an increasing number of nominal Christians in an increasingly unchurched society. Puritan ministers could no longer assume that people who attended church and generally assented to Christian doctrines had a personal, devotional commitment to God. And this presented a problem. By strict Puritan standards, such nominal Christians should not be allowed to participate in the political community or have their own children baptized (which marked infants as future members of the community). But enforcing such a high standard would leave a seriously contracted constituency for the Puritan enterprise. In a community of the saints, the number of fully committed saints was dwindling. And Puritan ministers feared that their own influence would eventually decline along with the size and influence of their flock. So the question naturally arose: How could these more loosely committed Christians be bound to Congregational churches and to the political community?

This was America's first major encounter with the fact of growing diversity (there would be many more). The Puritan response was both remarkably flexible and theologically risky. To keep more people engaged in the Puritan experiment (and to maintain their own relevance), Puritan leaders lowered the standards required for participation. Under what was known as the "Half-Way Covenant," people who held Christian beliefs but lacked a conversion experience could participate in public affairs and have their children baptized. Though Holy Communion was still denied to them, in all other respects they could be part of the Puritan enterprise. Over time, some Congregational churches even relaxed the restriction on receiving Communion. In the tension between personal piety and collective calling, the Puritans generally sided with maintaining the appearance of a covenant community, even if the rules had to be bent in the process.

This compromise, however, was only part of the Puritan response. Puritan leaders still longed and prayed for a return to the spiritual purity and intensity of earlier generations. When an earthquake shook New England in 1727, people streamed into churches, convinced they might be swallowed up by the earth. Ministers warned that it was a sign of God's displeasure with the colonists' lukewarm faith and prayed for a community-wide revival of religious conviction and passion. But the resulting earthquake of religious emotion helped end the Puritan experiment.

## TWO DEATHS

The western reaches of New England were America's first frontier. In the early eighteenth century, life there was laborious and complicated by occasional Indian raids. Drinking was the main pastime and, not coincidentally, violence was endemic. The region had seen sporadic signs of religious revival. But these had generally fizzled like sparks on wet ground. It was Edwards's preaching that finally put fire to tinder.

Edwards was not a natural candidate to be a spiritual arsonist. He had none of Wesley's frenetic energy or organization skills. He was not particularly likable, except to close friends. Edwards came from a distinguished clerical family. As a young man, he was subject both to fits of "melancholy" and periods of intense spiritual joy, often rooted in an appreciation of nature. He attended Yale and eventually settled into the pastorate of a prominent Northampton church. There he preached for four years with little obvious effect on his congregation, and worried (perhaps excessively) about the tavern-going and "frolicking" of local youth.

The most consequential days of his life, and the preface to the Great Awakening, began with a death in 1734 and effectively ended with another death the next year.

The first tragedy came in the tiny town of Pascommuck, not far from Northampton. As Edwards described it: "There happened a very sudden and awful death of a young man in the bloom of his youth; who being violently seized with pleurisy and taken immediately very delirious, died in about two days; which (together with what was preached publicly on that occasion) much affected many young people."

Edwards was referring to the sermon he gave to the grief-stricken mourners. At the service, after painting a picture of the joys of vigorous

youth, he asked the younger mourners in the audience to imagine themselves in the place of the corpse: "When others stand by your bedside and
see you gasping and breathing your last or come afterward and see you
laid out dead by the wall and see you put into the coffin and behold the
awful visage which death has given you, how shocking it will be them to
think that this is the person that used to be so vain and frothy in conversation. This is he that was so lewd a companion. This is he that used to
spend of his time in his leisure hours so much in frolicking."

From across the centuries, this may seem like a low spiritual blow at
a funeral. But Edwards, in the Puritan tradition, was blunt in preaching
about the things he considered most important. His method was to call
the bluff of the listener. If death is a fact, face it. If hell is real, avoid it.
If salvation is offered, grab it. Edwards ended his sermon by holding out
the Christian hope of a body that "will rise again a thousand times more
active and beautiful." But it was the combined warning of corpse and
preacher that seemed to sober the minds of local youth.

The religious stirrings that began among young people quickly spread.
In the following days more than three hundred people, young and old,
male and female, underwent dramatic conversions. Edwards was soon
referring to the Awakening in Northampton as "universal"—including
every white adult who lived in the town. And it quickly jumped racial
boundaries. "Several Negroes," reported Edwards, "appear to have been
truly born again."

Little of this could be attributed to Edwards's rhetorical performance. He spoke methodically and solemnly, and generally leaned on
one elbow as he preached. Early in his career he read his sermons from
3 7/8- by 4 1/8-inch cards sewn into booklets. But Edwards delivered the
revival message with the kind of utter conviction that stirred conviction
in others.

Edwards found himself riding a genuine spiritual phenomenon.
The Awakening took hold in more than thirty communities running
north and south along the Connecticut River. Other pastors added supportive voices or joined in the work. Revival sermons led to conversion

experiences that were often intensely emotional. A deepening sense of personal sinfulness might be accompanied by crying or wailing. A consciousness of God's grace and forgiveness could come in a rush of tearful joy. One revival witness observed several stout men swoon and fall "as if a cannon ball had been discharged."

Such religious "affections" were far from the normal, good order of the Congregationalist meetinghouse or the Anglican church. This was soon noticed by unamused critics. From early on, some of the rationalists who dominated Boston's establishment were dismissive of revival fervor. Timothy Cutler, an Anglican priest, described clerics who supported the revival as "men of the lowest Form in Learning and Judgement, contradicted in their Thoughts, and very apt to fall in with any thing whimsical and visionary." Elite condescension toward evangelicals began even before evangelicalism had fully congealed.

Cutler's criticisms were absurdly mistaken when applied to Edwards. The pastor who sparked the Awakening turned out to be a brilliant and subtle thinker. His thick books of theology on grace, free will, and the religious affections were groundbreaking and fully engaged with the intellectual trends of his time. Though not distinguished for his pastoral touch, Edwards was one of the greatest minds of eighteenth-century America. And his approach to the revival was hardly whimsical. While he could personally attest to the movement's spiritual authenticity, he also worried about the possibility of people "running wild." Edwards was convinced that the emotions he saw released came from God, but he was also concerned that emotional excesses might discredit the movement. So he spent the rest of his short life trying to understand what constituted a genuine experience of God.

Edwards's account of the Northampton revival, *A Faithful Narrative*, is precise, objective, and nearly scientific in tone—a kind of user's manual for revivalism. In subsequent works, he placed the Awakening in a larger historical frame. Human history, Edwards argued, was beginning to move at a quickened pace. Revivals such as Northampton's would soon "awaken whole countries of stupid and sleeping sinners," preparing the way for a golden millennial age. The revival in colonial America, he speculated, might play a special role as the first earthly foothold of Christ's kingdom. This view of the end times—this eschatology—is now referred to as postmillennialism. It is an ultimately optimistic conception of history as a rising path toward Christ's thousand-year reign on earth.

Yet just as the Northampton revival was reaching its height, a second death brought it to a gruesome halt. A prominent and well-liked figure in the community, Joseph Hawley II, cut his own throat and quickly bled out. The unfortunate man was Edwards's uncle. The nephew had seen Hawley fall deeper and deeper into depression, but the religious passion of the revival seemed to finally unhinge him. Edwards noted that the family was "very prone" to melancholy. But he ultimately blamed Satan for the situation, who seemed to be counterattacking the work of God. Other suicides followed. Edwards sensed that many distraught people had an invisible voice telling them: *Cut your own throat. Now is a good opportunity; now, NOW!* Whatever the explanation—genetic or supernatural—Hawley's death had the opposite effect of the earlier funeral. This was sobering in a very different manner. The air was out of the Awakening.

## MYSTICISM FOR THE MASSES

What had the Northampton revival really meant? Edwards was haunted and driven by the question. He considered himself a defender of the traditional Puritan order in a rapidly changing society. So he is probably better seen as the last Puritan reformer rather than the first evangelical—as a forerunner rather than a founder. But in that year between two deaths, Edwards glimpsed what faith—the kind of real faith that both burned and soothed—could be.

Edwards ended up rendering exceptional service to the cause of "experimental" religion. He set out to give a theoretical basis for religious experience, in much the same way John Locke had done for human understanding more broadly. In the process, Edwards became America's first psychologist of religion. He argued that human beings have an inherent capability—a sort of spiritual sixth sense—that allows them to perceive God's presence. He compared this capacity to the sense of taste. The taste of honey, Edwards observed, can't be conveyed by words alone, or perceived by reason alone. You can comprehensively describe honey's color, texture, and sweetness. But its flavor must be experienced in order to be really known. In a similar way, Edwards argued, the love of God can be intellectually described. Yet to fully comprehend it, one must feel it—bathe in it, be elevated and transformed by it. It is not enough to know that God is glorious; one must experience His glory. Only an encounter with God brings sufficient knowledge of God.

To learned men of religion in Edwards's time, this sounded like the dangerous surrender to subjectivity. The clerical establishment—as clerical establishments are wont to do—viewed religion mainly as a rational and ethical enterprise, and as a source of social stability and communal identity. Edwards, in contrast, was preaching universal, unmediated access to what he described as "a divine and supernatural light." The defining mark of a Christian, he argued, is not mere assent to Christian doctrine. "This Evidence, that they, that are spiritually *enlightened*, have the Truth of the things of Religion, is a Kind of *intuitive* and *immediate* Evidence."

When Edwards set out to describe this ineffable experience, he was driven to aesthetic language. The heart perceives "a kind of emanation of God's beauty" that is "related to God as the light is to the sun." We are drawn, he said, toward "the loveliness of God." When humans gain "the least Glimpse of the Glory of GOD," strong emotions are not only permissible but inevitable and essential. What else would you expect while being overwhelmed by the splendor of God's love?

Edwards was careful to insist that such experiences were subordinate to the teaching and authority of scripture, which remained the ultimate measure of orthodoxy. And he further contended that the quality of religious emotions must be judged by the influence conversion has in the daily lives of believers. The external evidence of this internal experience should be a new and lasting "taste" for biblical truth and right conduct. The focus of conversion, Edwards argued, should be on God and his saving power, not on the needs or emotions of the individual. But in these circumstances, obedience to God is not a chain or a chore. "The spiritual light is the dawning of the light of glory in the heart," said Edwards. "There is nothing so powerful as this to support persons in affliction, and to give the mind peace and brightness, in this stormy and dark world."

Though Edwards was a perfectly orthodox Calvinist, what he is describing is a mystical encounter with God. More than that, Edwards claimed that this encounter is not the rare mountaintop achievement of saints and sages, but rather a normal feature of a Christian life. The Awakening, in this sense, was mysticism for the masses.

## DEMONSTRATION, LIFE, POWER

It fell, however, to a different type of leader to turn God's surprising work into a new religious era.

George Whitefield's first trip from England to America, as we've seen, was to clean up the unholy mess left by his friend John Wesley in Georgia. Upon returning home, he was ordained as an Anglican priest, eagerly consumed Edwards's *Faithful Narrative*, began field preaching, and quickly emerged as a pietist prodigy. The momentum of Whitefield's ministry seemed to smack of divine origin. He was an entertaining speaker, but he also struck a deep spiritual tone that resonated in growing crowds of the poor and dispossessed. Near Bristol in early 1739 his audiences approached ten thousand. By May, he was preaching to London audiences double that size. By summer he embarked on his first preaching trip to the American colonies.

Whitefield's American revival tour was anticipated in colonial newspapers like the arrival of a rock star. This is an appropriate anachronism, given that Whitefield essentially invented the modern idea of celebrity. He was young, handsome (though cross-eyed), energetic, cheerful, entertaining, and utterly convinced of his cause. The young priest spoke extemporaneously, fluently, and passionately. Onstage, he was a show-man, melodramatically acting out the parts of biblical characters and placing his audience in the midst of the story. Benjamin Franklin (White-field's book publisher and eventual friend) was a frequent attendee at Whitefield's sermons and observed that "every Accent, every Emphasis, every Modulation of Voice, was so perfectly well turned and well placed that without being interested in the subject, one could not help being pleased with the Discourse, a Pleasure of much the same kind with that received from an excellent Piece of Music."

For a little over a month, Whitefield spoke to crowds in the thou-sands almost every day. People would sometimes wait outside churches at three in the morning to be assured a seat for his preaching. Many followed him from place to place like revival groupies. According to his-torian Henry Stout, Whitefield had quickly become "one of the best-known persons in Anglo-America, perhaps second only to King George III." The preacher at the center of it all was twenty-six years old.

To say that Whitefield's reception in America was warm is to mis-understand the whole concept of temperature. A reporter for the *New England Weekly Journal*, sent to cover one of Whitefield's revival services, described himself as initially skeptical, having heard "that some *Enthu-siasm* might have mix'd itself with his *Piety*." The resulting article about the event strained and sputtered in search of superlatives: "Mr. *White-field* spoke as one having authority: All he said was *Demonstration, Life and Power!* . . . *Surely God is with this Man of a Truth*." More important to Whitefield, the common people in his audience were caught up into his preaching. "He looked as if he were Clothed with authority from the Great God," said a poor farmer named Nathan Cole, "*and a sweet sollome solemnity sat upon his brow. And my hearing him preach, gave me a heart wound.*"

It is worth gaining a view of these events from Whitefield's perspec-tive, since he embodied so many traits of evangelical revivalism. His journal entries (in italics) provide a running commentary of that conse-quential month:

- **Philadelphia:** On his first evening of the tour, Whitefield preached to a crowd of about six thousand—a number equal to half the city's population. The next night it was more like eight thousand. He visited a local religious society of young women. *"A wonderful power was in the room, and with one accord, they began to cry out and weep most bitterly for the space of half an hour. . . . Five of them seemed affected as those who are in fits."* All of which brings to mind a much later British invasion. *"Near fifty negroes came to give me thanks for what God had done to their souls."* Whitefield's events were multiracial.

- **Nottingham:** Whitefield estimated an audience of two thousand. *"Oh what tears were shed and poured forth after the Lord Jesus. Some fainted; and when they had got a little strength, they would hear and faint again."* The young minister tried to describe his own experience while preaching. *With what power did a sense of His all-constraining, free, everlasting love flow in upon my soul."*

- **Boston:** Here he was officially greeted by the colonial governor. Meeting with a group of ministers who were trying to pin down his theological views, he responded that he *"saw regenerate souls among the Baptists, among the Presbyterians, among the Independents and among the [Anglican] Church folks—all children of God, and yet born again in a different way of worship."* Whitefield downplayed denominational distinctions to draw the broadest possible audience. At one church event, a creaking board caused a panic that the building was falling. *"Some threw themselves out of the windows; others threw themselves out of the gallery, and others trampled on each other."* Five people died, but the show went on in a nearby field. Whitefield is not impressed with a visit to Harvard. *"The college is scarce as big as one of our least colleges at Oxford. . . . Discipline is at a low ebb. Bad books are become fashionable."* This was not taken well at Harvard when Whitefield's journals were eventually published. Another meeting with local ministers got strained. *"The Lord enabled me to open my mouth boldly against unconverted ministers; I am persuaded, the generality of preachers talk of an unknown, unfelt Christ."* At his farewell address to the city, there were twenty thousand in attendance—the largest crowd ever gathered in British North America to that point. *"Numbers, great numbers, melted into tears, when I talked of leaving them."*

- **Northampton:** Whitefield visited Edwards's church. *"Northampton, where no less than 300 souls were saved about 5 years ago."* Whitefield had a warm stay with the Edwards family, though Edwards gently warned him against the practice of questioning the faith of other ministers. Whitefield's reflection had a faint odor of condescension. *"When I came to remind them of their former experiences, both minister and people wept much."*

It is difficult now to imagine the shocking novelty of Whitefield's method. The overwhelming majority of people who heard him in person were having experiences they had never had before. They were attending a religious event outside the walls of their own church. They were sharing that experience with strangers from multiple denominations. They were listening to a minister who was attempting to persuade (and entertain) them rather than just proclaiming religious dogmas. They were in a religious setting that welcomed and encouraged the expression of their emotion. For many, these events were so memorable, it shifted their expectations of what a religious leader could (or should) be—a change that, at varying rates, would influence every Protestant denomination in America.

Seldom does profound social change happen this quickly or comprehensively. Americans struggled to understand what they had just witnessed. Literary attempts to interpret the revival abounded. Books by Whitefield and about him nearly doubled the production of printed texts in America between 1738 and 1741.

Whitefield's tour inspired or emboldened ministers preaching the "New Birth" across New England and the Mid-Atlantic (the South would come later). In Puritan areas, the half-hearted commitment of the Halfway Covenant was a constant object of criticism by revival preachers. But this group of nominal Christians was also one of the main audiences for revival preaching. Many people within existing churches had their faith renewed or revolutionized. There is a lively academic debate over how many new converts were gained by churches in the period. (In Connecticut—one of the few states to keep good records—there was a yearly average of thirty-three new members per church at the height of the Awakening.) But the numbers are not really the point. The Awakening caused a tremendous spiritual churn, in which individuals, ministers, churches, and denominations were forced to determine, and sometimes declare, if they supported or opposed the revival.

This was not like a Billy Graham crusade coming into town in the 1950s (though they were also remarkable in their time). And it was also different from Wesley's Methodist revival, which generally burned on the social periphery. The Great Awakening in America shot through society from bottom to top, from small towns to Harvard. It challenged cultural assumptions at the deepest level. Writing in 1969, historian Richard Bushman tried to capture this level of social disruption: "The Awakening was more like the civil rights demonstrations, the campus disturbances, and the urban riots of the 1960s combined."

The evangelical view of religious commitment was highly disruptive to normal church order. Before the Great Awakening, if you had asked a colonist his or her definition of "church," you likely would have gotten a description of their local congregation—the institution that had baptized their children and was the focus of their communal life. But the Awakening involved a radically new definition of "church" as the invisible community of the saved—the sum of those who had accepted "heart religion." While this might lead to heavenly unity, it was bound to be a source of earthly division within communities, congregations, and families.

The very idea of being miraculously saved by God implied that others were not. It even implied that the pastor of a local congregation might lack a real knowledge of God. This type of assessment—a congregant pronouncing on the orthodoxy of his or her pastor—was almost unimaginable in the pre-Awakening social order. But Whitefield did not shy away from it. The title of one pamphlet he penned was indicative of his tact: *A Letter wherein he Vindicates his Asserting that Archbishop Tillotson knew no more of Christianity than Mahomet.*

Whitefield was not a theological innovator. Like Edwards (but unlike Wesley), Whitefield was a Calvinist, convinced that only God could draw sinners toward faith. But the practice of the Great Awakening adjusted Calvinism in unavoidable ways. Whitefield knew that tactics such as mass meetings and emotionally engaging sermons were more likely to produce conversions than the more arid expressions of Anglicanism. The whole point was to elicit certain intense reactions and individual choices. A Calvinist believes that the acceptance of grace is wholly predetermined by God. But the revival preacher must act as if every member of his audience is capable of making an individual decision of eternal consequence. In a revival, the theory of predestination—the belief that God alone chooses who is saved and who is damned—gives way to the practical assumption of human volition. This tonally modified, less forbidding form of Calvinism became the theological vernacular for much in the movement. This fit better with the spirit of the times, which increasingly celebrated individual autonomy and choice in the economic and philosophical realms.

Opponents of the Awakening warned that it would be socially destabilizing. And they were surely right. British colonial society was based on a rigid hierarchy in which everyone you met was either a social superior or inferior. Those in the lower classes were expected to take off their hat and generally defer in the presence of their betters. The evangelical message, in contrast, assumed absolute equality before God. And more than that, it called all human beings to a common standard of virtue that did not vary by background. "Evangelical religion," said historian Alan Heimert, "divested Americans of this quasi-feudal intellectual heritage by defining virtue not as a variety of deportments that differed from class to class and calling to calling but as a 'temper' essentially the same for all men, regardless of station."

Revivalism was spiritually egalitarian, at least in implication. And

unlike in England, there was no equivalent of Wesley to keep the movement within conservative social bounds (though Edwards tried at various
points). So the Awakening was often an untamed phenomenon. Revivalists had established a direct experience of God as the most important
qualification for spiritual leadership. And the Spirit sometimes moved
in mysterious, or at least unconventional, ways. One of the main revival
critics, Charles Chauncy, expressed his disgust that "Women and Girls;
yea, Negroes, have taken upon themselves to do the Business of preachers." Though not a universal practice, it was not unknown for women,
black Americans, and Native Americans to play the role of lay "exhorters"
in evangelical church services. In her diary, Mary Cooper of Oyster Bay,
for example, described attending a mixed-race revivalist church where
her sister Sarah was a leader and visiting another church to "hear a black
man preach." "In the revivals," according to historian Thomas Kidd, "the
world seemed to turn upside down as those with the very least agency in
eighteenth-century America felt the power of God surge in their bodies."

At this point, descriptive language of the emerging debate gets difficult for some modern readers. We are accustomed to thinking about
evangelicals as conservatives and theological liberals as more progressive
or radical (though this picture has seen some recent revision). In mid-
eighteenth-century New England, the defenders of the existing social
order were moving in the direction of rationalism and theological liberalism. It was evangelicals who were correctly regarded as progressive
social disrupters. Someone like Edwards was conservative in tone, temperament, and deportment. But he was teaching that any farmer working
in his fields had the same immediate access to God's presence—and the
same spiritual value—as any noble scion or distinguished scholar. Once
the establishment woke to the social implications of this doctrine, it did
not go down well in portions of Boston.

Or New Haven. In 1740, Whitefield made a visit to Yale and judged
it spiritually barren. In a later open letter to Yale students he wrote: "I
was obliged to say to your college, that 'your light has become darkness.' . . . A dead ministry will always make a dead people." At first, Yale's

conservative rector, Thomas Clap, welcomed the Awakening, as did most everyone. But as some of the itinerant revival preachers who arrived in New Haven after Whitefield became more radical, so did many Yale students. Soon the school was in an uproar. Students were having disorderly prayer meetings at all hours, featuring singing, exhorting, crying, and all the rest. What's more, a truly radical preacher, James Davenport, urged students to boycott New Haven's First Church, which Yale required its young men to attend.

During commencement week, Clap came down hard on the evangelical counterculture movement, expelling the brilliant but militant evangelical student David Brainerd. The Yale trustees instituted a campus speech code that forbade calling the rector, tutors, or trustees "Hypocrites, carnall or unconverted Men." Violators would be expelled on the second offense.

The commencement speaker that year was none other than Jonathan Edwards. Clap hoped that Edwards had the standing with evangelical students to calm the waters and restore some semblance of order. We have only Edwards's expanded version of the address, but it must have been a warning sign to Clap and his trustees when the speaker noted: "The end for which God pours out his Spirit, is to make men holy, and not to make them politicians." In his remarks, Edwards did urge the students to avoid spiritual pride, impulsive thinking, and radical preachers who rejected learning.

But Edwards's main message was a careful, systematic demolition of the arguments being made by traditionalists against the Awakening. Edwards strongly defended the role of emotion in religion, both "the apprehension of sin and death" and the "sweet sense of the greatness, wonderfulness, and excellency of divine things." Then he proceeded to warn the rector and trustees that insufficient enthusiasm for the revival put their own souls at risk. "If there be any who still resolutely go on to speak contemptibly of these things," he said, "I would beg them to take heed that they be not guilty of the unpardonable sin. When the Holy Spirit is much poured out, and men's lusts, lukewarmness, and hypocrisy are reproached by its powerful operations, then it is the most likely time of any, for this sin to be committed. . . . [M]any who are silent and inactive, especially ministers, will bring that curse of the angel of the Lord upon themselves." Translation: If you are not with the Awakening, you are against God.

This was probably not what Clap had in mind. A year later, the Boston *Evening Post* reported, "From Connecticut [comes a report] that in divers Parts of that Colony, they are in great Confusion on religious Accounts; and that at Yale College in New-Haven the Divisions are so great, that the students have all left it, and are gone home." Clap had actually sent the students home because the campus had become unmanageable. "I am quite Tired and Sick of all public controversies," he wrote in a letter to a friend. "They are destructive to all the natural and spiritual Comforts of Life."

The radical preacher Davenport became a cautionary tale of how "enthusiasm" could spill over into extremism. Davenport was a Yale graduate who came from one of the most prominent families in Connecticut. He was strongly influenced by Whitefield's preaching. But Davenport made a name for himself by personally accusing much of the local clergy of being unregenerate heretics. His confrontational style got him twice arrested and escorted out of the state. One witness said his services were so disorderly it was like "a visit to Bedlam." In 1743, acting on guidance he said was "received from the Spirit in Dreams," Davenport convinced his followers to have a book burning. A massive bonfire was built by the wharf in New London. Puritan classics, along with luxury clothing, were committed to the flames.

At this point, Davenport pulled off his pants and put them in the fire. According to a witness, a "young sister" pulled them out and "sent them at him, with as much Indignation as tho' they had been the Hire of a Whore." After Davenport had his pants thrown back into his face, another shocked participant accused him of having the "Devil in him." Davenport replied that "He tho't so too," adding "that he was under the influence of an evil Spirit, and that God had left him." Davenport, who clearly had some mental health issues, eventually apologized for his conduct. But it remained a cautionary tale of what can happen when the claim of direct, divine inspiration becomes untethered from ecclesial oversight.

The whole incident at Yale indicated how bitter these religious debates had quickly become. As the visibility of the Great Awakening grew, a kind of religious polarization took hold. Almost everyone felt compelled to choose a side between new and old. Congregationalists who embraced the Awakening were known as "New Light" believers—as opposed to "Old Light" Congregationalists who preferred traditional ways. (Presbyterians saw a similar split between "New Side" and "Old Side.") And the New Light was also increasingly divided between moderates (such as Edwards) and radicals (such as Davenport before his breakdown).

Whitefield was somewhere between the two New Light camps, though he would mellow over time. Looking back at his early sermons in America, he said, "I have been too bitter in my zeal. Wild-fire has been mixed in it." Edwards would eventually refer to Whitefield as "a person, concerning whom the Country is so much divided in the Sentiments, with Spirits so deeply and contrarily engaged." None of this hindered Whitefield, who made six more visits to America, lived free of scandal, and delivered more than fifteen thousand sermons during his life. Over time, as attitudes toward him mellowed as well, he became a kind of honorary American. Whitefield died in America and was buried there, making his final mission trip a permanent one. But it was not, as we'll see, the end of his service.

Following the arrival of Whitefield, nearly all the elements of American evangelicalism came together in a sudden, powerful rush: Celebrity preachers. Itinerant evangelists. Extemporaneous sermons. Dramatic, cathartic conversions. Outdoor services. The downplaying of denominationalism. New, popular hymns. These techniques were employed because they worked—reflecting a very practical, and very American, concern for outcomes. Evangelical leaders were leaving behind the institutional models of European Christianity and pioneering a type of faith that responded to the demands of the religious marketplace. And they found no shame in it. Would it be better, they asked, if people held dry, lifeless beliefs and continued to sleepwalk through empty religious rituals? Instead, evangelicals placed every person at the center of a divine drama, in which the urgent choices they faced had eternal consequences.

When the nature of this challenge to established religion was fully evident, some of the conservative elite sniffed rather than answering. They talked of evangelicalism as more appropriate to the "clownish and rustic" parts of the colonies. Or they boasted that their own congregations consisted "chiefly of families of honor." This not only indicated that they were out of touch with their times and their countrymen; it indicated they had lost all contact with real Christianity. There is no valid form of this faith that declares: "The first shall be first."

There was, however, a more consequential argument taking place over the proper place of emotion—or, as it was often called, "the affections"—in religion. The concern that serious Old Light thinkers had with the crying, laughing, and swooning at evangelical services was not merely stylistic; it was ethical. They believed that a properly ordered Christian life involved the restraint of destructive passions and a reasoned obedience to the moral law. The unseemly release of emotion, in their view, was actually a human failure. The conservatives, as Heimert argues, were "announcing the eighteenth-century principle—that man is, or ought to be, pre-eminently a rational creature."

It would be wrong to say that the evangelicals took the side of irrationality (especially given the example of Edwards). But they *were* loudly insisting that a direct experience of God, naturally accompanied by intense emotion, was essential to an adequate knowledge of God. The main point was not the sensations; but the sensations were evidence of the encounter. Any form of faith lacking this supernatural encounter, they argued, is inanimate. All that remains is some gutted candles and a dusty rule book. Not even the intellectual knowledge "of a Solomon, a Newton, or an Edwards" can make men holy or happy, explained New Light pastor Nathanial Whitaker. For that, you need to feel and know God's transforming love.

However you view the New Light position, it is clearly the more modern of the two options. The field of psychology, as it later developed, did not reveal a unitary mind, making rational choices based on ethical principles. It described layers of consciousness, in which choices we believe are rational actually reflect deep processes, needs, emotions, and experiences. Edwards's depiction of a theology based on sensation is fully compatible with a modern model of the mind. The spirit of evangelicalism, in some ways, anticipated the spirit of Romanticism, with its embrace of deep emotion and its emphasis on the feeling individual. The New Lights were announcing a principle of the nineteenth century—that human beings are preeminently feeling creatures.

Without a doubt, this type of religion encouraged American individualism. In the medieval worldview, the essence of human duty was to know and accept one's place and station in a divinely ordained social order. (This is the same argument—enforced by the whip—that would be made by slave owners to enslaved people.) But people who have chosen their own version of faith in defiance of elites are more likely to demand choices in other areas—how they work, where they live, whom they marry, how they govern themselves. Autonomy is transferrable. The powerful communal aspirations of Puritanism were giving way to the powerful individual expectation of choice. When Sarah Osborne wrote a spiritual memoir in 1743, she said, "God made with me an *everlasting covenant*." Not with the Puritan state, but with *her*. This was bound to leave a more fluid sense of personal identity.

But this left a dilemma. A country shaped by Christian assumptions cannot view autonomy as an end in itself. That would be inconsistent with the faith chosen in this case, which mandates sacrificial love of neighbor. And a descent into selfish individualism would erase America's communal mission as surely as invasion and occupation. So the questions naturally arose: What is the substitute for the fading Puritan vision? How could the country maintain public virtue, and generate common social purpose, in the absence of a powerful theocentric state?

Edwards—perhaps the only New Light thinker who might have done it—remained too much of a Puritan to directly offer a replacement for Puritanism. But many preachers—both New Light and Old Light—believed that the way for individuals to cohere and move forward was by serving as subjects of the Kingdom of God, even if that concept was not always clear.

The concept of the Kingdom comes directly from Christ's teaching in first-century Palestine. And it confused his followers from the start. It was said to be "at hand" with the start of Christ's ministry. But it was also "not of this world." It was, He said, "within you." Yet we pray "Thy Kingdom come." It is present and future; now and not yet.

It is easier to describe what it isn't than what it is. It is not a governmental entity (like a covenant commonwealth), or a voluntary organization. It does not involve coercion or hierarchy. Its subjects are not united, explained Edwards, by "Honour or Interest." Instead, Christians are bound by a mutual and active love that serves God's purposes in the world and hastens the arrival of Christ's earthly rule.

Most New Light figures were postmillennialists, believing that their world was on the verge of a new era of blessing and accomplishment. The Awakening was not a call to repent and be saved because the end of the world was near (as in premillennialism). It was a call to repent and be saved because a new world was about to begin, as the work of God moved forward. For Edwards and many of his peers the Kingdom was not political, but it was also not merely symbolic. At the height of the Awakening, Edwards believed that revival may well sweep the rest of the earth, inaugurating a new age of peace and progress that would last a thousand years. It would be "a time of great light and knowledge . . . universal peace and good understanding between nations . . . temporal prosperity . . . health and long life . . . wealth and a great increase in children." With the fading of revival fervor in 1744, this prospect looked less and less likely.

But the millennial hope was still powerful among American postmillennialists.

There is another way, however, to look at the idea of the Kingdom of God in America, which is less about eschatology and more about history. It can be seen not only as the description of a future state, but as the depiction of the deepest aspirations of those who seek and expect it. The idea of the Kingdom is a mental instrument by which individual faith is transformed into social vision. The content given to this ideal shows how Christians believe their influence should look in the world. The Kingdom, said theologian H. Richard Niebuhr, is "the hard, unyielding core which keeps religion from becoming a mere function of culture." It reveals where the outlines of an ideal coincide with a given society, and where those lines differ. If the patterns are identical, it would be a Kingdom of complacency. And it would make no difference if Christians had existed at all.

The Kingdom is admittedly a difficult, even dangerous, religious concept to introduce into a political context. The millennial hope can easily be abused in the cause of nationalism, or utopianism, or imperialism, or militarism, or socialism or capitalism. Or it can justify complete separation from the world. But in the aftermath of the Great Awakening, the question will often arise: "Whose Kingdom should come?"

# Isaac Backus and the American Revolution: "The Logic of Liberty"

A MONTH AFTER THE FIRST CONTINENTAL CONGRESS convened in Philadelphia in 1774, John Adams took the morning to visit an exhibition on human anatomy assembled by one Dr. Chovet. There were, Adams recorded in his diary, four complete skeletons, "a Leg with all the Nerves, Veins and arteries injected with Wax," and "Wax representations of all the Muscles, Tendons &c., of the Head, Brain, Heart, Lungs, Liver, Stomack, Gutts, Cawl-Bladder, Testicles." In the Enlightenment spirit, Adams found the whole thing both "admirable" and "exquisite."

The evening brought less compliant companions. Adams, along with his second cousin Samuel Adams and Robert Treat Paine—all members of the Massachusetts delegation to the Congress—were invited to Carpenter Hall, as Adams later recalled it, to do "a little business." Instead, they were faced by "a great number of Quakers seated at the long table with their broad brimmed beavers on their heads," along with some unhappy Baptists. For five hours the Massachusetts delegates were confronted on the gap between their state's support for liberty "in general," and its denial of religious liberty to Baptists in particular. Adams later called the group—which included Baptist pastor and activist Isaac Backus, Brown University president James Manning, and Quaker merchant Israel Pemberton—a "self-created tribunal, which was neither legal nor constitutional." Clearly the charge of hypocrisy had stung the famously thin-skinned founder.

Backus—a six-foot-tall, physically imposing former farmer with a diffident manner—was part of a (appropriately named) Baptist Committee of Grievances back home in Massachusetts that highlighted violations of religious conscience. He was also the author of *An Appeal to the Public on Religious Liberty, Against the Oppressions of the Present Day*. Those oppressions concerned the establishment of Congregationalism—the denomination of the colony's Puritan founders—as the official faith of Massachusetts. By law and tradition, the building of a Congregational meetinghouse and the support of a Congregational minister were considered duties of a whole community. So everyone, in theory, was subject to taxes for those purposes. People who refused to pay religious taxes could be jailed, or have property confiscated and sold to cover their tax bill.

Over time, religious dissenters in established sects such as the Baptists and Quakers had been granted the right to opt out of these taxes. But exemptions involved cumbersome bureaucratic certification. And these certifications were often ignored or invalidated by local tax collectors. Religious dissenters were unjustly dragged off to prison with some regularity, and often with complete impunity. Many dissenters, just to keep the peace, ended up paying for the promulgation of religious views they didn't share.

According to the Baptists' account of the Carpenter Hall meeting, the session started off with Manning—who helped found Brown University as a Baptist institution open to students of all faiths—reading a short statement he had written along with Backus. "The province of the Massachusetts Bay," the statement noted, "being settled by persons who fled from civil and religious oppression, it would be natural to imagine them deeply impressed by the value of liberty, and nobly scorning a domination over conscience." Instead of this, the statement cuttingly continued, "they fell from the unhappy state of being oppressed, to the more deplorable and ignoble one of becoming oppressors." The Baptists cited the "great Mr. Locke" on the proper limits of civil magistrates when it came to matters of conscience. But their appeal was ultimately theological.

"The care of souls," the statement said, "cannot belong to the civil magistrate, because his power consists only in outward force; but pure and saving religion consists in the inward persuasion of the mind, without which nothing can be acceptable to God."

At first, the politicians tried to minimize the problem. "The delegates from Massachusetts," Backus recounted, "used all their arts to represent that we complained without reason. John Adams made a long speech, and Samuel Adams another; both of whom said, 'There is, indeed, an ecclesiastical establishment in our province; but a very slender one, hardly to be called an establishment.'" The two Adamses went on to claim that the Massachusetts General Court stood ready to hear reasonable complaints and provide help. As the meeting wore on and tempers frayed, Samuel spoke his real mind. Both Backus and Manning were converts to Baptist belief as a result of the Great Awakening, which was viewed with suspicion by the Massachusetts establishment. "S.???? Adams tried to represent that *regular* Baptists were quite easy among us," said Backus, "and more than once insinuated that these complains [sic] came from enthusiasts who made it a merit to suffer persecution." Then Paine unhelpfully added: "There was nothing of conscience about the matter; it was only a contending about paying a little money."

Here Backus's diffidence gave way to anger. Backus's own mother had been imprisoned once for thirteen days when she refused to pay the religious tax. The problem for the dissenters was not the size of the assessment, he insisted, but the principle of the thing. "I told them they might call it enthusiasm or what they pleased; but I freely own, before all these gentlemen, that it is absolutely a point of conscience with me; for I cannot give in the certificates they require, without implicitly acknowledging that power in man which I believe belongs only to God."

"This shocked them," wrote Backus, with evident satisfaction. The meeting ended "with their promising to do what they could for our relief." But not before a warning about the likely obstacles from authorities back in Massachusetts. "John Adams," recounted Backus, "said we might as well expect a change in the solar system, as to expect they would give up their establishment." Backus's assessment was philosophical: "Such absurdities does religious tyranny produce in a great man."

Before returning home, the Baptists arranged for a copy of Backus's *An Appeal to the Public* to be distributed to every member of the First Continental Congress. But the aftermath of the meeting with the Massachusetts delegates was a debacle. The Quakers with whom the politically naive Baptists associated in Philadelphia were broadly seen as skeptical of the Patriot cause, and Backus and the others suffered from being identified with them. Paine spread a rumor that "Mr. Backus went to Philadelphia in order to prevent the colonies from uniting in defense of their liberties." The prominent Congregationalist minister and educator (later president of Yale College) Ezra Stiles claimed that the delegates to the Congress "expected only a private interview with some of the Baptists, but instead of that, when they came, they found a house full, etc.; that they were attacked and treated in the most rude and abusive manner; that the Baptists pretended they were oppressed, but after all their endeavors, they could only complain of a poor four-pence." Then Stiles added ominously: "When we have the power in our own hands, we will remember them."

Backus published a long letter in response to the vicious rumor campaign. "Must we be blamed for not lying still," he asked, "and thus let our countrymen trample upon our rights, and deny us the very liberty that they are ready to take up arms to defend for themselves?" After repeating his religious case against the establishment of religion, Backus observed that the much-hated tea tax imposed by the imperial authorities was roughly the same amount as the religious tax imposed on Baptists each year in their parishes. "All Americans are alarmed at the tea tax," he wrote, "though, if they please, they can avoid it by not buying the tea; but we have no such liberty."

John Adams turned out to be correct in one respect. The solar system did not quickly realign. When Backus died thirty-two years later—as the country's most prominent and tireless advocate of religious freedom—the state of Massachusetts still had an officially established faith. But Backus and other evangelicals of the Revolutionary generation were advancing a new and ultimately irresistible conception of religion in America. They saw the essence of Christianity as the voluntary, individual relationship between human beings and God, protected and respected by the state but not supported or imposed by it. This configuration of church and state defied seventeen hundred years of uniform precedent in the Christian world, in which the leaders of a country decided its official religion. Opponents gravely predicted that government neutrality would undermine both religion and public morals. In reality, it ignited in a wild competition for souls that both Christianized and democratized America in ways it had never been before.

The standoff between Adams and Backus in Philadelphia also contained broader symbolism. Men of the Enlightenment such as John Adams and products of the Great Awakening such as Backus were allies in the War for Independence. But their views and interests were not always identical, and not eventually compatible. Evangelicals became the vanguard of the Revolutionary political movement and adopted many of the civic republican views of the founders as their own. But a smaller number of activists—often religious outsiders and dissenters like Backus—raised fundamental questions about the nature and limits of the new nation's promise. Did the American Revolution merely secure freedom from Britain, or should it secure freedom of individual conscience? Was the spiritual dignity possessed by all human beings consistent with the cruel indignities of slavery? It fell to the children of the Great Awakening to help clarify the meaning of America in the realm of the spirit.

One of the odder moments in American religious history came on September 17, 1775, when a group of Continental Army volunteers camped in Newburyport, Massachusetts, preparing for a campaign to drive the British from Quebec. Members of the unit attended Sunday services at the First Presbyterian Church, which was pastored by a Separate evangelical who was a committed Patriot. The church also happened to be the final resting place of George Whitefield, who died there on his last visit to America in 1770. After the sermon and a military procession, some officers went down into the crypt where Whitefield lay. Rather than merely paying their respects, they opened his tomb and took from the decaying corpse his clerical collar and wristbands. They carried these tokens into battle—like medieval crusaders carrying holy relics—in the hope of inspiring their soldiers to righteous victory.

What actually followed was the first major American defeat of the Revolutionary War. Apart from the ineffectiveness of the gesture, the whole enterprise raises questions. Why would American soldiers turn to a deceased Anglican priest as their symbolic leader? Why would Patriots assume that the cause of evangelical religion and the cause of violent revolution were one and the same?

From the British perspective, this was not a religious struggle. Fresh from success in the Seven Years' War—in which they defeated France in a contest for global supremacy—the British were trying to bring some order to an accidentally acquired empire and pay back the enormous debt they had incurred. The Stamp Act was an attempt to have the colonists share the burden of defending their own western frontier. The Townshend Acts required British colonies to trade with the mother country. The Quebec Act gave the new British citizens of the Quebec province the right to practice their Catholic faith. These measures were designed to solve discrete imperial challenges, not impose a comprehensive political and religious tyranny.

In the colonies, most of the initial reasons for resistance were non-religious as well. Many colonists resented being the milk cow of British mercantilism, reacted angrily to the marginalization of their own colonial legislatures, and generally felt jerked around by distant, unaccountable power. For many decades, the British government had treated the American colonies with benign neglect. Now the colonies were getting unwanted attention. Even the most innocuous British actions were interpreted by the colonists as assaulting both their rights as Englishmen and their uniquely American identity. Every hostile British move seemed to the Americans like a further slide toward subjugation. The disposition of the colonists, said Heimert, was "to sniff the approach of tyranny in every tainted breeze."

Yet the social soil in which the Revolution flourished had been prepared by religious influences. While British ham-handedness did the most to unite the fractious and culturally divided colonies, religion had already promoted national cohesion of a different sort. Though the Great Awakening did not constitute a single denomination, it was undeniably a single movement—the first real mass movement of American history. Converts from Massachusetts, New Jersey, and Georgia who shared little else had a powerful, transformative experience and religious vocabulary in common. According to Heimert, Whitefield was "both instrument and symbol of the intercolonial union of the people of God"—a role that was later played in American imagination by political leaders such as George Washington. And the religious content of pietism—particularly its individualism and anti-institutionalism—meshed well with the Enlightenment's promise of a more open and equal society. These very different expressions of modernity shared the same starting point: the empowered, choosing individual. Now it would be the empowered, choosing, armed individual.

Not all religious people in the colonies, of course, favored armed revolution. According to centuries of Christian thinking on what constitutes a just war, the case for violence was not particularly strong. The list of British provocations cited by the colonists—interfering with locally passed laws, arbitrarily dismissing colonial legislatures, deploying British troops in peacetime, cutting off trade, employing foreign mercenaries, the rude dismissal of colonial petitions—hardly amounted to "slavery" (as they often hysterically claimed). Many of those loyal to the Church of England remained loyal to the Crown.

Yet the vast majority of American Christians—both New Light converts and Old Light traditionalists—ended up as Patriots. And the children of the Great Awakening developed a particular reputation for Revolutionary zeal. Many took part in organized campaigns to resist British taxes. Some became involved in the rowdy brutality of the Sons of

Liberty (even though tarring and feathering Loyalists and looting their homes were not particularly Christian methods of dispute resolution). Awakening preachers became some of the most outspoken supporters of the Revolutionary cause, as well as military chaplains and effective military recruiters. New Light revolutionaries essentially took over the government of Connecticut in the years leading up to the Revolution, and their tactics of intimidation managed to drive some Old Lights toward becoming Loyalists.

The revival of the 1740s blended easily—perhaps too easily—into the rebellion of the 1770s. The explosion of Revolutionary passion closely resembled the explosion of religious fervor that had preceded it. Whitefield's idiom previewed the emotive, confrontational rhetoric of the Revolution. In both style and substance, Patrick Henry's political rabble-rousing—"Give me liberty, or give me death!"—was unimaginable without the rabble Whitefield had first roused. After hostilities broke out, one Loyalist described the Revolution as the work of "Congregationalists, Presbyterians and Smugglers." A crown official reported back that the conflict had become "at Bottom very much a religious war."

In the decades leading up to the 1770s, the Puritan version of covenant theology essentially collapsed under the assault of religious individualism. Yet the Puritan sense of mission was reimagined to resume its revolutionary arc across history. The colonies still felt called by God to great purposes. But the ideological content of that calling changed. The Puritan social ideal was replaced by civic republicanism—the main ideology of America's founding. The religious search for a fully Christian society gave way to the nearly religious embrace of liberty as the highest social value.

Like the Puritan experiment, the republican tradition still sought to create a virtuous community. But the republican virtues were different. "What I distinguish by the name of virtue in a republic," said Montesquieu, "is the love of one's country, that is, the love of equality. It is not a moral, nor a Christian, but a political virtue." Most of America's founders embraced a conception of public virtue that would have been

more familiar to ancient Romans than colonial Puritans. Rather than
seeking a transformational encounter with God, republicanism honored
the exercise of reason and duty in the communal affairs of the country.
The American founders (in general) put their primary focus on worldly
rather than spiritual affairs. They emphasized self-sufficiency rather than
dependence on God. They saw human beings as self-interested, but not
inherently sinful. Their primary measure of goodness was public useful-
ness rather than divine approval. In this transition, the American calling
was effectively secularized. The "City on the Hill" was no longer the political embodiment of reformed Protestantism; it stood for the empowered free conscience that Protestantism implied.

This remarkable shift—the sacralization of a secular political ideal—
was embraced by religious leaders of every background, with little debate
or apparent struggle. "Far from removing political culture from the dominion of religious concepts," argues historian Nathan Hatch, "ministers
extended the canopy of religious meaning so that even the cause of liberty became sacred." This was the thinking that carried off evangelical
relics into battle against the British. The calling of faith was reconceived
as the ideology of political revolution.

There was nothing inevitable about the strong Christian embrace of
the Revolution's political philosophy. American civic republicanism had
roots in Whig ideas back in Britain. This approach to politics was more
a tendency than a formal ideology. Whigs believed that government has
a duty to protect individual rights, yet also has a natural tendency to
abuse power and violate individual rights. So Whigs looked to a strong
constitution (an unwritten one in Britain, eventually a written one in
America) to limit, divide, and balance political power. Whigs were offended by corruption and political factions. They feared both civil and
religious tyranny. They generally viewed religion not as the path to God,
but as a source of political and social stability. And they often supported
secular education to encourage free inquiry and cultivate the enlightened
spirit of the age.

In Europe, Whig politics tended to be associated with religious skepticism. Many of its strongest advocates ended up as Unitarians or atheists. "A republican spirit is injurious to religion among Methodists," Wesley warned his followers, "as I find most fallen Methodists . . . are Republicans." American figures such as Thomas Jefferson—who was highly suspicious of traditional Christianity and strongly supportive of secular education—were more typical of the breed. Many British pietists, including Wesley, found it more natural to assume a Tory or conservative political identity. Their faith led them to emphasize stability, respect for the traditional social order, and obedience to the divinely chosen monarch. Republican agitation, Wesley warned, was destined to end in chaos or despotism. Yet in colonial America, Whig political ideas became the default setting of serious Christianity. Resistance to tyranny was viewed as obedience to God.

One of the strongest advocates for this Christian-republican synthesis was also one of the most overtly religious of the founders, Dr. Benjamin Rush. After the war, Rush wrote to his friend Jefferson that Christianity was a "strong ground of republicanism." Both traditions of thought, he claimed, aimed at "republican liberty and equality." But Christianity was essential to republican virtue, Rush argued, because reason alone "affords motives too feeble to induce mankind to act agreeably upon them." This historical interpretation was also favored by Heimert, who claimed that while a "pure rationalism" might have declared the independence of the American people, "it could never have inspired them to fight for it." In the American Revolution, this inspiration often came in the form of faith. "It was the more orthodox clergymen of America," argued Heimert, "who infused the Lockean vocabulary with a moral significance, a severity and urgency, and thereby translated the ideas of social contract and natural law into a spur to popular activity." Rationalism set the ideological direction of the Revolution, but religion gave it wings.

Edwards and the founders were the most formidable Americans of the eighteenth century. But understanding the religious and political trends of the time requires a visit not to Thomas Jefferson's Monticello or

Adams's Braintree, but to a farm in Norwich, Connecticut, where Isaac
Backus was born and heard the call of God. Men such as Adams and Jefferson were exceptional for their learning and vision. But Backus—the
earnest Baptist who confronted John Adams about religious liberty during the First Continental Congress—was a more representative child of
his times. While others made the Enlightenment's case for natural rights,
Backus made the religious case for disestablishment, and relentlessly
pushed his state and country toward the recognition of religious rights.
In all this, he highlighted the pitfalls of religious social engagement by
being one of the few figures of the Revolutionary period who successfully
avoided them.

Young Isaac came to religion in the wake of tragedy. When he was
only a teen, his father died suddenly, and his mother Elizabeth fell into
a deep depression. The widow found solace in the revival preaching of
James Davenport, who was, at this point, in full possession of his wits
and his pants. In 1740, she was converted and opened her home to prayer
meetings. The strict piety of the group she gathered prevented its members from taking Communion with the unconverted, including people
admitted under the Half-Way Covenant in their local church. So the enthusiasts meeting in Backus's home became the core of an unauthorized,
Separate Congregationalist church.

Young Backus witnessed all this, but still struggled with a strong
sense of his own sinfulness. "I felt," he said, "like a stupid beast before
God." While working in the fields on August 22, 1741—evangelicals can
often chart their spiritual progress with great specificity—Backus was
"enabled by divine light to see the perfect righteousness of Christ and the
freeness and riches of his grace. . . . My heavy burden was gone, torment-
ing fears were fled, and my joy was unspeakable." Here was Edwards's
"divine and supernatural light" in action.

The services in the Backus household began attracting unfavorable attention from the local religious establishment, which was disturbed both
by the competition and the boisterous assemblies at irregular hours led
by "illiterate exhorters." Members of the nascent New Light congregation

were placed under formal sanction, which did little to dampen their enthusiasm. Persecution is often the fertilizer of new religious movements.

The most controversial New Light tenet was not their dim view of the Half-Way Covenant; it was their conviction that some Congregationalist ministers might not be converted Christians at all. But beneath this serious theological conflict was the beginning of a class conflict. Old Lights saw the New Lights as ignorant and captive to "animal affections." The New Lights resented Old Light clergymen for wearing finery, insisting on being called by their academic titles, and generally "lording it over" the humble. Backus wrote: "Does not the core of all this difficulty lie in this, that common people [justly] claim as good a right to judge and act for themselves in matters of religion as civil rulers or the learned clergy?"

Backus was soon to assert this claim for himself. Though other members of his extended family had attended Yale, Isaac was not college educated. Yet during a consequential walk in the woods, Backus had "such a converse with God as I never had before" and felt a pull toward Christian ministry. After protesting that he was too ignorant for the job, Backus heard God answer back: "Cannot he who formed man's mouth make him to speak?" (My grandfather had a very similar walk in the Kentucky woods where he heard the audible voice of God call him to ministry in the Nazarene Church, a later offshoot of Methodism.) For many pietists, such encounters were sources of an irresistible, lifelong sense of mission. It isn't easy to keep a young man down on the farm when he's heard the voice of the Deity.

Like many of his preaching peers, Backus started as an itinerant evangelist—a role that often caused tension when normal parish boundaries got crossed. But lively preaching was in high demand in the wake of Whitefield, and Backus reported "great shakeing [sic] among the dry bones." In such services, the shaking was often quite literal, as people groaned under divine conviction of guilt and deliverance. Eventually, Backus was asked to pastor a New Light congregation in Titicut, Massachusetts, where he settled down and served for the rest of his long life.

Demonstrating how bitter religious divisions were becoming, local Old Light forces promptly (and falsely) accused Backus of fathering several children by different women. This did not seem to faze him. During his first five months in Titicut, Backus preached 109 sermons with "about a dozen souls converted." This pace—about ten sermons per saved soul— was no threat to Edwards or Whitefield. But it previewed a certain stubbornness in causes Backus regarded as right.

One of those causes arrived swiftly. On his arrival in Titicut in 1749, Backus was assessed a five-pound tax to help build a Congregationalist meetinghouse—essentially being forced to promulgate beliefs he did not share. He, along with others in his New Light congregation, refused to pay. Backus described the resulting confrontation in his diary: "This morning I was seized by the officer and he threatened to carry me to prison for the precinct rate but Glory to God he gave men a sweet calm and serenity of [sic] should not to fear him nor to treat him with any bitterness—I told him that they were going on in an unscriptural way to support the gospel and therefore I could not do anything to countenance them in such a way—he told me if I would not pay him he would immediately carry me to jail."

Backus was spared prison when his tax was paid for him by a wealthy local. But one member of his church, Esther White, would not allow others to pay her assessment. She ended up in Plymouth jail for a year. In response to this unjust treatment, Backus felt the need to "go to our rulers, as Moses did to Pharaoh, to ask them to Let the People go"—not the last time we will see the story of the Exodus employed against oppression. So the young preacher organized a petition of protest to the state's general court signed by 187 people. It began: "God has given to every Man an Unalienable Right in Matters of His Worship to act for himself as his Conscience reserves ye Rule from God." The petition was the first of many in Backus's fifty-year struggle to redraw the boundaries of church and state in Puritan New England.

Perhaps the most important political crisis Backus faced concerned infant baptism. It may seem strange to modern sensibilities that the mode of Christian baptism should be a vital public matter. But in the Puritan commonwealth, infant baptism defined the covenant community. It was the founding act for both church and state. To reject infant baptism was to reject covenant theology. And to reject covenant theology was to deny the legitimacy of the Puritan enterprise. The alternative mode of baptism—baptism by immersion for believing adults—involved a different and modern way of thinking. The church, in this view, is assembled by the voluntary decisions of its members. The state is an entirely separate institution. Indeed, one of the primary purposes of the state is to protect free religious choices.

This transition was disorienting for people who grew up with Puritan assumptions. Even contemplating the baptism controversy, reported Backus, caused "such tossings in my mind as seemed as if they would have sifted and shaken me, as it were, to pieces." For years, he temporized and vacillated. But in the end, Backus came down on the side of adult baptism because the Bible—the ultimate source of evangelical authority—only records instances of adult baptism. He announced to his congregation that henceforward none should be baptized "except those who give evidence of having believed in him." Then he was immersed himself.

This act was a radical—and legally risky—break with the Puritan worldview. A New Light Congregationalist who rejected the basis of Puritan identity was no longer really a Congregationalist. Theologically, Backus remained as strong a Calvinist as the Puritans had been. But the new religious energy of revivalism could not be contained within establishment Congregationalism. Along with people in his church and many other Separates, Backus eventually became a Baptist. This much-persecuted tradition—born in the more radical reaches of the Reformation—believed that state churches were sources of spiritual corruption. They sought to reconstitute the church on the New Testament pattern as a community of believers whose conversion was attested by adult baptism. And they thought it absurd that God's grace should somehow pass "through the loins of saintly parents." Joining the community of the saved required an individual, conscious decision to accept Christ.

At the time of the Awakening, New England's "Old Baptists" were a weak, stagnant, complacent denomination with perhaps twenty-five churches in all of New England. Initially, Baptists were deeply suspicious about the influx of noisy and combative new pietists such as Backus. But the denomination ended up benefiting greatly from the Awakening's explosion of fervor. Backus went on to write the first comprehensive account of his adopted creed: *A History of New England Baptists*. In the book, he estimated that more than forty thousand people left Congregationalism during this period, with most taking the plunge and becoming Baptists. By 1804, New England had more than three hundred Baptist churches, which sent a wave of Separate Baptist preachers and missionaries to the American frontier and to the South.

Backus himself was one of the explanations for this growth. Those captured by the spirit of the Awakening were often tireless. In the decades till his death in 1806, Backus made 918 preaching trips along a twelve-hundred-mile circuit, traveling with a Bible and a container of rum in his saddlebags (this was before most Baptists found such spirits scandalous). His daily work was to organize a new denomination by binding Old Baptists with converts of the Awakening. In the midst of this, he conducted a running battle against religious oppression by the Standing Order, became a trustee of the education fund of Rhode Island College (later Brown University), wrote a steady stream of books and pamphlets, endorsed the American Revolution, and became the principal voice for religious freedom in the emerging republic.

As a religious matter, Backus believed he was pressing the Protestant Reformation to its logical conclusion—elevating the individual, informed by his or her own reading of the Bible, as the ultimate arbiter of religious truth. But in the process, pietist pastors such as Backus also were creating a new form of popular religion—anti-clerical, anti-institutional, anti-elitist, and sometimes anti-intellectual. By elevating individual decision-making above the traditions of the religious aristocracy, this movement became, in essence, a democratic revolt against the ecclesiastical and social order. Indeed, it was attacked by Old Light

Congregationalists as a "rebellion against the state." This commitment—
a belief in the free expression of the convicted heart—spilled out into
society in a variety of unpredictable ways.

As a pastor, Backus eventually was forced to push back against a
number of radical, antinomian ideas. Based on a less than orthodox
reading of the Bible, some converts declared their current bodies to be
immortal. Others claimed the right to leave their wives and live with
spiritual soulmates. One father allowed his daughter to enter such an
arrangement with a man, because the young couple had promised to "lay
with the Bible between them." Rather predictably, this form of theological birth control was ineffective. The girl ended up pregnant.

The orthodox children of the Awakening made a virtue not only of
avoiding sin but of abstinence from frivolous pleasures. They generally
regarded drunkenness, card playing, dancing, and other assorted frolicking as distractions from the eternal purposes of the soul. And they wanted
their way of life to be morally distinctive from the culture around them.
As a result, evangelicals sometimes straddled the line between sanctity
and sanctimony. When Backus married, for example, he forbade any
merrymaking after the service. "I have often Looked with abhorrence,"
he said, "upon the Common Practice of most people in this Point; mainly
their giving way to their Lusts and indulging themselves in vanity and
Carnality when they are about to Seek a Companion and to Enter into a
married State."

From the start, evangelicals were concerned to show that openness
to surging religious emotion did not imply carnal indiscipline. So sweet
release in one area of life was often accompanied by deep repression in
others.

Beneath such sententiousness, however, the new religious individualism implied and encouraged vast social changes. "The Puritans," argued historian William McLoughlin, "feared the depravity of man too
much to trust that God would be willing to save souls with sufficient
regularity to preserve Christian civilization without considerable support and assistance from the institutions of Church and State." Backus

and his fellow revivalists preached that common people could trust their own experiences on religious matters of ultimate importance. And some like Backus warned that the institutions of church and state could actually be obstacles to the spread of true religion and the saving of souls. This religious revolution prepared the way for revolutionary thinking of a different sort. The crisis of the church previewed the crisis of the nation.

Why did colonial religion shift so seamlessly into advocating revolution and embracing republican conceptions of liberty?

Certainly, there was a long libertarian streak in American religious culture. When British statesman Edmund Burke made his 1775 appeal in Parliament for conciliation with the colonists, he described them as "protestants; and of that kind, which is most averse to all implicit submission of mind and opinion." In the tradition of muscular nonconformity, the Puritans valued their political and theological autonomy and feared meddling by the Church of England, which they generally regarded as only one step removed from Catholicism. The deliberations of the Congregationalist community meeting created rudimentary habits of self-government (at least among male believers) that the British dismissed at their peril. And some Calvinists remained nostalgic about the Puritan and parliamentary revolt a century earlier in Britain that had decapitated a king and established a short-lived commonwealth. The most vivid Calvinists—Presbyterians—became some of the most vigorous advocates for republican political ideals. In North Carolina, a Loyalist officer referred to Presbyterian churches as "sedition shops."

One of the strongest motivators of the Revolution came at the crossroads of religious identity and geopolitics. It is easy to forget how precarious colonial Protestants believed their position to be, clinging to the Eastern seaboard, with enemies to the north, west, and south during much of the colonial era. Not only did they fear the imposition of Anglican bishops by their quasi-papist home country; they feared invasion and forced conversion by fully papist French and Spanish Catholic kings.

In colonial America, Catholicism played a similar role to Communism during the Cold War—as a foreign, aggressive, antidemocratic ideology that threatened a uniquely American way of life. Conquest by a Catholic power would not only undermine Anglo-American culture; it would terminate the colonies' divinely appointed mission. American Protestants were accustomed to feeling beleaguered, and they were naturally prickly and combative.

The Great Awakening supercharged such sentiments. The political energy of religious individualism that had been largely sublimated in Great Britain exploded in America. And one of the main reasons had to do with evangelical eschatology—its theory about the end of history.

All orthodox Christians at the time would have accepted that Christ would eventually return to earth in glory, establish a millennium of peace and human flourishing, and impose ultimate justice on the living and the dead. But the prophetic portions of the Bible leave the details and sequencing of those events notoriously unclear. Some throughout Christian history have been "premillennialists"—people who believe that the conflict between God and Satan in the world will grow worse and worse until Christ's sudden, decisive intervention to end history and begin his millennial rule. Others, as we saw with Edwards, have been "postmillennialists"—people who believe that the preaching of the gospel and the practice of Christian virtue will lead to a millennial golden age that culminates in Christ's return.

These views do not dictate any particular political doctrine. Yet each encourages a certain view of history and presents a different political temptation. Premillennialists have tended to search historical events for signs of the approaching apocalypse and to emphasize preparations for the Second Coming rather than the pursuit of social change in a doomed world. This can encourage an apocalyptic politics, in which history is perpetually on the verge of Armageddon. Postmillennialists, in contrast, have tended to view history as a hopeful record of progress, in which the expansion of authentic Christianity and advance of human excellence are signs of God's arriving rule. This can encourage a messianic or utopian politics, which confuses national goals with divine purposes. Colonial Christians managed to succumb to both temptations.

Back in England, eschatology had played a limited role in the Methodist revival. There was some prophetic speculation at the time, but it was largely apolitical and confined to a fringe. Wesley was a postmillennialist but regarded excessive eschatological speculation as a distraction from the central Christian work of soul winning. America, in contrast, had the Puritan sense of mission deeply ingrained in its self-conception. The colonies felt called to be not only a new England but a new Israel. So it was not enough for Patriot Christians to view the remarkable events of their time as a dramatic human struggle. They placed these developments at the very center of God's purposes in history.

In the initial task of inciting revolutionary passions, religious leaders were decidedly apocalyptic in tone. They often presented their struggle as the culminating contest between good and evil in the world. During the Reformation, the Catholic pope had generally been assigned the position of the Antichrist. In Puritan America, raucous crowds held annual Pope's Day festivities on November 5 in which they burned effigies of the pope and the devil. So it was a major shift when Patriot preachers began placing British political figures in this diabolical role. Speaking near a Liberty Tree in 1766, one anonymous Sons of Liberty orator proclaimed that previous critiques of the Stamp Act had been too narrow. America was facing, he said, not just "wicked policies," but "monsters in the shape of men." He went on to identify two British royal ministers, George Granville and the Earl of Bute, as the beasts depicted in the biblical book of Revelation. The Patriot speaker warned that colonists who even touched the tax stamps required by the British would "receive the mark of the Beast, and become infamous in your country throughout all generations." In 1777, Presbyterian Revolutionary leader and former pastor Abraham Keteltas described the Revolution as "the cause of heaven against hell—of the king Parent of the universe against the prince of darkness, and the destroyer of the human race."

Even given the strong emotions of the period, placing King George

III in the role of Satan was a bit of a stretch. But it was not uncommon. One widely distributed Revolutionary pamphlet argued that the Hebrew and Greek words for "Royal Supremacy in Great Britain" contained the hidden numerical value 666, the "number of the Beast." In 1776, the Baptist preacher Samuel Sherman described an invisible spiritual war taking place beneath America's Revolutionary struggle: "God Almighty, with all the powers of heaven, are on our side. Great numbers of angels, no doubt, are encamping round our coast, for our defense and protection. Michael stands ready; with all the artillery of heaven, to encounter the dragon, and to vanquish this black host." This was a distinctly American premillennialism.

As the Revolution moved along, and American victory seemed slightly less impossible, depictions of catastrophic struggle were increasingly paired with visions of millennial possibility. For many Patriot Christians, the Revolution offered the prospect not just of separation from Great Britain, but of a completely new work of God in the world. The defeat of tyranny and Satan would leave America at the threshold of Christ's arriving Kingdom. David Avery, the New Light chaplain at Bunker Hill, predicted that America would "become IMMANUEL'S land, a Mountain of Holiness, a Habitation of Righteousness! The Lord's spiritual Empire of Love, Joy and Peace will flourish gloriously in this Western World!" Another pastor claimed that God's Kingdom would come "to its perfection in America." This was a distinctly American postmillennialism.

Historian Nathan Hatch calls this mix of patriotic optimism and eschatology "civil millennialism." What might at first seem like the overflow of rhetorical zeal was actually a far more ambitious political and theological project. A generation of pastors—both Old Light and New Light—took the old Puritan conception of national calling and refilled it with the content of civic republicanism. Much of the Old Testament was transformed into an object lesson of how Israel had fallen from a state of civil and religious freedom into oppressive monarchy. Satan was reinterpreted not just as the father of lies but as the inspiration for tyranny. America was still the new Israel announced by the Puritans. But in the frame of civil millennialism, Israel became the prototype of a Whig commonwealth, and the Puritans were idealized as pioneers of religious and political liberty. The millennial hope was also ambitiously modified. God's Kingdom would arrive not, as Edwards saw it, through global revival, but through the global expansion of the principles of liberty brought to fruition in America. Britain's attack on America, said Samuel Sherwood, was one "of the last efforts and dying struggles of the man of sin." American victory would usher in a new era of freedom and progress. Preachers of all backgrounds during the Revolutionary period—almost en masse—adopted a republican conception of the millennium.

The details of this golden age were generally left vague. It was sometimes depicted as the arrival of "light and liberty," or the triumph of "truth and happiness." In both Old Light and New Light preaching, the new age often involved increasing commerce, growing population, cultural accomplishment, and territorial expansion. Christ's arriving Kingdom, it turned out, sounded a lot like a chamber of commerce promotional brochure. In such descriptions, one can hear both a typically American identification of God's blessing with national prosperity and a typically American sense of westward destiny.

Hatch calls civil millennialism "the first substantially new eschatology since the Reformation." And it served a vital purpose in Revolutionary ideology. Enlightenment analogies for the founding of a new nation tended to be theoretical and bloodless. Who wants to sacrifice their lives, fortunes, and sacred honor in order to enter a social contract? The process of breaking with an old—and in many ways admirable—political and social order for the sake of an uncertain future was more like taking a leap of faith than signing a lease agreement. And Christian millennialism justified this risky choice as both a blow against evil and the path to a dramatically better world. "The basis for this ideological transformation," argues historian Ruth Bloch, "did not lie in radical Whig political thought, with its fear of change, nor, for most Americans, in Enlightenment ideas of progress. The main connecting link that afforded this remarkably easy transition was rather the religious tradition of millennial prophecy."

The benefits of this wholesale revision of Christian eschatology were clear to all involved. The ideological architects of the Revolution—even the Deists and Unitarians—got a powerful source of religious legitimacy and urgency for their military and political task. The Patriot Christians—both Old Light and New Light—sanctified their own political cause and earned a central place in pursuing it. And both founders and religious leaders found a common language of aspiration, rooted in familiar historical concepts. When John Adams talked about fighting the spirit of the Antichrist, his evangelical listeners might have imagined a person; Adams was actually referring to the influence of Catholic and feudal law.

Christians looking back on these events for instruction and inspiration need to understand what was actually happening in this period. Patriot clergy, Hatch explains, were appropriating "the means of traditional religion to accomplish the ends of civic humanism." Civil millennialism did not originate in scholarly biblical study and reflection. It took shape in attempts to justify first the French and Indian War, and then the American War for Independence. This was as much a project of ideology as it was of theology—resulting in a kingdom very much of this world.

In 1774, a rural New England clergyman announced to his flock that anyone who didn't join an economic boycott of British goods was "not fit to approach" the Communion table. Edwards had wanted to restrict Holy Communion only to true Christian believers. Some now proposed to limit it only to true Patriots. Liberty had become, in the words of Revolutionary firebrand Patrick Henry, a "holy cause." Making this case involved the ambitious distortion of biblical passages for political purposes. When pastors quoted Galatians—"Ye have been called unto liberty"—to oppose the Stamp Act, it is difficult to imagine that colonial tax policy was what the Apostle Paul had in mind. But it indicated a certain mindset. For many supporters of the Revolution, its importance justified using whatever biblical and theological tools lay easily at hand.

In the course of one generation, the Great Awakening was repurposed to serve American nationalism. In the mainstream of Patriot Christianity, this endorsement was enthusiastic and uncritical. Pastors

not only supported the war; they drafted bad theology, tortured biblical
exegesis, and fevered eschatology into the service of their new country.
Not only did they reflect the political views of their cultural cohort, but
they also amplified, intensified, and legitimized those views.

In the process, Patriot Christians demonstrated the eternally recurring temptation of religion in America: to be derivative rather than
formative. For large numbers of evangelicals in this period, their religious views sacralized their political opinions rather than shaping, con-
straining, and judging those opinions. During the American Revolution,
Christians became the instruments of a good cause, even a great cause—
but still instruments nonetheless. Christian advocacy of nascent American nationalism, when combined with powerful cultural memories of the
Puritan mission, slipped easily into an unconstrained Christian nationalism. The political temptation of American evangelicalism began with the
founding of America itself.

Such Christian nationalism is the main story of late colonial Christianity, but not the whole story. A smaller number of colonial Christians—
whom historian Mark Noll calls "reforming patriots"—both supported
the Revolution *and* saw it as a chance to apply the ideal of freedom more
rigorously and consistently. Their embrace of the Patriot cause was sincere, but not uncritical. They applied ethical norms that stood outside
and above the conflict of Whig vs. Loyalist that dominated their historical moment. In the process of founding a new government, they proposed
to correct some of the moral failures of their own society. And precisely
because they pressed the full ethical implications of the Revolutionary
cause, they were sometimes attacked for insufficient loyalty to that cause.

The most obvious and immediate test of Christian social conscience
came on the enslavement of Africans—an issue that would continue to
challenge and divide American Christians for the next seven decades and
beyond. In its 1775 proclamation justifying armed rebellion against Britain, the Continental Congress began by denying it was proper for "a part
of the human race to hold an absolute property in, and an unbounded

power over others." It went on to accuse the British government of "enslaving these colonies by violence." The hypocrisy of such statements was jarringly self-evident. When American independence was declared, about 20 percent of the population of the thirteen mainland colonies was comprised of enslaved people. Plenty of Americans had unbounded power over other human beings, who were bought, sold, and abused as if they were property. And it was morally obscene—even by the standards of the late eighteenth century—to compare British tax and trade policy to the horrors of chattel slavery.

This issue did not begin high on the agenda of evangelical concerns in America, as it had in Britain. Many of the early leaders of the Great Awakening either ignored or accommodated the colonial practice of slavery. In a lifelong outpouring of words, Edwards hardly mentioned the topic. Whitefield viewed enslaved people as an important audience for the gospel and strongly condemned the abuse of slaves. He did not, however, oppose the institution of slavery and eventually owned several slaves himself.

Yet by the 1770s, there were evangelical leaders in every part of the thirteen colonies who viewed slavery as an inherent evil, as well as a potential provocation for divine judgment on their country. Take the case of Samuel Hopkins, who was a disciple and close friend of Edwards and pastor of a New Light church in Rhode Island. Hopkins was exposed to the horrors of slavery by seeing captive Africans unloaded like cargo at the docks of Newport. His outraged Christian conscience led him to write a 1776 pamphlet—*A Dialogue, Concerning the Slavery of the Africans; Shewing it To Be the Duty and Interest of the American Colonies to Emancipate All Their African Slaves*—which systematically considered and dismissed the various theoretical arguments in favor of the practice before making an argument for immediate abolition.

This work is particularly notable as an experiment in empathy. Hopkins tried to imagine how enslaved people might view the American obsession with freedom. "When they observe all this cry and struggle for liberty for ourselves and our children," he wrote, "and see themselves and their children wholly overlooked by us, and behold the sons of liberty oppressing and tyrannizing over many thousands of poor blacks, who have as good a claim to liberty as themselves, they are shocked with the glaring inconsistence." Hopkins also urged Americans to imagine how they would react if their own relations were taken into slavery. "If many thousands of our children were slaves in Algiers or any parts of the Turkish dominions," he wrote, "how would the attention of all the country turn to it! How greatly should we be affected by it! Would any cost or labour be spared, or any difficulty or hazard be too great to go through, in order to obtain their freedom?" The tract was dedicated to the Continental Congress and a copy was distributed to every member.

Hopkins's support for immediate abolition rose out of a moral theory he called "disinterested benevolence." Rather than focusing primarily on the interpretation of a few ambiguous scriptural texts dealing directly with slavery, Hopkins emphasized the spirit of love and benevolence that should accompany Christian conversion. The commandment to love our neighbor, Hopkins argued, requires "universal, disinterested good will," which "disposes us to do good to all." And this should lead us to work on God's behalf to alleviate the suffering of others, especially the marginalized.

In Hopkins's approach, the Golden Rule is not just a guide for personal behavior but a mandate for social reform. He wrote: "The following precept of our Lord and Savior, 'All things whatsoever ye would that men should do unto you, do ye even so to them,' which is included in loving our neighbor as ourselves, will set at liberty every slave." And the keeping of enslaved people, Hopkins concluded, is not just a personal but a corporate failure. "It is, therefore," he said, "become a national sin, and a sin of the first magnitude—a sin which righteous Heaven has never suffered to pass unpunished in this world." This type of indignation laid the groundwork for a coming wave of antislavery activism.

Another prominent evangelical critic of slavery, Presbyterian pastor Jacob Green, had been converted as a student at Harvard by hearing Whitefield preach. Green was a staunch republican, who opened his

home as a hospital for released prisoners of war. To his New Jersey congregation, he described the Revolution as a "glorious" cause, on which
"we may hope for a divine blessing." But he went on to say that he felt
"obliged to point out many crying sins among us." Chief among them, in
his view, was slavery. "Can it be believed," he pointedly asked, "that a people contending for liberty should, at the same time, be promoting and
supporting slavery?" Green stressed the shared aspirations of all human
beings, including Africans in America. "Are they not fond of liberty as
well as others of the human race? Is not freedom the natural, inalienable
right of all?" Green feared that Americans would lose the war as punish-
ment for allowing slavery to continue. But even if they won, he predicted
that the new country would see "convulsions, contentions, oppressions
and various calamities, so that our liberty will be uncomfortable, till we
wash our hands from the guilt of negro slavery."

This prophecy of America's uncomfortable liberty turned out to be
eerily correct. Those who argue that it is unfair to judge slave-owning
members of the founding generation by the moral standards of a later
time must contend with Green, Hopkins, antislavery Quakers, and other
religious critics of the practice. Many of the founders stood convicted of
rank hypocrisy by the moral standards of their own time. It was precisely
this obvious tension between the American ideal of human freedom and
the brutal practice of owning humans that led some to construct a more
elaborate rationale in favor of slavery based on racial inferiority. To justify their inconsistency in applying American ideals, they defined the
objects of their exploitation as subhuman. The advocates of this view
eventually found evangelical pastors who would baptize their bigotry.
But enslaved blacks also converted to evangelical Christianity, internal-
ized its teaching of radical equality, and became the clearest voices in
their own defense.

Backus's position on slavery was somewhere between Whitefield's accom-
modationism and Wesley's abolitionism. "No man abhors that wicked
practice more than I do," he said, "and would gladly make use of all lawful

means toward the abolishing of slavery in all parts of the land." But he thought that emancipation was likely to be gradual. Rather than being "struck by an apoplexy," Backus predicted, it would "die with a consumption," as more and more state governments ended the practice. This hope—similar to the one Abraham Lincoln initially held—would prove entirely unrealistic, as slavery became further entrenched in the economy and cultural identity of the white South.

Backus's more visionary contribution came on another issue emphasized by the reforming evangelicals: religious liberty. In the late eighteenth century, most Americans of European background (with the exception of some twenty-five hundred Jews) would have identified themselves as Christians of one sort or another. Many lived in states such as Massachusetts and Virginia that had officially established and tax-supported state religions, reflecting the nearly uniform practice back in Europe.

Yet late colonial America was experiencing its next stage of growing diversity, mainly because of immigration and the Great Awakening. There were substantial numbers of Lutherans, Presbyterians, Anglicans, Quakers, Baptists, Moravians, and Dutch Reformed. By the time American independence was declared, no single Christian denomination could claim majority support in any region outside New England. And even there, Rhode Island was a standing rebuke to the Standing Order. A century before, Cotton Mather had complained of Rhode Island that there had never been "such a variety of religions on so small a spot of ground." Mather compared the result to a cesspool. But such diversity—within the boundaries of Protestant Christianity—was increasingly characteristic of the nation as a whole. American society was being forced to deal with the undeniable fact of pluralism. And many religious groups, particularly those with shrinking influence, had not learned the basic habits of pluralism.

In this atmosphere, Baptists such as Backus played a particularly important part. The legal disadvantages imposed on their denomination provided them with a unique vantage point from which to make their cultural critique. While sharing the theological commitments of many of

their neighbors, they remained social outsiders. And while generally supporting the conflict with Britain, they had no illusions about the flaws
and failures of the society that was engaged in the Revolution—a society
that subjected them to constant indignities. Baptists had one step of
mental distance from the emerging nation. They demonstrated that it
was possible to criticize elements of colonial life without being Loyalists.
Unlike colonists who completely conflated Christianity with nationalism, Baptists believed the Patriot cause itself needed examination and
reform. They were determined to be formative, not derivative.

Backus exemplified this critical distance. In his mind, he had embraced the Reformation's logical conclusion—putting the responsibility
for eternal choices in the hands of every individual. Now he sought to
push the American Revolution to its logical conclusion—encouraging
government to respect such free choices as a legal and religious imperative. Backus was determined to press the logic of liberty.

Like many colonials, Backus had some early reservations about
the Revolution, which he initially saw as the fight of a hypocritical
Congregationalist elite against Great Britain. "We have lately been on
the borders of a civil war, for LIBERTY; hanging and burning were
not too bad for the enemies of LIBERTY! Ah! little do many see what
they are doing; for all this noise: *Whosoever committeth sin is the servant
of sin. . . .* Such harbour the worst enemies to liberty in their own
bosoms." But after push came to shove at Lexington and Concord,
Backus became a committed Patriot. His eldest son served in the Connecticut militia. Ultimately, the overwhelming majority of Baptists
decided they disliked Catholicism and political subjugation more
than they resented the Massachusetts legislature. But they did not
stop pushing back at their mistreatment, even during the Revolution.
Backus came to view the war as a just cause, as well as an act of Provi-
dence that could help sweep away an unjust religious establishment.
He joined the Revolution in part because he hoped it would hasten a
second revolution: the overthrow of the New England religious order.

The source of injustice, in Backus's view, was the offer of religious liberty as a matter of reluctant tolerance rather than a matter of legal right and religious principle. When King William III gave Massachusetts a new charter in 1691, its Congregationalist government was compelled to extend tolerance to a few, officially recognized minority groups: Anglicans, Quakers, and the Old Baptists. Later on, members of these groups were granted exemptions from religious taxation—if they received a certificate from their church demonstrating their status as religious dissenters. But the products of the Great Awakening—Separate Congregationalists and Separate Baptists—were generally dismissed as fanatics and "schismatics" who did not deserve this type of accommodation.

Such official prejudice had considerable public support in New England. Because local taxes were imposed to build a Congregationalist meetinghouse and support a Congregationalist minister, those claiming religious exemption narrowed the tax base. It was a common jibe that Separate Baptists such as Backus were "getting dipped to wash away their taxes." There were cases in which Congregationalists moved rather than live in areas infested by Separate Baptists who drove up tax assessments for everyone else. As a result, Massachusetts made the process of gaining an exemption onerous, humiliating, and uncertain. No dissenter was exempted from religious taxes in a newly settled area until the meetinghouse was constructed. Separate Baptists were forced to get written certification of authenticity of their views from Old Baptist congregations (which sometimes resented the newcomers). Some local officials just ignored the exemption process entirely. State courts (comprised entirely of Congregationalists) were often biased against the dissenters.

The case of Ashfield, Massachusetts, in 1769 was a vivid case in point, as well as a well-set trap. After religious taxes were levied on local Baptists to construct a meetinghouse, they predictably refused to pay. So constables sold their land in an obvious effort to run them out of town. The Tory lieutenant governor of Massachusetts urged the Baptists to take their appeal to King George III. This, the colonial official calculated, would insert the king into the affairs of the colony, while turning churches against each other over the wisdom of involving the highly resented monarch. The plan worked. With appeals to the colonial legislature at a dead end, Backus and others petitioned the king, explaining that 398 acres had been forcibly put up for sale to meet the tax assessment. The king eventually sided with the Baptists, but they were never given back all that was due to them. And suspicions about the Baptists' loyalty grew again.

Through all this, Backus became the most creative and active member of the Baptist Grievance Committee. He began writing articles advocating religious freedom in newspapers. He was a frequent defense witness at the trials of dissenters. In the spirit of an ACLU civil rights lawyer, Backus began searching for other legal test cases. An advertisement he placed in the *Boston Evening-Post* asked for any Baptists "who are or have been oppressed" to collect documents on their "cases of suffering," and forward them to the committee. Backus found hundreds of instances where exemptions had been denied because Baptists turned in material a day or two late, or sent it to the wrong address, or didn't follow precise bureaucratic wording.

Backus previewed the motivations and manner of generations of religious social activists who would follow him. He was inspired by the defiant, here-I-stand spirit of the Protestant Reformation. But he also previewed the democratic populism that would sweep the new country in successive waves. The Great Awakening was multiplying a certain kind of American citizen: unawed by tradition, skeptical of elites, called to public duties, and utterly convinced of the righteousness of his or her cause.

Backus's frustrations with the Massachusetts system reached a boiling point in 1773, which was also a turning point in Baptist activism. His fellow believers, he felt, had exhausted their options in a legal system that was stacked against them. So rather than focusing on individual test cases, Backus urged mass civil disobedience against the entire structure of state-sponsored religion. Backus sent a letter to all Baptist congregations affiliated with his association, urging them to refuse any compliance with the existing tax system, including the exemption process. If everyone resisted at once, Backus reasoned, it would reveal the immense growth among Separate Congregationalists and Separate Baptists. And the penalties of imprisonment and distraint would become impossible to enforce against so large a number of violators. The American colonists had engaged in civil disobedience against Britain; now Backus wanted to employ the same tactics against the Massachusetts establishment. What had started as a request for accommodation became an assault on the remaining stronghold of the Puritan governing project.

The effort largely failed. Many Baptists were skittish about being on the wrong side of the law. To accommodate disagreements on strategy within its own ranks, the Baptist association left participation in the protest up to the discretion of individual congregations. Participation was uneven. Enthusiasm quickly faded. Backus did succeed in creating a legal defense fund to help resisters. But the disestablishment of Congregationalism in Massachusetts would not happen until the presidency of Andrew Jackson.

For Backus, however, the whole experience served to refine and sharpen his arguments in favor of religious liberty, which would resonate well beyond his state and time. In 1773, Backus wrote his pamphlet *An Appeal to the Public for Religious Liberty Against the Oppression of the Present Day*, the single most influential presentation of pietist arguments for religious freedom in the eighteenth century. While the Enlightenment case for separating church and state started with the assertion of individual rights, Backus was most concerned about creating an atmosphere in which true religion could flourish. His case for freedom of conscience was ultimately rooted in the nature of religion itself.

Backus began by disputing the founding Puritan myth: the identification of Protestant New England with biblical Israel. The Puritans looked at the Old and New Testaments and saw a single, continuing covenant at work between God and His people. The composition of the chosen, in their view, had expanded beyond the Jews to include the Christian church. The coming of Christ had obviated the need for practices such as animal sacrifice and Temple worship. But the Puritans believed that key elements of the Abrahamic covenant still applied to their own circumstance. God—as with ancient Israel—had set apart their community to demonstrate His love and faithfulness. As with ancient Israel, corporate obedience would bring communal blessing, and corporate disobedience would bring divine judgment. For the Puritans, the story of Israel was not just an inspiration or an analogy. While the outward signs of God's covenant community had changed, the spiritual reality continued.

Backus argued that this was a fundamental misunderstanding of salvation itself. In his reading of the Bible, he saw two covenants at work. The initial covenant with biblical Israel—what Backus called the "covenant of works"—applied to one community as a birthright and was fulfilled by communal obedience. This was superseded by what Backus called the "covenant of grace," which was foreshadowed in the Old Testament but fully revealed in the life, death, and resurrection of Jesus. This second covenant community was defined by voluntary, individual belief in Christ as Savior, witnessed by adult baptism. Rather than being restricted to one people or nation, this new Israel could be found among every people, in every nation, as the gospel advanced across the world. Backus faulted his Puritan forebearers "for jumbling the constitution of the Old Testament church and the New together; whereas if we take them distinct, the limits of each are expressed very plain."

This innocuous-sounding shift in theological position was actually social and political gelignite. If the two-covenant theory was true, the claim of any human government to be the heir to Israel's status as God's chosen people was an exegetical blunder of the first order. And any religious establishment created as a result of that claim was artificial and illegitimate.

This break between the old dispensation of enforced religious conformity and the new dispensation of free religious choice ran parallel to other intellectual developments of the eighteenth century. "That Americans were ready to grasp this new outlook after 1740," argued historian William McLoughlin, "and to pursue it to its logical conclusions marks the real break with the Old World, the medieval mind, and the Puritan

ethos. The Baptist doctrine of the two covenants was the pietistic formu-
lation of the Enlightenment's rejection of the past, its willingness to cut
all traditional ties with the old order and begin anew."

This change had implications in every layer of American life:

- **The Individual:** Backus asserted the priority of personal conscience
  precisely because the stakes of religious choices are so high. Just as
  everyone will face God's final judgment as an individual, so he or she
  must embrace God's grace as an individual. A personal relationship
  with God is the result of consent, which can't be compelled by the
  state. "By the law of Christ," argued Backus, "every man is not only
  allowed but required to judge for himself concerning the circum-
  stantials as well as the essentials of religion, and to act according to
  the full persuasion of his own mind." The Awakening's elevation of
  individual religious choice implied and required the advance of civil
  liberty. "God alone is the Lord of the conscience," Backus wrote, "and
  hath left it free from the doctrines and commandments of men."

- **The Church:** In Backus's view, the Christian church should be comprised only of converted, baptized believers, who submit to religious
  leaders on religious matters. When civil authorities meddled in religious affairs—by preferring a certain sect or imposing taxes to support one denomination—the result was to dilute the purity of the
  church while disregarding individual conscience. For Enlightenment
  thinkers such as Jefferson and Madison, the disestablishment of the
  church protected the state from clerical interference. For Backus, the
  disestablishment of the church protected the church from human
  control, manipulation, and corruption.

- **The State:** According to Backus, God established two distinct forms
  of government: ecclesiastical and civil. The church—serving a kingdom not of this world—is charged with encouraging right belief and
  applying appropriate church discipline. The state is charged with
  maintaining a healthy social environment where Christianity is free
  to spread. The problem comes—as in Puritan New England—when

the two roles are combined or confused. Both Puritans and the Baptists believed that religion is essential to the good ordering of society. But Backus argued that state support of religion produced both an oppressive state and a diluted faith. The Puritans, he said, had managed "to destroy the means in order to accomplish the end!" The good social influence of the Christian church would come, in Backus's view, not through its privileged political standing, but through the overflowing benevolence of the truly converted.

Backus was careful to note that the state would still often need to act on the basis of shared morality, as when it forbids murder or theft. The Baptists wanted a nonsectarian state; they did not recommend or foresee an entirely secular state. Governing, in their view, would always be informed by basic ethical principles. And those who govern should be people of integrity. But understanding the basic, moral ground rules necessary to self-government, Backus insisted, does not require the teaching of a specific sect. Such principles are discoverable by the application of reason alone. This type of "general revelation" is available to everyone who reasons with good intention. But religious truths—truths about salvation and the nature of the church—are not discernible by unaided reason. And this type of "special revelation" is beyond the scope of the state to embrace or enforce. The role of government that Backus describes is not demoted, but it is constrained.

This was not Jefferson's high "wall of separation" between church and state. Backus had no problem with Bible reading in schoolhouses, days of public thanksgiving, and other ritual recognitions of generic Protestantism. His view was more like the original version of the metaphor by Roger Williams, who spoke of a "wall of separation between the garden of the Church and the wilderness of the world." Jefferson was concerned about breaches of the wall from the clerical side. Backus was not focused on keeping the garden out of the wilderness; he was determined to keep the wilderness out of the garden.

•    •    •

Backus's Puritan opponents saw this as the path to irreligion and social chaos. A leading Congregationalist minister, Phillips Payson, told the Connecticut legislature: "Let the restraints of religion once be broken down, as they inevitably would be by leaving the subject of public worship to the humors of the multitude, and we might well defy all human wisdom and power to support and preserve order and government of the state." Another Puritan leader, Samuel West, bluntly claimed: "If there is no law to support religion, farewell meetinghouses, farewell ministers, and farewell religion."

This pessimism about the results of pluralism—about leaving religious matters "to the humors of the multitude"—was foreign to everything Backus believed. The advance of Christ's Kingdom, he said, "does not receive its support from earthly power, but from *truth*." In Backus's mind, God is perfectly capable of building and sustaining his church without the support of the state. The title of one pamphlet Backus penned summarized his view: *Truth Is Great and Will Prevail*. Having experienced a great, transforming truth in his own life, he was disposed to trust the power of unvarnished truth in the social and religious affairs of his state and country.

What Backus did not, perhaps, take with sufficient seriousness was the effect his model would have on churches themselves. When ministers were chosen for their theological education, paid by the state, and granted an elevated social status, they had some independence from the views of their community. Congregationalist pastors could be fired after a broad and determined revolt of their congregation, as Edwards discovered. But there was usually a degree of deference to clerical opinions. The churches that resulted from the Awakening, in contrast, were dramatically more democratic. Congregations were increasingly assembled through the popularity of their preaching. And the salaries of clergy were paid by the free contributions of the church's members. While a particularly charismatic minister could hold great sway over his flock, this remained a market-oriented model of church organization. A pastor who defied the social views of his congregation—say, on an issue such as slavery—was also defying the source of his livelihood. A more democratic church is not always a more principled church.

Backus spent much of the rest of his pastoral career trying to calm and steady people who had become intoxicated by religious freedom. When the individualism inherent in pietism was combined with the weak authority of new churches and the lack of theological sophistication among many laymen, the resulting situation was religiously volatile. While Backus generally supported the democratization of religion, one of that trend's predictable outcomes was a spike in heresy. The American religious marketplace was becoming more diverse and raucous.

On his extensive travels in New England as a kind of theological troubleshooter, Backus found that a significant number of Separate Baptists were moving onward to join new religious movements. Some—believing that a benevolent God would not condemn anyone to eternal damnation—were becoming Universalists. Others were shifting away from Calvinism toward a Methodist emphasis on free will in accepting God's grace. Still others were attracted to Shakerism—a sect founded by Ann Lee that practiced celibacy, farmed communally, and worshiped through dancing and speaking in tongues. Some of Lee's followers hinted that she was the female incarnation of Christ. Backus was less impressed, dismissing her as "a common prostitute." The leaders of the Shaker movement, according to Backus, "delight themselves much in feasting and drinking spiritous liquor." Some Shakers, he added, "carried matters so far this year as for men and women to dance together entirely naked, to imitate the primitive state of perfection." After more than a century of New England Puritanism, drinking, feasting, and naked dancing must have had a certain appeal. But Backus was having none of it.

In his own life, Backus experienced both the burden and glory of his evangelical beliefs. When his daughter Sibel became ill (probably from cancer) at age twenty, he did all he could to encourage her deathbed conversion. But Sibel, in terrible pain, never seemed to find the spiritual comfort he had found at a similar age. "She had a very deep sense of sin upon her mind," Backus later wrote, "and distressing fears that she had no true conviction, because her heart was so vile and hard." When Backus asked if she thought God would accept her soul, she could only reply, "I think I do." This lack of confidence intensified her father's suffering: "I saw my dear daughter pass through the dark valley, without such a manifestation of light as I longed for, which grieved my heart." For evangelicals, the prospect of heavenly reunions after death also entailed the possibility of eternal partings.

The death of Backus's wife, Susanna, from a lingering illness, after more than fifty years of marriage, demonstrated the contrasting comforts of faith. Backus wrote in his diary: "Elder Rathbun was here on the 12th, and prayed with her, and when he asked her what she would have him pray for, she said, 'I am not so much concerned about living or dying, as to have my will swallowed up in the will of God.'" It was an elegant restatement of the Great Awakening's greatest hope: for any man or woman to be consumed by the presence and purpose of the living God.

Backus did not live to see the final overthrow of the Massachusetts religious establishment. But he did see a broad religious tolerance take root in his state. In many towns and parishes, Congregationalists ended up granting a general and permanent exemption from religious taxation to their Baptist neighbors. And Backus—noted in his later years for his "venerable countenance, his large features, his imposing wig"—was broadly revered in his old age. The town of Middleboro elected him as a delegate to the state convention that debated the federal constitution. Many of his parishioners opposed ratification, fearing that the move toward a stronger central government would threaten individual rights. Backus ended up in alliance with his traditional rivals of the Standing Order and voted for the document, choosing republican order over democratic chaos.

Around this time, Backus was sent by his Baptist association to see and encourage the progress of a fresh revival that was stirring in the South—a region that the Great Awakening had largely missed in its initial pass. Backus spent five months traveling in North Carolina and Virginia, delivered 170 sermons, and found rapidly growing and multiplying

Baptist churches in areas that "had shown but little regard to religion but a few years before." Virginia in particular had become an example and battleground of religious pluralism. The recently disestablished Church of England in Virginia was religiously stagnant and hurt by its association with British rule. (Backus described its ministers as "drunkards, card-players, and swearers.") New Light Presbyterians, led by Samuel Davies, had gained many converts in the wealthier and better-educated eastern part of the state. The Methodists, initially stigmatized by Wesley's opposition to the Revolution, were just beginning a period of remarkable growth. And the Baptists were making gains everywhere. "Before 1768," Backus reported, "there were but 5 Baptist churches [in Virginia] . . . and now they have more than a hundred churches, some of which have 5 or 600 members."

It surprised and pleased Backus that Baptist circuit riders were counting conversions in every class of Virginia society. His oft-reviled church tradition "was a much, if not the most esteemed of any religious denomination." This meant that most of the Baptists he encountered were slave owners. Some high-profile converts became convinced that their newly found faith was inconsistent with slavery. Robert Carter of Nomini Hall—one of the most prominent and politically influential men in Virginia—freed more than five hundred enslaved people. The South's most visible and radical Baptist elder, John Leland, was a supporter of abolition. But the overwhelming majority of Virginia Baptists were trying to square the new birth with the ownership of slaves. Backus attended an association meeting in Virginia where Baptists discussed the ethics of separating a husband and wife owned by different masters. The group also debated the rules when disciplining a house slave who was also a member of the master's church. Baptist slave owners were attempting to reconcile the irreconcilable. But most managed just fine.

What Backus was witnessing in the South was the start of the Second Great Awakening. The first had sprinkled America with revivalism; the second would fully immerse it, and essentially create the nation that fought the Civil War.

For Backus, another distinction came when he was offered an honorary degree from Rhode Island College in 1797. He was deeply conflicted about accepting it. Backus was concerned that Baptists were taking on airs as they became more mainstream. Some Baptist churches displayed silver candlesticks. Some preachers presided in black robes (and forced him to be enrobed when he spoke from their pulpits). Backus missed the Christian simplicity of the early days of his ministry. He was eventually persuaded by friends to accept the academic honor. But it must have come as a surprise for him to learn that, at the same ceremony, Rhode Island College was also granting an honorary degree to his old rival, John Adams.

Adams had risen to become the second president of the United States. Yet it was Backus who had clearly won the debate they engaged in at the Continental Congress. The cause of religious liberty had gained not only respectability, but a sense of inevitability. For the next two centuries, America would essentially follow Backus's model of church-state relations—with a nonsectarian government but a moralistic public square. Backus's revolt against religious taxes had failed. But the title of another of his pamphlets summarized his influence: *A Door Opened for Equal Christian Liberty and No Man Can Shut It.*

# The Appeal of Saint Dorothy

*The Washington Post*, December 9, 2012

The RECENT VOTE BY AMERICA'S CATHOLIC BISHOPS to move Dorothy Day toward canonization was controversial, but mainly among those who manufacture controversy for a living. The media have enjoyed pointing out that Day's main advocate, Cardinal Timothy Dolan, is a traditionalist, while Day was a socialist who once had an abortion. It must be something like a conservative president nominating a raging liberal to the Supreme Court, except with eternal tenure at stake.

The application of political categories to theological matters is usually a mistake. In this case, it exceeds the media's usual quota of religious ignorance.

Day, to be sure, would make for an interesting chapter in *Lives of the Saints for Children*. She began her pilgrimage as a left-wing journalist in 1920s New York, writing for journals with names like *The Masses*. Day interviewed Leon Trotsky, was friendly with John Reed, picked up pocket money by modeling nude, and drank to excess with playwright Eugene O'Neill. One boyfriend promised to leave her unless she got an abortion—and left her anyway after she did.

In Day's late twenties came the birth of a daughter and a decisive Catholic conversion, complete with rosaries, devotion to the saints, and daily Mass. Her common-law husband at the time, a militant atheist, could not abide the change and left her as well. He accused her of "absorption in the supernatural"—a pretty good description of sainthood. Day set out to serve the poor, hungry, and homeless while criticizing the "filthy, rotten system" that seemed to produce so many of them. She founded dozens of communal farms and "Houses of Hospitality," where those in need were treated as humans and guests, not merely as the masses. She also protested for workers' rights and against nuclear weapons and got arrested with the best of them. In 1980, at the age of eighty-three, Day died at a House of Hospitality in Manhattan that she shared with the indigent.

Not being a Catholic, I'm not sure how the posthumous duties of saints are assigned. But Day is qualified for an interesting range. She could be the patron saint of Greenwich Village bohemians. Or of intense, combative New Yorkers. Or of women with jackass boyfriends.

Those who are surprised that this could be the story of a saint haven't been paying much attention for, well, more than two thousand years. According to church tradition, Mary Magdalene had an interesting past. Saint Paul had the blood of saints on his hands. Saint Augustine had been the party boy of Hippo. "It is not the healthy who need a doctor," explained Jesus, "but the sick."

The most inspiring, accessible saints are not models of piety but models of grace. They provide at least a faint hope that the road to spiritual excellence might begin at any moment—even now—in our flawed and tangled lives.

Sainthood for Day—still a long procedural road—would also be a reminder that the Christian church is not defined or bounded by political ideology. The views of Day's Catholic Worker Movement resist easy categorization. Her pacifism was of the muscular variety that opposed World War II. She criticized the profit motive but also distrusted all concentrations of governmental power. Her socialism was patterned on the communal provision of the early Christian church and medieval religious orders. Day's ideology might best be called localism—a vision she described as consisting of "land, bread, work, children, and the joys of community in play and work and worship."

It is a tribute to the breadth of Catholicism that Day shared the same faith, at the same time, in the same city, with another prominent Catholic layman: William F. Buckley Jr. The church is an institution strengthened by such political contradictions—between pacifists and just-war theorists, distributionists and free marketeers, establishment figures and impatient prophets—because they serve to highlight the place of overlap. The Eucharistic altar is large—as large as politics and the world.

Above all, Saint Dorothy would be a reminder of the radical, shocking demands of human dignity. Day was gobsmacked by the notion. "The mystery of the poor," she said, "is this: that they are Jesus, and what you do for them you do for him." It may be pious overstatement. If true, however, we yawn at duties that should cause us to tremble. And those who take those duties literally and seriously are already saints.

# America Is Cursed with Tribal Morality

*The Washington Post*, November 27, 2017

AMERICA IS CURRENTLY CURSED, not only with tribal politics, but with tribal morality. Some liberals tend to minimize or excuse offenses against a few women in the broader cause of women's rights. What is a politician's wandering hand in comparison to maintaining legal abortion? Some conservatives tend to minimize or excuse offenses against women in the cause of conservative governance. What are a few old accusations compared to cementing a conservative Supreme Court or passing tax reform?

Both sides give personal failings less weight than a compelling public good. It is not always an unserious argument, but in this case, it is a cruel and dangerous one.

This description may sound like a columnist's caricature. But, on occasion, a caricature becomes incarnate. Alabama governor Kay Ivey (R) has admitted she has "no reason to disbelieve" any of Republican Senate candidate Roy Moore's accusers. Yet Ivey has announced she will vote for Moore anyway. "We need to have a Republican in the United States Senate," she explained, "to vote on the things like Supreme Court justices."

This is worth a pause. One of the accusers in this case says that in the late 1970s Moore, then a county prosecutor, offered to drive her home. Instead, she alleges, he parked behind the restaurant where she worked, touched her breasts, tried to pull off her shirt, grabbed her neck, and pushed her head toward his crotch, leaving nasty bruises and a lifetime of trauma. The victim was sixteen years old at the time. If Ivey truly believes this accusation, she is voting for someone who committed sexual assault on a teenage girl, in order to help secure one Senate vote on a prospective Supreme Court nominee.

This has the virtue, at least, of philosophic clarity. It is utilitarianism, unadorned. Ivey believes she is pursuing Jeremy Bentham's imperative, achieving the greatest good for the greatest number of people. It is a simple, easily stated moral rule.

There are many varieties of utilitarianism, but they share some weaknesses. While the principle is easy to state, it is not easy to apply. It always involves speculative judgments about the future. What if, as a senator, Moore becomes a rolling scandal of misogyny and intolerance? What if this deepens the image of the GOP as the party of prejudice and male dominance? And what if this costs Republicans control of the House of Representatives and a few other Senate seats? How would this affect Ivey's utilitarian calculation?

This scenario is not unlikely. During his recent defeat in the Virginia governor's race, Ed Gillespie—a comparatively good GOP candidate— lost female voters by 22 percentage points. Is the three-ring spectacle of Roy Moore in the Senate going to improve Republican electoral performance with women?

But the main problem with utilitarian calculation in politics reaches deeper. By definition, it means that the rights of the few can be sacrificed to the interests of the many. It is a theory that has always been plagued by hypothetical questions: What if punishing a few innocent people would, on balance, have a good social result? What if keeping a few people in slavery clearly benefited the many? What if a politician who is *currently* abusing teenagers demonstrably served a greater public good? At what point does the "but he'll vote right on Supreme Court nominees" argument end? Three rapes? Four murders? Wouldn't utilitarian calculations still apply?

In the cases before us—if you believe the credible testimony of the accusers—the rights and dignity of women have already been violated. Ignoring or playing down those violations in the pursuit of other social goals—conservative or liberal—is an additional form of victimization, this time by the broader society. By politicians such as Ivey. By voters willing to downplay the abuses on their own ideological team. All are making the statement that some lives, when weighed in the balance, really don't matter.

None of this is to make light of the difficult task of applying appropriate punishments for differing degrees of guilt. But various traditions of ethics rooted in religion—as well as the Enlightenment theories that informed America's founding—place a primary emphasis on the rights and dignity of individuals protected against the shifting interests of the majority.

This is the firm moral ground upon which our debate on sexual harassment should be conducted. Political figures guilty of coercion, exploitation, dehumanization, cruelty, and the abuse of power should not be trusted with power. Even on our own side.

PART 2

# Faith

# The Last Temptation

*The Atlantic*, April 2018

How evangelicals, once culturally confident, became an anxious minority seeking political protection from the least traditionally religious president in living memory

ONE OF THE MOST EXTRAORDINARY THINGS about our current politics—really, one of the most extraordinary developments of recent political history—is the loyal adherence of religious conservatives to Donald Trump. The president won four-fifths of the votes of white evangelical Christians. This was a higher level of support than either Ronald Reagan or George W. Bush, an outspoken evangelical himself, ever received.

Trump's background and beliefs could hardly be more incompatible with traditional Christian models of life and leadership. Trump's past political stances (he once supported the right to partial-birth abortion), his character (he has bragged about sexually assaulting women), and even his language (he introduced the words "pussy" and "shithole" into presidential discourse) would more naturally lead religious conservatives toward exorcism than alliance. This is a man who has cruelly publicized his infidelities, made disturbing sexual comments about his elder daughter, and boasted about the size of his penis on the debate stage. His lawyer reportedly arranged a $130,000 payment to a porn star to dissuade her from disclosing an alleged affair. Yet religious conservatives who once blanched at PG-13 public standards now yawn at such NC-17 maneuvers. We are a long way from *The Book of Virtues*.

Trump supporters tend to dismiss moral scruples about his behavior as squeamishness over the president's "style." But the problem is the distinctly non-Christian substance of his *values*. Trump's unapologetic materialism—his equation of financial and social success with human achievement and worth—is a negation of Christian teaching. His tribalism and hatred for "the other" stand in direct opposition to Jesus's radical ethic of neighbor love. Trump's strength-worship and contempt for "losers" smack more of Nietzsche than of Christ. *Blessed are the proud. Blessed are the ruthless. Blessed are the shameless. Blessed are those who hunger and thirst after fame.*

And yet, a credible case can be made that evangelical votes were a decisive factor in Trump's improbable victory. Trump himself certainly acts as if he believes they were. Many individuals, causes, and groups that Trump pledged to champion have been swiftly sidelined or sacrificed during Trump's brief presidency. The administration's outreach to white evangelicals, however, has been utterly consistent.

Trump-allied religious leaders have found an open door at the White House—what Richard Land, the president of the Southern Evangelical Seminary, calls "unprecedented access." In return, they have rallied behind the administration in its times of need. "Clearly, this Russian story is nonsense," explains the megachurch pastor Paula White-Cain, who is not generally known as a legal or cybersecurity expert. Pastor David Jeremiah has compared Jared Kushner and Ivanka Trump to Joseph and Mary: "It's just like God to use a young Jewish couple to help Christians." According to Jerry Falwell Jr., evangelicals have "found their dream president," which says something about the current quality of evangelical dreams.

Loyalty to Trump has involved progressively more difficult, self-abasing demands. And there appears to be no limit to what some evangelical leaders will endure. Figures such as Falwell and Franklin Graham followed Trump's lead in supporting Judge Roy Moore in the December Senate election in Alabama. These are religious leaders who have spent their entire adult lives bemoaning cultural and moral decay. Yet they publicly backed a candidate who was repeatedly accused of sexual misconduct, including with a fourteen-year-old girl.

In January, following reports that Trump had referred to Haiti and African nations as "shithole countries," Pastor Robert Jeffress came quickly to his defense. "Apart from the vocabulary attributed to him," Jeffress wrote, "President Trump is right on target in his sentiment." After reports emerged that Trump's lawyer paid hush money to the porn star Stormy Daniels to cover up their alleged sexual encounter, Graham vouched for Trump's "concern for Christian values." Tony Perkins, the president of the Family Research Council, argued that Trump should be given a "mulligan" for his past infidelity. One can only imagine the explosion of outrage if President Barack Obama had been credibly accused of similar offenses.

The moral convictions of many evangelical leaders have become a function of their partisan identification. This is not mere gullibility; it is utter corruption. Blinded by political tribalism and hatred for their political opponents, these leaders can't see how they are undermining the causes to which they once dedicated their lives. Little remains of a distinctly Christian public witness.

As the prominent evangelical pastor Tim Keller—who is not a Trump loyalist—recently wrote in the *New Yorker*, "'Evangelical' used to denote people who claimed the high moral ground; now, in popular usage, the word is nearly synonymous with 'hypocrite.'" So it is little wonder that last year the Princeton Evangelical Fellowship, an eighty-seven-year-old ministry, dropped the "E word" from its name, becoming the Princeton Christian Fellowship: Too many students had identified the term with conservative political ideology. Indeed, a number of serious evangelicals are distancing themselves from the word for similar reasons.

I find this desire understandable but not compelling. Some words, like strategic castles, are worth defending, and "evangelical" is among them. While the term is notoriously difficult to define, it certainly encompasses a "born again" religious experience, a commitment to the authority of the Bible, and an emphasis on the redemptive power of Jesus Christ.

I was raised in an evangelical home, went to an evangelical church

and high school, and began following Christ as a teen. After attending
Georgetown University for a year, I transferred to Wheaton College in
Illinois—sometimes called "the Harvard of evangelical Protestantism"—
where I studied theology. I worked at an evangelical nonprofit, Prison
Fellowship, before becoming a staffer for Senator Dan Coats of Indiana (a fellow Wheaton alum). On Capitol Hill, I found many evangelical
partners in trying to define a "compassionate conservatism." And as a
policy adviser and the chief speechwriter to President George W. Bush, I
saw how evangelical leaders such as Rick and Kay Warren could be principled, tireless advocates in the global fight against AIDS.

Those experiences make me hesitant to abandon the word "evangelical." They also make seeing the defilement of that word all the more painful. The corruption of a political party is regrettable. The corruption of
a religious tradition by politics is tragic, shaming those who participate
in it.

How did something so important and admirable become so disgraced? For many people, including myself, this question involves both
intellectual analysis and personal angst. The answer extends back some
150 years, and involves cultural and political shifts that long predate
Donald Trump. It is the story of how an influential and culturally confident religious movement became a marginalized and anxious minority
seeking political protection under the wing of a man such as Trump, the
least traditionally Christian figure—in temperament, behavior, and evident belief—to assume the presidency in living memory.

Understanding that evolution requires understanding the values that
once animated American evangelicalism. It is a movement that was dam-
aged in the fall from a great height.

My alma mater, Wheaton College, was founded by abolitionist
evangelicals in 1860 under the leadership of Jonathan Blanchard, an
emblematic figure in mid-nineteenth-century northern evangelicalism.
Blanchard was part of a generation of radical malcontents produced by
the Second Great Awakening, a religious revival that had touched millions of American lives in the first half of the nineteenth century. He was

a Presbyterian minister, a founder of several radical newspapers, and an antislavery agitator.

In the years before the Civil War, a connection between moralism and a concern for social justice was generally assumed among northern evangelicals. They variously militated for temperance, humane treatment of the mentally disabled, and prison reform. But mainly they militated for the end of slavery. Indeed, Wheaton welcomed both African-American and female students, and served as a stop on the Underground Railroad. In a history of the 39th Regiment of the Illinois Volunteer Infantry, the infantryman Ezra Cook recalled that "runaway slaves were perfectly safe in the College building, even when no attempt was made to conceal their presence."

Blanchard had explained his beliefs in an 1839 commencement address given at Oberlin College, titled "A Perfect State of Society." He preached that "every true minister of Christ is a universal reformer, whose business it is, so far as possible, to reform all the evils which press on human concerns." Elsewhere he argued that "slave-holding is not a solitary, but a social sin." He added: "I rest my opposition to slavery upon the one-bloodism of the New Testament. All men are equal, because they are of one equal blood."

During this period, evangelicalism was largely identical to mainstream Protestantism. Evangelicals varied widely in their denominational beliefs, but they uniformly agreed about the need for a personal decision to accept God's grace through faith in Christ. The evangelist Charles G. Finney, who was the president of Oberlin College from 1851 to 1866, described his conversion experience thusly: "I could feel the impression, like a wave of electricity, going through and through me. Indeed it seemed to come in waves and waves of liquid love."

In politics, evangelicals tended to identify New England, and then the whole country, with biblical Israel. Many a sermon described America as a place set apart for divine purposes. "Some nation," the evangelical minister Lyman Beecher said, "itself free, was needed, to blow the trumpet and hold up the light." (Beecher's daughter Harriet Beecher Stowe was among the founders of this magazine.) The burden of this calling was a collective responsibility to remain virtuous, in matters from ending slavery to ending Sabbath-breaking.

This was not advocacy for theocracy, and evangelical leaders were not blind to the risks of too close a relationship with worldly power. "The injudicious association of religion with politics, in the time of Cromwell," Beecher argued, "brought upon evangelical doctrine and piety, in England, an odium which has not ceased to this day." Yet few evangelicals would have denied that God's covenantal relationship with America required a higher standard of private and public morality, lest that divine blessing be forfeited.

Perhaps most important, prior to the Civil War, evangelicals were by and large postmillennialists—that is, they believed that the final millennium of human history would be a time of peace for the world and of expansion for the Christian Church, culminating in the Second Coming of Christ. As such, they were an optimistic lot who thought that human effort could help hasten the arrival of this promised era—a belief that encouraged both social activism and global missionary activity. "Evangelicals generally regarded almost any sort of progress as evidence of the advance of the kingdom," the historian George Marsden observes in *Fundamentalism and American Culture*.

In the mid-nineteenth century, evangelicalism was the predominant religious tradition in America—a faith assured of its social position, confident in its divine calling, welcoming of progress, and hopeful about the future. Fifty years later, it was losing intellectual and social ground on every front. Twenty-five years beyond that, it had become a national joke.

The horrors of the Civil War took a severe toll on the social optimism at the heart of postmillennialism. It was harder to believe in the existence of a religious golden age that included Antietam. At the same time, industrialization and urbanization loosened traditional social bonds and created an impression of moral chaos. The mass immigration of Catholics and Jews changed the face and spiritual self-conception of the country. (In 1850, Catholics made up about 5 percent of the population. By 1906, they represented 17 percent.) Evangelicals struggled to envision a diverse, and some believed degenerate, America as the chosen, godly republic of their imagination.

But it was a series of momentous intellectual developments that most effectively drove a wedge between evangelicalism and elite culture. Higher criticism of the Bible—a scholarly movement out of Germany that picked apart the human sources and development of ancient texts—called into question the roots, accuracy, and historicity of the book that constituted the ultimate source of evangelical authority. At the same time, the theory of evolution advanced a new account of human origins. Advocates of evolution, as well as those who denied it most vigorously, took the theory as an alternative to religious accounts—and in many cases to Christian belief itself.

Religious progressives sought common ground between the Christian faith and the new science and higher criticism. Many combined their faith with the Social Gospel—a postmillennialism drained of the miraculous, with social reform taking the place of the Second Coming.

Religious conservatives, by contrast, rebelled against this strategy of accommodation in a series of firings and heresy trials designed to maintain control of seminaries. (Woodrow Wilson's uncle James lost his job at Columbia Theological Seminary for accepting evolution as compatible with the Bible.) But these tactics generally backfired, and seminary after seminary, college after college, fell under the influence of modern scientific and cultural assumptions. To contest progressive ideas, the religiously orthodox published a series of books called *The Fundamentals*. Hence the term *fundamentalism*, conceived in a spirit of desperate reaction.

Fundamentalism embraced traditional religious views, but it did not propose a return to an older evangelicalism. Instead it responded to modernity in ways that cut it off from its own past. In reacting against higher criticism, it became simplistic and overliteral in its reading of scripture. In reacting against evolution, it became anti-scientific in its general orientation. In reacting against the Social Gospel, it came to regard the whole concept of social justice as a dangerous liberal idea. This last point constituted what some scholars have called the "Great Reversal," which took place from about 1900 to 1930. "All progressive social concern," Marsden writes, "whether political or private, became suspect among revivalist evangelicals and was relegated to a very minor role."

This general pessimism about the direction of society was reflected in a shift away from postmillennialism and toward *premillennialism*. In this view, the current age is tending not toward progress, but rather toward decadence and chaos under the influence of Satan. A new and better age will not be inaugurated until the Second Coming of Christ, who is the only one capable of cleaning up the mess. No amount of human effort can hasten that day, or ultimately save a doomed world. For this reason, social activism was deemed irrelevant to the most essential task: the work of preparing oneself, and helping others prepare, for final judgment.

The banishment of fundamentalism from the cultural mainstream culminated dramatically in a Tennessee courthouse in 1925. William Jennings Bryan, the most prominent Christian politician of his time, was set against Clarence Darrow and the theory of evolution at the Scopes "monkey trial," in which a Tennessee educator was tried for teaching the theory in high school. Bryan won the case but not the country. The journalist and critic H. L. Mencken provided the account accepted by history, dismissing Bryan as "a tin pot pope in the Coca-Cola belt and a brother to the forlorn pastors who belabor half-wits in galvanized iron tabernacles behind the railroad yards." Fundamentalists became comic figures, subject to world-class condescension.

It has largely slipped the mind of history that Bryan was a peace activist as secretary of state under Woodrow Wilson and that his politics foreshadowed the New Deal. And Mencken was eventually revealed as a racist, an anti-Semite, and a eugenics advocate. In the fundamentalist–modernist controversy, there was only one winner. "In the course of roughly thirty-five years," the sociologist James Davison Hunter observes in *American Evangelicalism*, "Protestantism had moved from a position of cultural dominance to a position of cognitive marginality and political impotence." Activism and optimism were replaced by the festering resentment of status lost.

The fundamentalists were not passive in their exile. They created a web of institutions—radio stations, religious schools, outreach ministries—that eventually constituted a healthy subculture. The country, meanwhile, was becoming less secular and more welcoming of religious influence. (In 1920, church membership in the United States was 43 percent. By 1960, it was 63 percent.) A number of leaders, including the theologian Carl Henry and the evangelist Billy Graham (the father of Franklin Graham), bridled at fundamentalist irrelevance. Henry's book *The Uneasy Conscience of Modern Fundamentalism* was influential in urging greater cultural and intellectual engagement. This reemergence found its fullest expression in Graham, who left the fundamentalist ghetto, hobnobbed with presidents, and presented to the public a more appealing version of evangelicalism—a term that was deliberately employed as a contrast to the older, narrower fundamentalism.

Not everyone was impressed. When Graham planned mass evangelistic meetings in New York City in 1957, the theologian Reinhold Niebuhr editorialized against his "petty moralizing." But Niebuhr's attack on Graham provoked significant backlash, even in liberal theological circles. During a sixteen-week "crusade" that played to packed houses, Graham was joined one night at Madison Square Garden by none other than Martin Luther King Jr.

Over time, evangelicalism got a revenge of sorts in its historical rivalry with liberal Christianity. Adherents of the latter gradually found better things to do with their Sundays than attend progressive services. In 1972, nearly 28 percent of the population belonged to mainline-Protestant churches. That figure is now well below 15 percent. Over those four decades, however, evangelicals held steady at roughly 25 percent of the public (though this share has recently declined). As its old theological rival faded—or, more accurately, collapsed—evangelical endurance felt a lot like momentum.

With the return of this greater institutional self-confidence, evangelicals might have expected to play a larger role in determining cultural norms and standards. But their hopes ran smack into the sexual revolution, along with other rapid social changes. The Moral Majority appeared at about the same time that the actual majority was more and more comfortable with divorce and couples living together out of wedlock. Evangelicals experienced the power of growing numbers and healthy subcultural institutions even as elite institutions—from universities to courts to Hollywood—were decisively rejecting traditional ideals.

As a result, the primary evangelical political narrative is adversarial, an angry tale about the aggression of evangelicalism's cultural rivals. In a remarkably free country, many evangelicals view their rights as fragile, their institutions as threatened, and their dignity as assailed. The single largest religious demographic in the United States—representing about half the Republican political coalition—sees itself as a besieged and disrespected minority. In this way, evangelicals have become simultaneously more engaged and more alienated.

The overall political disposition of evangelical politics has remained decidedly conservative, and also decidedly reactive. After shamefully sitting out (or even opposing) the civil rights movement, white evangelicals became activated on a limited range of issues. They defended Christian schools against regulation during Jimmy Carter's administration. They fought against Supreme Court decisions that put tight restrictions on school prayer and removed many state limits on abortion. The sociologist Nathan Glazer describes such efforts as a "defensive offensive"—a kind of morally indignant pushback against a modern world that, in evangelicals' view, had grown hostile and oppressive.

This attitude was happily exploited by the modern GOP. Evangelicals who were alienated by the pro-choice secularism of Democratic presidential nominees were effectively courted to join the Reagan coalition. "I know that you can't endorse me," Reagan told an evangelical conference in 1980, "but I only brought that up because I want you to know that I endorse you." In contrast, during his presidential run four years later,

Walter Mondale warned of "radical preachers," and his running mate, Geraldine Ferraro, denounced the "extremists who control the Republican Party." By attacking evangelicals, the Democratic Party left them with a relatively easy partisan choice.

The leaders who had emerged within evangelicalism varied significantly in tone and approach. Billy Graham was the uncritical priest to the powerful. (His inclination to please was memorialized on one of the Nixon tapes, in comments enabling the president's anti-Semitism.) James Dobson, the founder of Focus on the Family, was the prickly prophet, constantly threatening to bolt from the Republican coalition unless social-conservative purity was maintained. Jerry Falwell Sr. and Pat Robertson (the latter of whom ran for president himself in 1988) tried to be political kingmakers. And, following his dramatic conversion, Chuck Colson, of Watergate infamy, founded Prison Fellowship in an attempt to revive some of the old abolitionist spirit as an advocate of prison reform. Yet much of this variety was blurred in the public mind, with *religious right* used as a catchall epithet.

Where did this history leave evangelicals' political involvement?

For a start, modern evangelicalism has an important intellectual piece missing. It lacks a model or ideal of political engagement—an organizing theory of social action. Over the same century from Blanchard to Falwell, Catholics developed a coherent, comprehensive tradition of social and political reflection. Catholic social thought includes a commitment to solidarity, whereby justice in a society is measured by the treatment of its weakest and most vulnerable members. And it incorporates the principle of subsidiarity—the idea that human needs are best met by small and local institutions (though higher-order institutions have a moral responsibility to intervene when local ones fail).

In practice, this acts as an "if, then" requirement for Catholics, splendidly complicating their politics: If you want to call yourself pro-life on abortion, then you have to oppose the dehumanization of migrants. If you criticize the devaluation of life by euthanasia, then you must criticize the devaluation of life by racism. If you want to be regarded as pro-family, then you have to support access to health care. And vice versa. The doctrinal whole requires a broad, consistent view of justice, which—when it is faithfully applied—cuts across the categories and clichés of American politics. Of course, American Catholics routinely ignore Catholic social thought. But at least they have it. Evangelicals lack a similar tradition of their own to disregard.

So where do evangelicals get their theory of social engagement? It is cheating to say (as most evangelicals probably would) "the Bible." The Christian Bible, after all, can be a vexing document: At various points, it offers approving accounts of genocide and recommends the stoning of insubordinate children. Some interpretive theory must elevate the Golden Rule above Iron Age ethics and apply that higher ideal to the tragic compromises of public life. Lacking an equivalent to Catholic social thought, many evangelicals seem to find their theory merely by following the contours of the political movement that is currently defending, and exploiting, them. The voter guides of religious conservatives have often been suspiciously similar to the political priorities of movement conservatism. Fox News and talk radio are vastly greater influences on evangelicals' political identity than formal statements by religious denominations or from the National Association of Evangelicals. In this Christian political movement, Christian theology is emphatically not the primary motivating factor.

The evangelical political agenda, moreover, has been narrowed by its supremely reactive nature. Rather than choosing their own agendas, evangelicals have been pulled into a series of social and political debates started by others. Why the asinine issue of spiritually barren prayer in public schools? Because of Justice Hugo Black's 1962 opinion rendering it unconstitutional. Why such an effort-wasting emphasis on a constitutional amendment to end abortion, which will never pass? Because in 1973 Justice Harry Blackmun located the right to abortion in the constitutional penumbra. Why the current emphasis on religious liberty? Because the 2015 *Obergefell v. Hodges* decision legalizing same-sex marriage has raised fears of coercion.

It is not that secularization, abortion, and religious liberty are trivial issues; they are extremely important. But the timing and emphasis of evangelical responses have contributed to a broad sense that evangelical political engagement is negative, censorious, and oppositional. This funneled focus has also created the damaging impression that Christians are obsessed with sex. Much of the secular public hears from Christians only on issues of sexuality—from contraceptive mandates to gay rights to transgender bathroom usage. And while religious people do believe that sexual ethics are important, the nature of contemporary religious engagement creates a misimpression about just how important they are relative to other crucial issues.

The upside potential of evangelical social engagement was illustrated by an important, but largely overlooked, initiative that I witnessed while working at the White House. The President's Emergency Plan for AIDS Relief (PEPFAR)—the largest initiative by a nation in history to fight a single disease—emerged in part from a sense of moral obligation informed by George W. Bush's evangelical faith. In explaining and defending the program, Bush made constant reference to Luke 12:48: "To whom much is given, much is required." PEPFAR also owes its existence to a strange-bedfellows political alliance of liberal global-health advocates and evangelical leaders, who had particular standing and sway with Republican members of Congress. Rather than being a response to secular aggression, this form of evangelical social engagement was the reaction to a massive humanitarian need and displayed a this-worldly emphasis on social justice that helped save millions of lives.

This achievement is now given little attention by secular liberals or religious conservatives. In the Trump era, evangelical leaders have seldom brought this type of issue to the policy front burner—though some have tried with criminal-justice reform and the fight against modern slavery. Individual Christians and evangelical ministries fight preventable disease, resettle refugees, treat addiction, run homeless shelters, and care for foster children. But such concerns find limited collective political expression.

Part of the reason such matters are not higher on the evangelical agenda is surely the relative ethnic and racial insularity of many white evangelicals. Plenty of African Americans hold evangelical theological views, of course, along with a growing number of Latinos. Yet evangelical churches, like other churches and houses of worship, tend to be segregated on Sunday. Nearly all denominations with large numbers of evangelicals are less racially diverse than the country overall.

Compare this with the Catholic Church, which is more than one-third Hispanic. This has naturally stretched the priorities of Catholicism to include the needs and rights of recent immigrants. In many evangelical communities, those needs remain distant and theoretical (though successful evangelical churches in urban areas are now experiencing the same diversity and broadening of social concern). Or consider the contrasting voting behaviors of white and African-American evangelicals in last year's Senate race in Alabama. According to exit polls, 80 percent of white evangelicals voted for Roy Moore, while 95 percent of black evangelicals supported his Democratic opponent, Doug Jones. The two groups inhabit two entirely different political worlds.

Evangelicals also have a consistent problem with their public voice, which can be off-puttingly apocalyptic. "We are on the verge of losing" America, proclaims the evangelical writer and radio host Eric Metaxas, "as we could have lost it in the Civil War." Franklin Graham declares, a little too vividly, that the country "has taken a nosedive off of the moral diving board into the cesspool of humanity." Such hyperbole may be only a rhetorical strategy, employing the apocalypse for emphasis. But the attribution of depravity and decline to America also reflects a consistent and (so far) disappointed belief that the Second Coming may be just around history's corner.

The difficulty with this approach to public life—other than its insanely pessimistic depiction of our flawed but wonderful country—is that it trivializes and undercuts the entire political enterprise. Politics in a democracy is essentially anti-apocalyptic, premised on the idea that an active citizenry is capable of improving the nation. But if we're already mere minutes from the midnight hour, then what is the point? The normal avenues of political reform are useless. No amount of negotiation or compromise is going to matter much compared with the Second Coming.

Moreover, in making their case on cultural decay and decline, evangelicals have, in some highly visible cases, chosen the wrong nightmares. Most notable, they made a crucial error in picking evolution as a main point of contention with modernity. "The contest between evolution and Christianity is a duel to the death," William Jennings Bryan argued. "If evolution wins . . . Christianity goes—not suddenly, of course, but gradually, for the two cannot stand together." Many people of his background believed this. But their resistance was futile, for one incontrovertible reason: Evolution is a fact. It is objectively true based on overwhelming evidence. By denying this, evangelicals made their entire view of reality suspect. They were insisting, in effect, that the Christian faith requires a flight from reason.

This was foolish and unnecessary. There is no meaningful theological difference between creation by divine intervention and creation by natural selection; both are consistent with belief in a purposeful universe, and with serious interpretation of biblical texts. Evangelicals have placed an entirely superfluous stumbling block before their neighbors and children, encouraging every young person who loves science to reject Christianity.

What if Bryan and others of his generation had chosen to object to eugenics rather than evolution, to social Darwinism rather than Darwinism? The textbook at issue in the Scopes case, after all, was titled *A Civic Biology*, and it urged sterilization for the mentally impaired. "Epilepsy, and feeble-mindedness," the text read, "are handicaps which it is not only unfair but criminal to hand down to posterity." What if this had been the focus of Bryan's objection? Mencken doubtless would still have mocked. But the moral and theological priorities of evangelical Christianity would have turned out differently. And evangelical fears would have been eventually justified by America's shameful history of eugenics, and by the more rigorous application of the practice abroad. Instead,

Bryan chose evolution—and in the end, the cause of human dignity was not served by the obscuring of human origins.

The consequences, especially for younger generations, are considerable. According to a recent survey by Barna, a Christian research firm, more than half of churchgoing Christian teens believe that "the church seems to reject much of what science tells us about the world." This may be one reason that, in America, the youngest age cohorts are the least religiously affiliated, which will change the nation's baseline of religiosity over time. More than a third of millennials say they are unaffiliated with any faith, up 10 points since 2007. Count this as an ironic achievement of religious conservatives: an overall decline in identification with religion itself.

By the turn of the millennium, many, including myself, were convinced that religious conservatism was fading as a political force. Its outsize leaders were aging and passing. Its institutions seemed to be declining in profile and influence. Bush's 2000 campaign attempted to appeal to religious voters on a new basis. "Compassionate conservatism" was designed to be a policy application of Catholic social thought—an attempt to serve the poor, homeless, and addicted by catalyzing the work of private and religious nonprofits. The effort was sincere but eventually undermined by congressional Republican resistance and eclipsed by global crisis. Still, I believed that the old evangelical model of social engagement was exhausted, and that something more positive and principled was in the offing.

I was wrong. In fact, evangelicals would prove highly vulnerable to a message of resentful, declinist populism. Donald Trump could almost have been echoing the apocalyptic warnings of Metaxas and Graham when he declared, "Our country's going to hell." Or: "We haven't seen anything like this, the carnage all over the world." Given Trump's general level of religious knowledge, he likely had no idea that he was adapting premillennialism to populism. But when the candidate talked of an America in decline and headed toward destruction, which could be returned to greatness only by recovering the certainties of the past, he was strumming resonant chords of evangelical conviction.

Trump consistently depicts evangelicals as they depict themselves: a mistreated minority, in need of a defender who plays by worldly rules. Christianity is "under siege," Trump told a Liberty University audience. "Relish the opportunity to be an outsider," he added at a later date. "Embrace the label." Protecting Christianity, Trump essentially argues, is a job for a bully.

It is true that insofar as Christian hospitals or colleges have their religious liberty threatened by hostile litigation or government agencies, they have every right to defend their institutional identities—to advocate for a principled pluralism. But this is different from evangelicals regarding themselves, hysterically and with self-pity, as an oppressed minority that requires a strongman to rescue it. This is how Trump has invited evangelicals to view themselves. He has treated evangelicalism as an interest group in need of protection and preferences.

A prominent company of evangelical leaders—including Dobson, Falwell, Graham, Jeffress, Metaxas, Perkins, and Ralph Reed—has embraced this self-conception. Their justification is often bluntly utilitarian: All of Trump's flaws are worth his conservative judicial appointments and more-favorable treatment of Christians by the government. But they have gone much further than grudging, prudential calculation. They have basked in access to power and provided character references in the midst of scandal. Graham castigated the critics of Trump's response to the violence during a white supremacist rally in Charlottesville, Virginia ("Shame on the politicians who are trying to push blame on @POTUS"). Dobson has pronounced Trump a "baby Christian"—a political use of grace that borders on blasphemy. "Complaining about the temperament of the @POTUS or saying his behavior is not presidential is no longer relevant," Falwell tweeted. "[Donald Trump] has single-handedly changed the definition of what behavior is 'presidential' from phony, failed & rehearsed to authentic, successful & down to earth."

It is remarkable to hear religious leaders defend profanity, ridicule, and cruelty as hallmarks of authenticity and dismiss decency as a dead language. Whatever Trump's policy legacy ends up being, his presidency has been a disaster in the realm of norms. It has coarsened our culture, given permission for bullying, complicated the moral formation of children, undermined standards of public integrity, and encouraged cynicism about the political enterprise. Falwell, Graham, and others are providing religious cover for moral squalor—winking at trashy behavior and encouraging the unraveling of social restraints. Instead of defending their convictions, they are providing preemptive absolution for their political favorites. And this, even by purely political standards, undermines the causes they embrace. Turning a blind eye to the exploitation of women certainly doesn't help in making pro-life arguments. It materially undermines the movement, which must ultimately change not only the composition of the courts but the views of the public. Having given politics pride of place, these evangelical leaders have ceased to be moral leaders in any meaningful sense.

But setting matters of decency aside, evangelicals are risking their faith's reputation on matters of race. Trump has, after all, attributed Kenyan citizenship to Obama, stereotyped Mexican migrants as murderers and rapists, claimed unfair treatment in federal court based on a judge's Mexican heritage, attempted an unconstitutional Muslim ban, equivocated on the Charlottesville protests, claimed (according to the *New York Times*) that Nigerians would never "go back to their huts" after seeing America, and dismissed Haitian and African immigrants as undesirable compared with Norwegians.

For some of Trump's political allies, racist language and arguments are part of his appeal. For evangelical leaders, they should be sources of anguish. Given America's history of slavery and segregation, racial prejudice is a special category of moral wrong. Fighting racism galvanized the religious conscience of nineteenth-century evangelicals and twentieth-century African-American civil rights activists. Perpetuating racism indicted many white Christians in the South and elsewhere as hypocrites. Americans who are wrong on this issue do not understand the nature of their country. Christians who are wrong on this issue do not understand the most basic requirements of their faith.

Here is the uncomfortable reality: I do not believe that most evangelicals are racist. But every strong Trump supporter has decided that racism is not a moral disqualification in the president of the United States. And that is something more than a political compromise. It is a revelation of moral priorities.

If utilitarian calculations are to be applied, they need to be fully applied. For a package of political benefits, these evangelical leaders have associated the Christian faith with racism and nativism. They have associated the Christian faith with misogyny and the mocking of the disabled. They have associated the Christian faith with lawlessness, corruption, and routine deception. They have associated the Christian faith with moral confusion about the surpassing evils of white supremacy and neo-Nazism. The world is full of tragic choices and compromises. But for *this* man? For *this* cause?

Some evangelical leaders, it is worth affirming, are providing alternative models of social engagement. Consider Tim Keller, who is perhaps the most influential advocate of a more politically and demographically diverse evangelicalism. Or Russell Moore, the president of the Ethics and Religious Liberty Commission of the Southern Baptist Convention, who demonstrates how moral conservatism can be both principled and inclusive. Or Gary Haugen, the founder of the International Justice Mission, who is one of the world's leading activists against modern slavery. Or Bishop Claude Alexander of the Park Church in North Carolina, who has been a strong voice for reconciliation and mercy. Or Francis Collins, the director of the National Institutes of Health, who shows the deep compatibility of authentic faith and authentic science. Or the influential Bible teacher Beth Moore, who has warned of the damage done "when we sell our souls to buy our wins." Or the writer Peter Wehner, who has ceased to describe himself as an evangelical even as he exemplifies the very best of the word.

Evangelicalism is hardly a monolithic movement. All of the above leaders would attest that a significant generational shift is occurring: Younger evangelicals are less prone to political divisiveness and bitterness and more concerned with social justice. (In a poll last summer, nearly half of white evangelicals born since 1964 expressed support for gay marriage.) Evangelicals remain essential to political coalitions advocating prison reform and supporting American global-health initiatives, particularly on AIDS and malaria. They do good work in the world through relief organizations such as World Vision and Samaritan's Purse (an admirable relief organization of which Franklin Graham is the president and CEO). They perform countless acts of love and compassion that make local communities more just and generous.

All of this is arguably a strong foundation for evangelical recovery. But it would be a mistake to regard the problem as limited to a few irresponsible leaders. Those leaders represent a clear majority of the movement, which remains the most loyal element of the Trump coalition. Evangelicals are broadly eager to act as Trump's shield and sword. They are his army of enablers.

It is the strangest story: how so many evangelicals lost their interest in decency, and how a religious tradition called by grace became defined by resentment. This is bad for America, because religion, properly viewed and applied, is essential to the country's public life. The old "one-bloodism" of Christian anthropology—the belief in the intrinsic and equal value of all human lives—has driven centuries of compassionate service and social reform. Religion can be the carrier of conscience. It can motivate sacrifice for the common good. It can reinforce the nobility of the political enterprise. It can combat dehumanization and elevate the goals and ideals of public life.

Democracy is not merely a set of procedures. It has a moral structure. The values we celebrate or stigmatize eventually influence the character of our people and polity. Democracy does not insist on perfect virtue from its leaders. But there is a set of values that lends authority to power: empathy, honesty, integrity, and self-restraint. And the legitimation of cruelty, prejudice, falsehood, and corruption is the kind of thing, one would think, that religious people were born to oppose, not bless. This disfigurement of evangelical faith squanders the reputation of something valuable: not just the vision of human dignity that captured Blanchard, but also Finney's electric waves of grace. At its best, faith is the overflow of gratitude, the attempt to live as if we are loved, the fragile hope for something better on the other side of pain and death. And this feather of grace weighs more in the balance than any political gain.

It is difficult to see something you so deeply value discredited so comprehensively. Evangelical faith has shaped my life, as it has the lives of millions. Evangelical history has provided me with models of conscience. Evangelical institutions have given me gifts of learning and purpose. Evangelical friends have shared my joys and sorrows. And now the very word is brought into needless disrepute.

This is the result when Christians become one interest group among many, scrambling for benefits at the expense of others rather than seeking the welfare of the whole. Christianity is love of neighbor, or it has lost its way. And this sets an urgent task for evangelicals: to rescue their faith from its worst leaders.

# Trump Should Fill Christians with Rage. How Come He Doesn't?

*The Washington Post*, September 1, 2022

IN MANY AMERICAN PLACES ON a pleasant Sunday afternoon it is possible, as I recently did, to have coffee in the city at a bohemian cafe draped with rainbow banners, then to drive thirty or forty-five minutes into the country to find small towns where Confederate and Trump flags are flown. The United States sometimes feels like two nations, divided by adornments defiantly affirming their political and cultural affinities.

Much of cosmopolitan America holds to a progressive framework of bodily autonomy, boundless tolerance, and group rights—a largely post-religious morality applied with near-religious intensity. But as a religious person (on my better days), what concerns me are the perverse and dangerous liberties many believers have taken with their own faith. Much of what considers itself Christian America has assumed the symbols and identity of white authoritarian populism—an alliance that is a serious, unfolding threat to liberal democracy.

From one perspective, the Christian embrace of populist politics is understandable. The disorienting flux of American ethical norms and the condescension of progressive elites have incited a defensive reaction among many conservative religious people—a belief that they are outsiders in their own land. They feel reviled for opposing gender ideology that seems to have arrived just yesterday, or for stating views on marriage that Barack Obama once held. They fear their values are under assault by an inexorable modernity, in the form of government, big business, media, and academia.

Leaders in the Republican Party have fed, justified, and exploited conservative Christians' defensiveness in service to an aggressive, reactionary politics. This has included deadly mask and vaccine resistance, the discrediting of fair elections, baseless accusations of gay "grooming" in schools, the silencing of teaching about the United States' history of racism, and (for some) a patently false belief that Godless conspiracies have taken hold of political institutions.

Some religious leaders have fueled the urgency of this agenda with apocalyptic rhetoric, in which the Christian church is under Neronian persecution by elites displaying Caligulan values. But the credibility of religious conservatives is undermined by the friends they have chosen to keep. Their political alignment with MAGA activists has given exposure and greater legitimacy to once-fringe ideas, including Confederate nostalgia, white nationalism, anti-Semitism, replacement theory, and QAnon accusations of satanic child sacrifice by liberal politicians.

Surveying the transgressive malevolence of the radical right, one is forced to conclude: If this is not moral ruin, then there are no moral rules.

The division between progressive and reactionary America does not fall neatly along the urban-rural divide. There are conservative megachurches in liberal strongholds, and Democratic-leaning minority groups in parts of rural America. But the electoral facts reveal a cultural conflict worsened by geographic sorting.

For decades, population density has been increasingly associated with partisan identification—the more dense, the more Democratic; the less dense, the more Republican. America might be united by its highways, but it is politically split along its beltways. Islands of urban, liberal blue dot a vast sea of rural, conservative red. And because the mechanisms that produce U.S. senators and electoral college electors skew in favor of geography over population, rural and small-town America starts with a distinct political advantage—the ability to transform fewer votes into better outcomes.

All this leaves portions of the nation boiling with righteous resentment. Many progressives feel cheated by a political system rigged by the founders against them. Many religious conservatives feel despised by the broader culture and in need of political protection. In the United States, grievance is structural and is becoming supreme.

Anxious evangelicals have taken to voting for right-wing authoritarians who promise to fight their fights—not only Donald Trump, but increasingly, his many imitators. It has been said that when you choose your community, you choose your character. Strangely, evangelicals have broadly chosen the company of Trump supporters who deny any role for character in politics and define any useful villainy as virtue. In the place of integrity, the Trump movement has elevated a warped kind of authenticity—the authenticity of unfiltered abuse, imperious ignorance, untamed egotism, and reflexive bigotry.

This is inconsistent with Christianity by any orthodox measure. Yet the discontent, prejudices, and delusions of religious conservatives helped swell the populist wave that lapped up on the steps of the Capitol on January 6, 2021. During that assault, Christian banners mixed with the iconography of white supremacy, in a manner that should have choked Christian participants with rage. But it didn't.

Conservative Christians' beliefs on the nature of politics, and the content of their cultural nightmares, are directly relevant to the future of our whole society, for a simple reason: The destinies of rural and urban America are inextricably connected. It matters greatly if evangelicals in the wide, scarlet spaces are desensitized to extremism, diminished in decency, and badly distorting the meaning of Christianity itself—as I believe many are.

To grasp how, and why, it's important to begin at the beginning.

History can be a strange and foreign place to visit. But Palestine in the first century AD, when Jesus gathered his movement, holds a mirror to our times: It was a period of social unrest in which relatively minor provocations could lead to mass protests and violence—and when Christianity (initially the Jesus movement within Judaism) was founded as a revolt against the elites.

The Holy Land was riven by a culture war. On one side were Greek cultural imperialism and Rome's brutal occupation. On the other was a Jewish people committed to preserving their identity but divided between accommodation and violent resistance. Conflict often played out along an urban-rural divide. Cities were relatively cosmopolitan. The countryside was religiously conservative. And it was from the latter—the Galilean cultural backwater—that Jesus emerged.

Residents of Galilee, who spoke their native Aramaic with a distinct accent, were sometimes dismissed as hicks. More sophisticated Jews thought them ignorant of the Torah. But Galileans were highly religious and respectful of the Temple cult in Jerusalem. Most were peasants who engaged in agriculture and fishing and lived in small villages. Jesus's hometown, Nazareth, probably counted four hundred residents. When the future disciple Bartholomew first heard about Jesus, his response was revealingly dismissive: "Can anything good come out of Nazareth?"

The lower classes in Galilee, according to recent studies, were routinely exploited by the wealthy, creating an undercurrent of economic discontent. The people resented the tribute paid to Rome, the Jewish officials paid to collect it, and the whole idea of being dominated and defiled by a pagan power.

Roman officials, as elites are wont to do, fed these resentments by arrogantly, or stupidly, violating local and religious customs. Pontius Pilate, the Roman prefect of Judea—whom we know from the criminal sentencing of Jesus—brought military standards decorated with images of the Roman emperor into Jerusalem in the dead of night, inciting a throng of offended Jewish protesters to bare their necks for execution rather than live to see such sacrilege. Pilate also stole money from the treasury of the Jerusalem Temple to build an aqueduct—and dispersed an angry, unarmed crowd with bloody blows.

Full-scale, armed rebellion by the Jewish people was still decades away. And during this period, the rule of Rome's proxy in Galilee, Herod Antipas, was relatively benign. Yet before and after Jesus, a line of holy men and malcontents gathered supporters to challenge Roman control.

They usually got quashed by marching legions. But most Jews lived in aching longing for Israel's national restoration, brought about by a revolutionary leader or a messianic king.

Put another way: People were primed for a militant, populist uprising to take back the Holy Land for God. This was the milieu entered by Jesus, in about AD 28.

Jesus did not spend any time (according to the records we have) spreading his message in the Romanized cities. This might have reflected a desire to avoid immediate conflict with Roman authorities and their Jewish proxies—the kind of clash that cost Jesus's prophetic predecessor John the Baptist his head. Yet Jesus also preached in the countryside because it was where He received his most enthusiastic reception. Rather than cultivating connections to the wealthy, He sought the company of people of low social status. And they appreciated it.

In the present day, the frightening fervor of our politics makes it resemble, and sometimes supplant, the role of religion. And a good portion of Americans have a fatal attraction to the oddest of political messiahs—one whose deception, brutality, lawlessness, and bullying were rewarded with the presidency. But so it is, to some extent, with *all* political messiahs who make their gains by imposing losses on others and measure their influence in increments of domination.

Jesus consciously and constantly rejected this view of power. While accepting the title "Messiah," He sought to transform its meaning. He gathered no army. He skillfully avoided a political confrontation with Rome. He said little about history's inevitably decomposing dynasties. He declared instead a struggle of the human heart—and a populist uprising, not in the sense of modern politics, but against established religious authorities.

His rhetorical sparring partners were often the Pharisees, who sometimes don't get a fair shake in the Gospels. They were part of a lay movement teaching that the piety and purity expected of priests should apply to the whole Jewish people. According to the Gospels, they occasionally invited Jesus to their homes for an evening of dinner and debate. One gets the impression that Jesus argued so adamantly with them because they had so many convictions in common: They shared beliefs in the importance of the Torah, in outreach to average people, and in the eventual resurrection of the dead. But it was Jesus's reinterpretation of these commitments that eventually (many years later) split Christianity from Judaism.

Jesus tested the boundaries of his faith. He intensified the moral demands of Jewish law by teaching that God expected the full transformation of *inner* motives. At the same time, He de-emphasized the ritual distinctives of the law, including Sabbath observance and dietary restrictions. "The Sabbath was made for man," He said, "not man for the Sabbath." And: "A man is not defiled by what enters his mouth, but by what comes out of it."

Jesus was an observant Jew, but one who redirected the meaning of observance. Rather than emphasizing the elements of his faith that set God's people apart from other nations, He focused on the elements of Judaism with universal application: to love God, to love one's neighbor, to love enemies and strangers. These themes were previewed by Hebrew prophets such as Isaiah; Jesus pressed them further. This was not the abandonment of Israel's God, but an unmediated, intimate way to understand and approach Him—one that circumvented the Temple and its burnt offerings.

This earned Jesus the enmity of the religious establishment and the Roman administration, both of which feared the social and political dislocation that often accompanies religious reform. It was enough to secure for Jesus a shameful execution in the company of thieves. But the inclusive faith He taught went on to resonate with people throughout the centuries and across the globe.

The ethos of the Jesus movement was anti-elitist. But it is the substance of its critique that mattered (and still matters) most:

- **Jesus preached against religious hypocrisy**—the public display of piety that hides inner corruption and imposes a merciless virtue on others. The Pharisees, at one point, were subjected to seven "woes" by Jesus, in the spirit of this one: "Woe to you, scribes and Pharisees, hypocrites! For you tithe mint and dill and cumin, and have neglected the weightier matters of the law: justice and mercy and faithfulness." The idea was not only that religious figures should practice what they preach. It was that religious observance could divert them from God's true priorities, convincing them they were righteous even when they missed the main points of their faith.

- **Jesus welcomed social outcasts whom polite society rejected**—people with leprosy, prostitutes, the mentally disabled, tax collectors, and those in the catchall category of "sinners." He elevated the status of women, who traveled with Him throughout Galilee. And He commended religious and ethnic outsiders—Romans, Samaritans, Canaanites—who displayed genuine faith. In one of his vivid parables, the town's most "respectable" people are invited to a wedding feast. When they beg off en masse, the host fills the banquet hall with "the poor, the crippled, the lame, and the blind"—a dramatic, even offensive, inversion of social status. The insiders were locked out. The outsiders joined the party. This was the announcement not only of a new age but of a new order, in which the last shall be first. And the reverse.

- **Most important, Jesus proclaimed the arrival of a kingdom**—the Kingdom of God—demanding first loyalty in the lives of believers. The word "kingdom" led to immediate misunderstandings, even among Jesus's closest followers, who expected a messianic kingdom that would liberate the Holy Land. The disciples even argued over who among them would be given greatest precedence in this earthly realm, provoking a firm rebuke from Jesus: "Whoever wishes to become great among you must be your servant." Like other Jews, Jesus believed in a future age in which God's sovereignty would be directly exercised on earth. But He came to believe that his life and ministry had inaugurated this kingdom in an entirely novel way.

Jesus rejected the role of a political messiah. In the present age, He insisted, the Kingdom of God would not be the product of Jewish nationalism. It would not arrive through militancy and violence, tactics that would contribute only to a cycle of suffering. Instead, God's kingdom would grow silently, soul by soul, "among you" and "within you," across every barrier of nation or race—in acts of justice, peacemaking, love, inclusion, meekness, humility, and gentleness.

When we act according to this counterintuitive conception of influence, a greater power achieves its aims through our seemingly aimless lives. But such a countercultural path, Jesus warned his followers, might lead to persecution or even death. And this was the path Jesus took as He walked, step by step, toward Jerusalem and the cross.

What brought me to consider these historical matters is a disturbing realization: In both public perception and evident reality, many white, conservative Christians find themselves on the wrong side of the most cutting indictments delivered by Jesus of Nazareth.

Christ's revolt against the elites could hardly be more different from the one we see today. Conservative evangelicalism has, in many ways, become the kind of religious tradition against which followers of Jesus were initially called to rebel. And because of the pivotal role of conservative Christians in our politics, this irony is a matter of urgency.

Having known evangelicals who live lives of moral integrity and serve others across lines of race and class, I have no intention of pronouncing an indiscriminate indictment. But all conservative Christians must take seriously a sobering development in America's common life. Many who identify with Jesus most loudly and publicly are doing the most to discredit his cause. The main danger to conservative churches does not come from bad laws—it comes from Christians who don't understand the distinctives, the demands, and the ultimate appeal of their own faith.

This development deserves some woes of its own:

- **Woe to evangelical hypocrisy.** Given the evidence of sexual abuse in the Southern Baptist Convention, the corruption and sexual scandal at Liberty University, the sex scandal in the Hillsong ministry, the sexual exploitation revealed in Ravi Zacharias's ministry, and the years of sexual predation at the (Christian) Kanakuk summer camps, Americans increasingly identify the word "evangelical" with pretense, scandal, and duplicity. In the case of the SBC, victims (mostly women) were ignored, intimidated, dismissed, and demeaned. Many of the most powerful Southern Baptist leaders betrayed the powerless, added cruelty on top of suffering, and justified their cover-up as essential to Christian evangelism. How can hearts ostensibly transformed by Christ be so impervious to mercy?

- **Woe to evangelical exclusion.** In their overwhelming, uncritical support of Trump and other nationalist Republicans—leaders who could never win elections without evangelical votes—white religious conservatives have joined a political movement defined by an attitude of "us" vs. "them," and dedicated to the rejection and humiliation of social outsiders and outcasts. From the start, the Trump-led GOP dehumanized migrants as diseased and violent. It attacked Muslims as suspect and dangerous. Even when evangelical Christians refuse to mouth the words of racism, they have allied themselves with the promoters of prejudice and white grievance. How can it be that believers called to radical inclusion are the most hostile to refugees of any group in the United States? How can anyone who serves God's boundless kingdom of love and generosity ever rally to the political banner "America First"?

- **And woe, therefore, to Christian nationalism.** Evangelicals broadly confuse the Kingdom of God with a Christian America, preserved by thuggish politicians who promise to prefer their version of Christian rights and enforce Christian values. The political calculation of conservative Christians is simple, and simply wrong.

Many perceive that their convictions and institutions are under assault by "woke" liberalism. Despite a judicial environment generally favorable to religious freedom, some view this tension as a death struggle for American identity. Their sources of information (such as conservative talk radio and Fox News) make money by inflating anecdotes into the appearance of systematic anti-religious oppression. And this led religious conservatives to seek and support a certain kind of leader. "I want the meanest, toughest SOB I can find to protect this nation," Southern Baptist pastor Robert Jeffress explained in his 2016 defense of Trump.

This view of politics is closer to *Game of Thrones* than to the Beatitudes. Nowhere did Jesus demand political passivity from his followers. But his teachings are entirely inconsistent with an approach to public engagement that says: "This Christian country is mine. You are defiling it. And I will take it back by any means necessary."

By assaulting democratic and religious pluralism, this agenda is at war with the constitutional order. By asserting self-interested rights, secured by lawless means, this approach has lost all resemblance to the teachings of Christ. A Christianity that does not humanize the life of this world is not Christianity.

The theological roots of this error run deep. Evangelicals often think that being a Christian means the individualistic acceptance of Jesus as their personal Savior. But this is quite different from following the example of Jesus we find in the Gospels. "He never asks for admirers, worshipers, or adherents," Søren Kierkegaard observed. "No, he calls disciples. It is not adherents of a teaching but followers of a life Christ is looking for."

What might an outbreak of discipleship look like? It would not bring victory for one ideological side or to one policy agenda. Christ did not deliver a manifesto or provide a briefing book. He called human beings to live generously, honestly, kindly, and faithfully. Following this way—which the Apostle Paul later called "the Way"—is not primarily a political choice, but it has unavoidable public consequences.

Imagine if today's believers were to live out the full implications of their faith.

Instead of fighting for narrow advantage, they would express their love of neighbor by seeking the common good and rejecting a view of greatness that makes others small.

Instead of being entirely captive to their cultural background, they would have enough critical distance to sort the good from the bad, the gold from the sand. This might leave them uncomfortable within their own tribe or their own skin—but the moral landscape is often easier to see from the periphery.

Instead of being ruled by anger and fear, they would live lightly, free from grudges and ready to offer forgiveness—thus preserving the possibility of future reconciliation and concord.

Instead of turning to violence in word or deed, they would assert the power of unarmed truth. They would engage in argument without slander or threats—demonstrating not wokeness or weakness, but due regard for our shared dignity.

Instead of being arrogant and willful, they would approach hard issues with humility, recognizing that even the most compelling principles are applied by fallible men and women. They would know that people who esteem the same ideal can come to different policy conclusions—and be open to the possibility of changing their own mind.

Instead of ignoring the cries of the ill, poor, and abused, they would honor the unerasable image of God we see in one another. Believers don't accept a society divided by rank or dominated by the illusion of merit—they seek to subvert such stratification in constructive ways, to prioritize justice and common provision for people in need.

Instead of giving in to half-justified despair, they would assert that there is hope at the end of a twisting road. Even when their strength is drained by long struggle and the bitterness of incoming attacks, they would live confidently rather than desperately, with faith in God's mercy and hope for a tearless morning.

Other noble religions and ethical systems come to similar conclusions. But for a Christian, one moment near the beginning of Jesus's ministry draws the distinction between BC and AD. Jesus stood up in a Nazareth synagogue and read from the scroll of the prophet Isaiah: "The Spirit of the Lord is upon me, because He has anointed me to proclaim good news to the poor. He has sent me to proclaim liberty to the captives

and recovering of sight to the blind, to set at liberty those who are oppressed, to proclaim the year of the Lord's favor."

These are some of the most hopeful words in history. Jesus thought
He could implant a new way of life on earth. Defying most historical
practice and precedent, He sought to reform human affairs in ways that
privilege the poor, the prisoner, the blind, the oppressed. He wanted to
put the joy, freedom, and healing of outcasts at the center of a new era.
At least trying to live under the inspiration of this good news lends purpose to our days and nobility to our failure.

This call is not merely political. Many are haunted by Jesus's words,
are drawn to emulate his person, and find Him mysteriously present
in their lives. Billions of human beings—Roman emperors and Celtic
tribesmen, Byzantine artists and medieval peasants, Puritan settlers
and enslaved Africans, Honduran farmers and Chinese house church
leaders—have claimed to feel Christ's comfort in their suffering, his guidance in their confusion, his company in their loneliness, and his welcome
at the hour of their death. If this is not the work of God, it is among the
strangest developments in the human story.

But the soul's trust is only the beginning of the heart's quest: to value
those whom Jesus valued, and to serve those whom Jesus served.

I know that people inspired by this vision have done great things in
the past—building hospitals for the poor, improving the rights of women
and children, militating against slavery, caring for the mentally disabled,
working for a merciful welfare state, fighting prejudice, improving global
health. But precisely because these things have happened, it is difficult
for me to comprehend why so many American evangelicals have rejected
the splendor and romance of their calling and settled for the cultural and
political resentments of the hard right. It is difficult for me to understand why so many believers have turned down a wedding feast to graze
in political dumpsters.

Are churches failing to teach an authentic Christian vision to Christian people? Have pastors domesticated the Christian message into something familiar, unchallenging, and easily ignored? Do the dark pleasures

of resentment and anger simply have a stronger emotional appeal than the virtues of compassion and self-sacrifice?

Or maybe it just feels impossible to judge your own upbringing and cultural background. It is hard to question the aggressive, predominant views of your community or congregation. It is far easier to seek belonging, even if it means accepting a lie or ignoring a wrong. Thus, moral courage is often a solitary stand.

What I am describing, however, is not a chain or a chore. When we are caked with the mud of political struggle, and tired of Pyrrhic victories that seed new hatreds, and frightened by our own capacity for contempt, the way of life set out by Jesus comes like a clear bell that rings above our strife. It defies cynicism, apathy, despair, and all ideologies that dream of dominance. It promises that every day, if we choose, can be the first day of a new and noble manner of living. Its most difficult duties can feel much like purpose and joy. And even our halting, half-hearted attempts at faithfulness are counted by God as victories.

God's call to us—while not simplifying our existence—does ennoble it. It is the invitation to a life marked by meaning. And even when, as mortality dictates, we walk the path we had feared to tread, it can be a pilgrimage, in which all is lost, and all is found.

Before such a consummation, Christians seeking social influence should do so not by joining interest groups that fight for their narrow rights—and certainly not those animated by hatred, fear, phobias, vengeance, or violence. Rather, they should seek to be ambassadors of a kingdom of hope, mercy, justice, and grace. This is a high calling—and a test that most of us (myself included) are always finding new ways to fail. But it is the revolutionary ideal set by Jesus of Nazareth, who still speaks across the sea of years.

# The Defiant Hope of Christmas: God Is with Us

*The Washington Post*, December 24, 2020

ONE OF THE STRANGER ELEMENTS of the strange Nativity narrative is the way an angel addresses Mary: "You who are highly favored." As a teen mother, pregnant before marriage and destined to give birth among barn animals, she might have been forgiven for regarding this as angelic sarcasm. Fast-forward three decades, and the most favored one will see her son executed among thieves before a jeering crowd.

The whole Christmas story is pregnant with enigma and violated expectations. The Creator pulls on a garment of blood and bone. Almighty God is somehow present in a fragile newborn. The deliverer of humankind is delivered, slimy with vernix, in a place smelling of dung. If God can come here, amid the shame and straw, he can come anywhere. If God came here, he has come everywhere.

As we pull back from these events, an odd violation of perspective kicks in. The largest figures of the time—King Herod, Emperor Tiberius—grow smaller. The smaller figures—Mary, Joseph, and some random shepherds—loom large. The smallest, most helpless figure blots out sun and moon and fills the whole sky with song: "Glory to God in the highest. Peace on Earth. Good will toward men."

Many in first-century Palestine—as in every time since—were looking for political deliverance. They had every right to resent the brutal rule of Rome and its proxies. But the Christmas story overturns that expectation. It asserts that the most important things—the things that last and count—are not political or social but personal and human. Instead of influence based on coercion, the birth of Jesus points to a power found in vulnerability, service, and humility. Humankind is offered not a new way of organizing society but a new way of being human, marked by compassion, purpose, dignity, and kindness.

Imagine if Jesus had been a political revolutionary. Even if he had miraculously succeeded in humbling Rome, he would be a historical footnote—someone on par with Judah Maccabee. Precisely because Christ's kingdom is not of this world, it was not limited to his time. Those who politicize religion are also miniaturizing it. Their faith is as fresh and relevant as last week's newspaper.

None of this is to dismiss the importance of politics. We are still working out the massive social implications of honoring God's image in every life. But in the Nativity story, political figures only appear as tax collectors and murderers. At the center of history lies a domestic drama. The universe held its breath as a baby drew his first. God arrived not as a conqueror, but as a child in a stable. A teacher on a hillside. A man nailed to a cross. And his achievement—bringing God's presence to humankind—makes every victory achieved by force look trifling in comparison.

If the Nativity story is true, God is not merely a philosophical or theological postulate. In the Scriptures, Jesus is given the name Emmanuel, which is Hebrew for "God with us." He entered the bowels of human existence for the sake of every human soul. The implications are remarkable. It means there are no insignificant or pointless lives. It means that the events and choices of an average day can carry eternal significance. It means that a journey of meaning and purpose—a life of courage and generosity—can begin from whatever desolate place we find ourselves.

This emphasis on the personal—this glorification of the human—has sometimes been captured in art. Consider the luminous domestic spaces of Vermeer. A milkmaid, a lacemaker, or a geographer shines with dignity and grace. A girl with a pearl earring and limpid eyes is as radiant as a Madonna.

Or consider James Wright's brief poem "Trouble," dealing with a young woman named Roberta who is pregnant out of wedlock. She is taunted on the street by a boy, Crum Anderson, who says she looks like she has swallowed a watermelon. The poem ends:

*All that time she thought she was nothing*
*But skin and bones.*

None of us—no matter what Crum Anderson says—is merely skin and bones. We are skin and bones and the life of God within us. Even lives that feel relentlessly ordinary or hopelessly broken are vessels of divine purpose. We are embraced, elevated, and dignified by God's astounding humility.

This should be a source of hope. I am not speaking here of optimism, which is more like a genetic gift than the foundation of a life. Some of us, in contrast, have the genetic affliction of depression, which can bathe life's wonders in dirty dishwater, making our days appear gray and two-dimensional. Depression tries to convince us that hope itself is a fiction. Sometimes the only comfort lies in knowing your mind is a vicious liar and in managing to endure another day.

But when we are thinking clearly, most of us can recall glimpses of purpose, beauty, and glory in our lives. In the overwhelming calm and joy of holding our child close. In the majesty and marvelous internal order of nature. In art or music that touches our deepest being. In the undeserved, sacrificial love of a friend. And maybe, if we are silent and open, in the sense that a benign God is speaking to us in the seemingly random events of our lives.

These are not logical proofs; they are signposts pointing in the direction of grace. And they culminate in the defiant hope of Christmas: God is for us. God is in us. God is with us.

In enforced isolation and loneliness, God is with us. In chronic pain and degenerative disease, God is with us. In a shattered relationship or a cancer diagnosis, God is with us. In an intensive care unit or a mental ward, God is with us. In life and in death, God will not leave us or forsake us.

It is possible, of course, that none of this is true. Such Christmas hope may well be a pleasing myth or projection of our own desires. If we had been there on the night in question, walking the Judean hills, would we have seen and heard the angels? I have no idea. But I do know that the civilization I inhabit is unimaginable without the birth of the Christ child. I know that billions in the last two millennia have claimed communion with Him. And I have faith that this extraordinary person, who knew God's heart so intimately, can be born into our hearts as well.

Such faith does not promise release from suffering, but it can bring deliverance from fear. It means that every moment we are blessed to inhabit, even in a difficult and shortened life, can be infused with God's presence and ennobled by His calling. The hope that began on Christmas Day still shines like a star and swells like a song, carried across the centuries by chanting monks and gospel choirs, filling great cathedrals and revival tents, but clearest in the quiet of our hearts: God is with us.

# What Good Friday Teaches Us About Cynicism

*The Washington Post*, April 13, 2017

THE STORY OF GOOD FRIDAY—the garden, the bloody sweat, the sleeping friends, the torch-carrying crowd, the kiss, the slash of a sword, the questioning, the scourging, the mocking, the beam, the nails, the despair of a good man—is an invitation to cynicism. Nearly every human institution is revealed at its worst.

Government certainly comes off poorly, giving Jesus the bureaucratic shuffle, with no one wanting to take responsibility, until a weak leader gives in to the crowd in the name of keeping the peace. "What is truth?" asks Pontius Pilate, with a sneer typical of politics to this day.

Professional men of religion do not appear in their best light. They are violently sectarian and judgmental and turn to the state to enforce their beliefs. "Jesus was not brought down by atheism and anarchy," theologian Barbara Brown Taylor sharply observes. "He was brought down by law and order allied with religion, which is always a deadly mix."

The crowd does not acquit itself well, turning hostile and cruel as quickly as an Internet mob, first putting palms beneath his feet, then thorns upon his brow.

Even friendship comes in for a beating. The men closest to Jesus sleep while his enemies are fully awake. There is betrayal by a close, disgruntled associate. And then Peter's spastic violence and cowardly denials. The women—all the assorted Marys—come off far better in the narrative. But Jesus is essentially abandoned to face his long, suffocating death alone.

And, for a moment, even God seems to fail, vanishing into a shocking silence. "My God, my God, why have you forsaken me?" says Jesus, in words that many of his followers would want to erase from the Bible. How could the Son of God be subject to despair? G. K. Chesterton called Christianity the only religion in which "God seemed for an instant to be an atheist."

Consider how the world appeared at the finish of Good Friday. It would have seemed that every source of order, justice, and comfort—politics, institutional religion, the community, friendship—had been discredited. It was the cynic's finest hour. And God Himself seemed absent or unmoved, turning cynicism toward nihilism. Every ember of human hope was cold. And there was nothing to be done about it.

Then something happened. There was disagreement at the time, as now, on what that something was. According to the story, Pilate posted a guard at the tomb with the instruction: "Make it as secure as you can." Then the cynics somehow lost control of the narrative. There was an empty tomb and wild reports of angels and ghosts. And the claim of resurrection.

Even those who believe the body was moved must confront certain facts. Faith in the figure whom Rome executed has far outlasted the Roman Empire. The cowardly friends became bold missionaries, most dying torturous deaths (according to tradition) for the sake of a figure they had once betrayed in their sleep. The faith thus founded has given the mob—all of us, even the ones who mock, especially the ones who mock—the hope of pardon and peace.

For believers, the complete story of Good Friday and Easter legitimizes both despair and faith. Nearly every life features less-than-good Fridays. We grow tired of our own company and travel a descending path of depression. We experience lonely pain, unearned suffering, or stinging injustice. We are rejected or betrayed by a friend. And then there are the unspeakable things—the death of a child, the diagnosis of an aggressive cancer, the steady advance of a disease that will take our minds and dignity. We look into the abyss of self-murder. And given the example of Christ, we are permitted to feel God-forsaken.

And yet ... eventually ... or so we trust ... or so we try to trust: God is forever on the side of those who suffer. God is forever on the side of life. God is forever on the side of hope.

If the resurrection is real, death's hold is broken. There is a truth and human existence that cannot be contained in a tomb. It is possible to live lightly, even in the face of death—not by becoming hard and strong, but through a confident perseverance. Because cynicism is the failure of patience. Because Good Friday does not have the final word.

# The Strange Tension Between Theology and Science

*The Washington Post*, April 24, 2014

IN THE LATE 1920S, ASTRONOMER EDWIN HUBBLE established that the light we detect from galaxies is shifted toward the redder colors of the spectrum, indicating that they are moving away from us at enormous speeds. And the farther away galaxies are, the faster they are fleeing. Rewinding that expansion through mathematics—dividing distance by speed—indicates that something extraordinary happened about 14 billion years ago, when the entire universe was small, dense, and exceedingly hot.

Scientists such as Alexander Friedmann and Georges Lemaître had anticipated the big bang—which Lemaître described as a "Cosmic Egg exploding at the moment of creation." Others theorized that such an event would have left a detectable residue of hydrogen plasma grown cold over time. In the 1960s, Arno Penzias and Robert Wilson duly detected it—finding microwave background radiation in every direction they pointed their telescope. The whole sky glows faintly at a temperature of about three degrees above absolute zero. Part of the static between channels on broadcast television is an echo of the big bang.

These are some of the most regularly confirmed, noncontroversial findings of modern science. Yet a recent poll found that a majority of Americans are "not too" or "not at all" confident that "the universe began 13.8 billion years ago with a big bang."

Some of this skepticism, surely, reflects the inherent difficulty of imagining unimaginable scales of time and space. And some fault must lie with American scientific education, which routinely transforms the consideration of wonders into a chore and a bore. But the poll also found that confidence in the big bang declines as belief in a Supreme Being increases.

This is not easy to explain. The predominant cosmological picture that predated the big bang—a static universe without beginning or end—would have pleased the ancient Greeks, who preferred their cosmos orderly and eternal. People influenced by the book of Genesis should feel more at home in a universe with a dramatic, cataclysmic beginning. Lemaître, in fact, was a priest, whom some suspected of sneaking theological assumptions into his science. He didn't, and carefully (and correctly) insisted that the big bang is consistent with both materialist and religious convictions. But the idea of a universe that began in a flash that flung stars, galaxies, and clusters of galaxies across the vast canvas of space is, to put it mildly, compatible with Jewish and Christian belief: "Let there be light."

So why this theological resistance to scientific assertions that are intuitively consistent with Christian theological views? The polls don't settle this question, but I can hazard a guess. Many conservative Christians equate modern science with materialism—a view conditioned by early twentieth-century debates over evolution and human origins. Science is often viewed as an alternative theology, with a competing creation story. Some religious communities define themselves by resisting this rival faith—and filter evidence to reinforce their identity.

This approach raises two protests. First, it will eventually fail. It is a deep weakness for any theology or ideology to be wrong about the scientific nature of the universe. The children of believers are presented with a cruel and false choice: In order to accept the scientific method, they must abandon the beliefs of their community. And many will naturally choose science. If theological conservatives define themselves by their skepticism about the (marvelous, breathtaking, compelling) findings of modern science, they will eventually lose—not only in public debates but in the minds of their own children.

Second, this strategy is completely unnecessary. The scientific method is the proper way—actually the only way—to understand the physical universe. There is no philosophical or theological method to study the structure of a star or a starfish. But this does not mean that the knowledge revealed by the physical sciences is the only valid type of human knowledge. There is ethical reasoning. There is also theological belief—involving the possibility that the Creator might suspend the laws of nature in certain circumstances, such as the parting of the Red Sea or the Resurrection.

The problem comes when materialism, claiming the authority of science, denies the possibility of all other types of knowledge—reducing human beings to a bag of chemicals and all their hopes and loves to the firing of neurons. Or when religion exceeds its bounds and declares the earth to be six thousand years old. In both cases, the besetting sin is the same: the arrogant exclusive claim to know reality.

# Pope Francis Challenges the Faithful

*The Washington Post*, November 17, 2014

POPE FRANCIS'S AMERICAN HONEYMOON IS OVER (though the whole idea of a papal honeymoon smacks of Borgia-era excess).

At first, some political conservatives complained that Francis was showing insufficient respect for distinguished Catholic theologians such as Adam Smith and Milton Friedman. But now, more thoughtful Catholic writers wonder if the pope (who conspicuously marries cohabiting couples) is laying the groundwork for more substantive changes on the sacrament of marriage and access to the Eucharist for the divorced and remarried. This, argues Ross Douthat of the *New York Times*, would "sow confusion among the church's orthodox adherents" and raise the (undesired) prospect of "schism."

The event occasioning these concerns was the recent Extraordinary Synod on the Family, which lived up to its billing. The pope invited participants to speak their mind "without fear," which revealed a series of divisions between the theological left and right, as well as between the developed and the developing worlds. "Francis," says journalist Christina Odone, "achieved miracles with his compassionate, off-the-cuff comments that detoxified the Catholic brand. He personifies optimism—but when he tries to turn this into policy he isn't in command of the procedures or the details. The result is confusion."

This seems to be the main concern of Catholic traditionalists: confusion. Francis is cultivating debate within the church about an essential social institution—and the value of relationships outside it—even as that institution is under assault by the world (at least in parts of the world where the sexual revolution continues its relentless march). In the middle of an important cultural conflict, Francis sounds an uncertain trumpet.

The pope himself seems unconcerned, continuing his unpredictable riff. He embraces the big bang. He appears in selfies. He criticizes euthanasia. He invites Patti Smith, the godmother of punk, to perform at the Vatican. He cashiers opponents. He calls the kingdom of God "a party" (which is precisely how the founder of the Christian faith referred to it). He is a man, by his own account, with no patience for "sourpusses."

As a Protestant, I have no particular insight into the internal theological debates of Catholicism. But the participants seem to inhabit different universes. One side (understandably) wants to shore up the certainties of an institution under siege. Francis begins from a different point: a pastoral passion to meet people where they are—to recognize some good, even in their brokenness, and to call them to something better. That something better is not membership in a stable institution, or even the comforts of ethical religion; it is a relationship with Jesus, from which all else follows.

Instead of being a participant in a cultural battle, Francis says, "I see the church as a field hospital after battle." First you sew up the suffering (which, incidentally, includes all of us). "Then we can talk about everything else. Heal the wounds." The temptation, in his view, is to turn faith into ideology. "The faith passes," he recently said, "through a distiller and becomes ideology. And ideology does not beckon [people]. In ideologies there is not Jesus; in his tenderness, his love, his meekness. And ideologies are rigid, always. . . . The knowledge of Jesus is transformed into an ideological and also moralistic knowledge, because these close the door with many requirements."

The message seems simple. It actually highlights a complexity at the heart of Christianity: Its founder coupled a call for ethical heroism (don't even lust in your heart) with a disdain for institutional religion and self-righteous clericalism. And this has been disorienting to institutionalists from the start.

Francis has devoted serious attention to reforming the institutional expression—particularly the finances—of the Catholic Church. But he has chosen to emphasize the most subversive and challenging aspects of Christian faith. He really does view rigidity, clericalism, and hypocrisy as just as (or more) damaging as sexual matters. Liberals want to incorporate this into their agenda. But the pope has his own, quite different agenda—which has nothing to do with our forgettable ideological debates. It is always revolutionary, and confusing to the faithful, when a religious leader believes that the Sabbath (including all the rules and institutions of religion) was made for man, and not the other way around.

Perhaps Francis is destined to be a divisive force within his church and an inspiration outside it (a theory that may be tested during his upcoming U.S. visit). But I am inclined to defend his influence with all the zeal of a non-convert. While popes may or may not be infallible, this one is marvelously wise and human.

# PART 3

# Family

# National Cathedral Sermon on Depression

February 17, 2019

WHEN YOUR DEAN AND I WERE conspiring about when I might speak, I think he mentioned February 3 as a possibility. A sermon by me on that date would have been considerably less interesting, because I was, at that point, hospitalized for depression. Or maybe it would have been more interesting, though less coherent.

Like nearly one in ten Americans—and like many of you—I live with this insidious, chronic disease. Depression is a malfunction in the instrument we use to determine reality. The brain experiences a chemical imbalance and wraps a narrative around it. So the lack of serotonin, in the mind's alchemy, becomes something like "Everybody hates me." Over time, despair can grow inside you like a tumor.

I would encourage anyone with this malady to keep a journal. At the bottom of my recent depression, I did a plus and minus, a pro and con, of me. Of being myself. The plus side, as you'd imagine, was short. The minus side included the most frightful clichés: "You are a burden to your friends." "You have no future." "No one would miss you."

The scary thing is that these things felt completely true when I wrote them. At that moment, realism seemed to require hopelessness.

But then you reach your breaking point—and do not break. With patience and the right medicine, the fog in your brain begins to thin. If you are lucky, as I was, you encounter doctors and nurses who know parts of your mind better than you do. There are friends who run into the burning building of your life to rescue you, and acquaintances who become friends. You meet other patients, from entirely different backgrounds, who share your symptoms, creating a community of the wounded. And you learn of the valor they show in lonely rooms.

Over time, you begin to see hints and glimmers of a larger world outside the prison of your sadness. The conscious mind takes hold of some shred of beauty or love. And then more shreds, until you begin to think maybe, just maybe, there is something better on the far side of despair.

I have no doubt that I will eventually repeat the cycle of depression. But now I have some self-knowledge that can't be taken away. I know that—when I'm in my right mind—I choose hope.

The phrase—"in my right mind"—is harsh. No one would use it in a clinical setting. But it fits my experience exactly.

In my right mind—when I am rested and fed, medicated and caffeinated—I know that I was living within a dismal lie.

In my right mind, I know I have friends who will not forsake me.

In my right mind, I know that chemistry need not be destiny.

In my right mind, I know that weeping may endure for the night, but joy comes in the morning.

This may have direct relevance to some here today. But I also think this medical condition works as a metaphor for the human condition.

All of us—whatever our natural serotonin level—look around us and see plenty of reason for doubt, anger, and sadness. A child dies, a woman is abused, a schoolyard becomes a killing field, a typhoon sweeps away the innocent. If we knew or felt the whole of human suffering, we would drown in despair. By all objective evidence, we are arrogant animals, headed for the extinction that is the way of all things. We imagine that we are like gods, and still drop dead like flies on the windowsill.

The answer to the temptation of nihilism is not an argument—though philosophy can clear away a lot of intellectual foolishness. It is the experience of transcendence we cannot explain, or explain away. It is the fragments of love and meaning that arrive out of the blue—in beauty that leaves a lump in your throat . . . in the peace and ordered complexity of nature . . . in the shadow and shimmer of a cathedral . . . in the unexplained wonder of existence itself.

I have one friend, John, who finds God's hidden hand in the habits and coloring of birds. My friend Catherine, when her first child was born, discovered what she calls "a love much greater than evolution requires." I like that. "A love much greater than evolution requires."

My own experience is tied to this place. Let me turn to an earlier, happier part of my journals, from May 2, 2002:

"It has probably been a month," I wrote, "since some prompting of God led me to a more disciplined Christian life. One afternoon I was led to the Cathedral, the place I feel most secure in the world. I saw the beautiful sculpture in the Bishop's Garden—the prodigal son melting into his father's arms—and the inscription of how he fell on his neck, and kissed him. I felt tears and calm, like something important had happened to me and in me. . . . My goals are pretty clear. I want to stop thinking about myself all the time. I want to be a mature disciple of Jesus, not a casual believer. I want to be God's man."

I have failed at these goals in a disturbing variety of ways. And I have more doubts than I did on that day. These kind of experiences may result from inspiration . . . or indigestion. Your brain may be playing tricks. Or you may be feeling the beating heart of the universe. Faith, thankfully, does not preclude doubt. It consists of staking your life on the rumor of grace.

This experience of pulling back the curtain of materiality, and briefly seeing the landscape of a broader world, comes in many forms. It can be religious and nonreligious, Christian and non-Christian. We sometimes search for a hidden door when the city has a hundred open gates. But there is this difference for a Christian believer: At the end of all our striving and longing we find not a force, but a face. All language about God is metaphorical. But the metaphor became flesh and dwelt among us.

Becoming alert to this reality might be called "enlightenment," or the work of the Holy Ghost, or "conversion." There really is no formula. Historically, there was Paul's blinding light on the road to Damascus. There was Augustine, instructed by the voice of a child to "take up and read." There was Pascal sewing into his jacket: "Since about half-past ten in the evening until about half-past midnight. FIRE. Certitude. Feeling. Joy. Peace." There was Teresa of Ávila encountering the suffering Christ with an "outpouring of tears." There was John Wesley's heart becoming "strangely warmed."

It is impossible for anyone but saints to live always on a mountain-top. I suspect that there are people here today—and I include myself—who are stalked by sadness, or stalked by cancer, or stalked by anger. We are afraid of the mortality that is knit into our bones. We experience unearned suffering, or give unreturned love, or cry useless tears. And many of us eventually grow weary of ourselves—tired of our own sour company.

At some point, willed cheerfulness fails. Or we skim along the surface of our lives, afraid of what lies in the depths below. It is a way to cope, but no way to live.

I'd urge anyone with undiagnosed depression to seek out professional help. There is no way to will yourself out of this disease, any more than to will yourself out of tuberculosis.

There are, however, other forms of comfort. Those who hold to the wild hope of a living God can say certain things:

In our right minds—as our most sane and solid selves—we know that the appearance of a universe ruled by cruel chaos is a lie and that the cold void is actually a sheltering sky.

In our right minds, we know that life is not a farce but a pilgrimage—or maybe a farce and a pilgrimage, depending on the day.

In our right minds, we know that hope can grow within us—like a seed, like a child.

In our right minds, we know that transcendence sparks and crackles around us—in a blinding light, and a child's voice, and fire, and tears, and a warmed heart, and a sculpture just down the hill—if we open ourselves to seeing it.

Fate may do what it wants. But this much is settled. In our right minds, we know that love is at the heart of all things.

Many, understandably, pray for a strength they do not possess. But God's promise is somewhat different: That even when strength fails, there is perseverance. And even when perseverance fails, there is hope. And even when hope fails, there is love. And love never fails.

So how do we know this? How can anyone be so confident?

Because we are Lazarus, and we live.

# Saying Goodbye to My Child, the Youngster

*The Washington Post*, August 19, 2013

EVENTUALLY, THE COSMOLOGISTS ASSURE US, our sun and all suns will consume their fuel, violently explode, and then become cold and dark. Matter itself will evaporate into the void and the universe will become desolate for the rest of time.

This was the general drift of my thoughts as my wife and I dropped off my eldest son as a freshman at college. I put on my best face. But it is the worst thing that time has done to me so far. That moment at the dorm is implied at the kindergarten door, at the gates of summer camp, at every ritual of parting and independence. But it comes as surprising as a thief, taking what you value most.

The emotions of a parent, I can attest, are an odd mix: part pride, part resignation, part self-pity, even a bit of something that feels like grief. The experience is natural and common. And still planets are thrown off their axes.

Our ancestors actually thought this parting should take place earlier. Many societies once practiced "extrusion," in which adolescents were sent away to live with friends or relatives right after puberty. This was supposed to minimize the nasty conflicts that come from housing teenagers and their parents in close proximity. Some nonhuman primates have a similar practice, forcibly expelling adolescents from the family group.

Fat lot did our ancestors know. Eighteen years is not enough. A crib is bought. Christmas trees get picked out. There is the park and lullabies and a little help with homework. The days pass uncounted, until they end. The adjustment is traumatic. My son is on the quiet side—observant, thoughtful, a practitioner of companionable silence. I'm learning how empty the quiet can be.

I know this is hard on him as well. He will be homesick, as I was (intensely) as a freshman. An education expert once told me that among the greatest fears of college students is they won't have a room at home to return to. They want to keep a beachhead in their former life.

But with due respect to my son's feelings, I have the worse of it. I know something he doesn't—not quite a secret, but incomprehensible to the young. He is experiencing the adjustments that come with beginnings. His life is starting for real. I have begun the long letting go. Put another way: He has a wonderful future in which my part naturally diminishes. I have no possible future that is better without him close.

There is no use brooding about it. I'm sure my father realized it at a similar moment. And I certainly didn't notice or empathize. At first, he was a giant who held my hand and filled my sky. Then a middle-aged man who paid my bills. Now, decades after his passing, a much-loved shadow. But I can remember the last time I hugged him in the front hallway of his home, where I always had a room. It is a memory of warmth. I can only hope to leave my son the same.

Parenthood offers many lessons in patience and sacrifice. But ultimately, it is a lesson in humility. The very best thing about your life is a short stage in someone else's story. And it is enough.

The end of childhood, of course, can be the start of adult relationships between parents and children that are rewarding in their own way. I'm anxious to befriend my grown sons. But that hasn't stopped the random, useless tears. I was cautioned by a high-powered Washington foreign policy expert that he had been emotionally debilitated for weeks after dropping off his daughter at college for the first time. So I feel entitled to a period of brooding.

The cosmologists, even with all their depressing talk about the eventual heat death of the cosmos, offer some comfort. They point out that we live in the briefest window—a fraction of a fraction of the unimaginable vastness of deep time—in which it is physically possible for life to exist. So we inhabit (or are chosen to inhabit) an astounding, privileged instant in the life span of the universe.

Well, eighteen years is a window that closed too quickly. But, my son, those days have been the greatest wonder and privilege of my life. And there will always be a room for you.

# After Cancer Diagnosis, Seeing Mortality in the Near Distance

*The Washington Post*, December 5, 2013

In my mid-twenties, I had a new bride, a plum job on Capitol Hill, and, apparently, the beginnings of a cancerous tumor on my right kidney. For twenty or twenty-five years—the best estimate of my doctors—it accompanied me at birthdays and on holidays and at the delivery of my children. It was quiet and kept to itself. Undiscovered, it would have donned camouflage and killed me in the end.

A cancer diagnosis is the experience of about 13 million Americans. Mine came early enough for surgery to make a difference. There were weeks of testing, waiting, and attempting to focus on other things. At the hospital, cheerful young nurses ask you to pull down your pants at odd moments—which is not nearly as pleasant as it sounds. Then six hours on the table, the haze of narcotics, the clockwork routine of poking and prodding, the welcome visits of family and friends. Then a growing desire to escape the pervasive, repulsive smell of cleanliness and to go home.

As an instinctual Calvinist, I'm not prone to ask "why me?"—as though mortality were carrying out some kind of personal vendetta. But my first impression was the apparent arbitrariness of it all. I have no family history of kidney cancer. I've never smoked. I haven't worked in a uranium mine. Any philosophy of life must take into account that random, witless developments—a tumor, an aneurism, a drunken driver—can be highly consequential. At some point, many of us will feel "as flies to wanton boys."

In my case, this realization of the radical contingency of events gave way to more constructive thoughts. They are not observations I can universalize. They don't apply to those in constant pain, or address the incomprehensible suffering of children with cancer. My experience left me less able to understand such horrors.

I was fortunate to see mortality in the near distance. Stepping outside that experience, as writers tend to do, it had elements of a physics experiment. As I waited to learn my fate, I noticed an effect on matter— an odd intensification of physical experience. Things around you offer more friction and hold your attention longer. Commonplace things like the bumps on tree bark. The light filtering through floating dust. The wetness of water. A contrast knob is turned, revealing the vivid pleasures of merely existing.

This heightened awareness applies to strangers in the street, who suddenly have faces. An unsolicited smile, the obvious creases of worry or pain, engage your emotions. There is nothing more democratic than mortality. Even if we are insects, we are insects (said Dickens) on the same leaf.

All of this is a function of a shifting perception of time. When the days seem limited, we more fully inhabit them. The arrow of time makes decay inevitable—and each moment unrecoverable. So we gain in appreciation for things as they are when we realize they will eventually be otherwise.

I'm sorry to report these effects are temporary. Perhaps they fade when you stop taking the Percocet. But I don't think the impressions are illusions. The healthy (rather than morbid) recognition of our mortality is realism. Cancer is a horror, but it is also a metaphor. Each of us is conceived with a seed of mortality that can't be surgically removed. It grows until it kills us, hopefully after a long life that honors the incredible, temporary privilege of living. We are, as W. B. Yeats harshly put it, "fastened to a dying animal."

That, but not only that. At every stage, even in the manner of their dying, people can demonstrate they are something more. I recall my Italian, New Yorker grandmother—full of years and full of cancer (the result of a lifelong smoking habit)—telling me through some of her last, gasping breaths: "You have made me so very happy." Such are the gifts human beings can give each other, even when there is nothing else to give.

It was not my time, thank God, to demonstrate such generosity. I'm left, for the moment, to experience some additional moments and to hope there is a plot behind random and witless events. But I've gained—along with many given a cancer diagnosis—a greater appreciation for the familiar words of the psalmist: "Teach us to number our days."

# Why I Will Never Live Without a Dog Again

*The Washington Post*, January 4, 2022

EVERYONE MUST TAKE A SUMMER BREAK from the relentless negativity of the news, which unfortunately reflects the relentless negativity of reality. So let me introduce you to Jack.

Jack is a puppy I picked up last week, eight months after the death of my much-loved Havanese, Latte. As soon as I brought Jack home—a powder puff of black and white, curvetting in the grass, all fluff and playful fury—I was reminded of the quandary and question that greets dog owners: Why do we take new dogs into our lives, knowing we will be decimated by their deaths?

I grieved hard for my Latte, who was the dog equivalent of St. Francis of Assisi—a little hairy mammal (Latte, not Francis) who radiated universal benevolence. She was a consoling, healing presence during the worst of my struggles against depression and cancer. In a very real sense, Latte was a better person than I am—a daily practitioner of the hardest parts of the Sermon on the Mount. She was meek, merciful (except to those godless squirrels), peaceable, and pure of heart. At her departure, I was the one who mourned.

I can still feel the ache at night. Not long ago, my wife told me I had been crying in my sleep. I don't usually recall my dreams. But in this case I remembered dreaming about the last time I saw Latte, after she was taken out of my arms to be euthanized at the veterinary hospital. She lifted her head and looked back at me with her large, sad eyes. And then one of the most steadfast, lavish, uncomplicated sources of affection in my life was gone. (Even now I can hardly write the words.) She died, aptly, of an enlarged heart.

The eighteenth-century evangelist John Wesley gave a sermon, "The General Deliverance," on the survival of animals in the afterlife—a very English line of theological argument. (Many Brits regard the Westminster Kennel Club Dog Show as a preview of heaven.) The Creator, said Wesley, "saw, with unspeakable pleasure, the order, the beauty, the harmony, of all the creatures." Wesley believed that during the end-time renewal of the world (a basic Christian doctrine), the "whole brute creation will then, undoubtedly, be restored, not only to the vigour, strength and swiftness which they had at their creation, but to a far higher degree of each than they ever enjoyed."

For most of my life, I lived in dogless ignorance and would have mocked such sentiments. (It is so typical of Homo sapiens to regard heaven as their own exclusive club.) I now hope that cross-species friendships of such intensity do not end in permanent partings. Everything truly good in life must leave some eternal imprint. Or pawprint. When I am not crying in my sleep, I now feel such gratitude for an animal willing to comfort another animal during some of the most trying days of his life. All without expectation of reward—except the occasional dried pig's ear.

In human relationships, the transforming presence of love is worth the inevitability of grief. Can dogs really love? Science might deny that the species possesses such complex emotions. But I know dogs can act in a loving fashion and provide love's consolations. Which is all we really know about what hairless apes can manage in the love department as well.

So I—who once saw dogs as dirty and dangerous—am resolved to never live without one again. This led to the gift from my kind wife of Jack, the Havanese fuzzball. After my dreary brushes with mortality, I needed new life in my life. And Jack is the bouncy incarnation of innocent joy. Waking up on the day of his arrival was like Christmas when I was nine.

On brief acquaintance, Jack is the best dog in the universe. During his first night with us, he slept for eight hours in the crate in our bed-room. There were a few bleats of homesick protest, but they were quickly stilled by my voice, by his knowing I was near. Why would a puppy just torn from his home, his litter, and his parents place immediate faith in us? This is one thing that makes the abuse of such animals so monstrous. It is not only the expression of the human capacity for sick cruelty; it is the violation of a trust so generously given.

There is an obstacle in training Havanese dogs. When you try to instill discipline, they employ a thermonuclear cuteness that melts all intentions of firmness. But what other object can you bring into your home that makes you smile every time you see it? Jack is a living, yipping, randomly peeing antidepressant. He improves the mental health of all who encounter him.

Why do we take in new dogs? Because their joy for living renews our own.

# Harry Potter and the Power of Myth

*The Washington Post*, July 18, 2011

ARGUABLY THE MOST FAMOUS LIVING ENGLISHMAN IS, technically, not alive. But Harry Potter now determines the American conception of Britishness as thoroughly as Sherlock Holmes ever did. Rather than making the disappointing pilgrimage to Baker Street, a generation will visit King's Cross station asking for Platform 9 3/4 and expect to exchange dollars for Galleons at Gringotts. The mythic geography of England—always as important as its actual hills and streets—has been reshaped by J. K. Rowling.

Young Potter is invariably taken either too seriously or not seriously enough. Modern witch-hunters believe his spells and potions are an invitation to the occult—forgetting the equally potent magic of Narnia or Middle Earth. Literary critics dismiss Rowling's writing as banal, her stories as derivative—a rummage sale of mythological creatures and conventional themes.

Neither snobs nor fundamentalists have prevented the sale of 450 million Harry Potter books, which places the series in the best-selling company of the Book of Mormon and *Quotations from Chairman Mao*.

The books, in fact, are gloriously derivative, providing an introduction not to magic but to mythology. Harry's world is populated by centaurs, dragons, werewolves, grindylows, veela, Cornish pixies, sphinxes, phoenixes, goblins, and hippogriffs. It is as though Egyptian, Greek, and Roman mythology, European folklore, and Arthurian legend suddenly discovered the same playground. "I'm one of the very few," Rowling has observed, "who has ever found a practical application for their classics degree."

The world's great stories—of heroic journeys, of peril, testing and courage, of nature enchanted, of happy endings—get reincarnated for a reason. Created to explain the world, myths eventually began to explain us and our prerational values and culture. When these strings are touched, we feel the vibrations deep down. And we know that myths are not the same as lies.

In his essay "On Fairy-Stories," J. R. R. Tolkien—who knew something of the subject—describes the highest achievement of the teller of stories as "sub-creation." The sub-creator fashions "a Secondary World which your mind can enter. Inside it, what he relates is 'true': it accords with the laws of that world." Tolkien calls this "a special skill, a kind of elvish craft." The creator of Harry Potter practices this craft well— an achievement her detractors cannot understand or duplicate. To read Rowling is to pack a bag and make a visit.

Tolkien describes the distinguishing climax of a fairy story as the "turn"—the moment when fantastic and terrible adventures are transformed by sudden grace, "giving a fleeting glimpse of Joy, Joy beyond the walls of the world, poignant as grief." "A tale that in any measure succeeds in this point," he continues, "has not wholly failed, whatever flaws it may possess."

In the last of the series, *Harry Potter and the Deathly Hallows*, and in the current movie based on it, Rowling reaches the turn. A boy who has played Quidditch, discovered girls, broken curfew, and cheated death again and again discovers that he was intended for death, "marked for slaughter," all along. A scarred hero—his birth prophesied, his character tested by the temptation of dark power—realizes he must sacrifice himself for the sake of his friends. The "chosen one," it turns out, was not chosen for honor but for extermination. Death, he finds, can be defeated only when it is embraced. Harry's destiny requires a "cold-blooded walk to his own destruction."

These are the ambitions of Rowling's brand of children's literature.

Harry's walk toward the Forbidden Forest gains the reflected emotional power of the walk from Gethsemane to Golgotha. It is the recycling of the greatest myth—a myth that some also regard as true. And the final delivery from death is the culmination of all happy endings.

Rowling seems to anticipate the objections of those who dismiss myths as lies. Harry's enemy, Voldemort, does the same. "That which Voldemort does not value," she writes, "he takes no trouble to comprehend. Of house-elves and children's tales, of love, loyalty and innocence, Voldemort knows and understands nothing. Nothing. That they all have a power beyond his own, a power beyond the reach of any magic, is a truth he has never grasped."

Rowling's children's tale—like the best that came before it—has a sliver, a glimpse, of that power, beyond the reach of magic.

# Crying at the Movies

*The Washington Post*, January 7, 2013

Following the *les miserables* incident on Christmas Day, I suspect I will never persuade my teenage sons to attend a movie with me again. At various moments of high emotion—and there are few other kinds in the movie—their father was a sobbing, embarrassing mess. And I agree with them that weeping for the imaginary suffering of fictional characters played by highly paid actors requires explanation.

I could blame biology. There is a neurochemical basis for empathy. People who view a hand being touched respond with the same sensory portion of their brain as if they had been touched themselves. Humans have an extraordinary talent for feeling the distress expressed in other faces—particularly when Anne Hathaway's gaunt, anguished face is two stories high, crying tears that could fill a baby pool. Hormones spike, unable to distinguish between real and imagined images. The lacrimal system produces and drains tears. Charles Darwin, that old sentimentalist, said that weeping is "an incidental result, as purposeless as the secretion of tears from a blow outside the eye."

But this is not quite true. Emotional tears, it turns out, have a different chemical composition from the tears that moisten our eyes. And empathetic tears, so far as we know, are not expressed by any other species. Showing vulnerability appears to serve the evolutionary purpose of building communities of cooperation and mutual support. We would help poor Fantine if we possibly could.

This may explain empathy, but it does not explain it away. The great temptation of modern science is reductionism. Because transcendence is experienced in a certain portion of the brain, the argument goes, the universe must be an impersonal void. Because religion serves an evolutionary purpose, religion is somehow an illusion. Because empathy has a physical basis, it is as purposeless as the response to a blow to the eye. Evolutionary biology and neuroscience deal in facts. Reductionism is a philosophy, and not a very sophisticated one.

People have been attracted to Victor Hugo's *Les Miserables* for more than 150 years precisely because it is a comprehensive rejection of such skepticism. At fourteen hundred pages of suffering, vulgarity, pity, fury, revolution, worship, and self-sacrifice, comprehensive is the right adjective. Other great romantics reveled in nihilism. Hugo gave the brief for life.

Part of Hugo's message of empathy was political, calling attention to people—especially poor women and orphans—who seemed "as though they were on a planet much further from the sun than we." When Hugo took in refugees from the Paris Commune of 1871, a conservative mob besieged his house chanting, "Death to Jean Valjean!" That is the reality a fictional character can assume.

But the main purpose of *Les Miserables*, says the writer Mario Vargas Llosa, is "to demonstrate the existence of a transcendent life, of which life on earth is a mere transient part." Hugo himself was not an orthodox anything, much less an orthodox Christian. But his great book is a vivid description of the workings of grace. Valjean begins as a hardened prisoner. He is shown mercy and learns to show it. He is hunted through a series of resurrections—emerging from a live burial, from the sewers of Paris. His nemesis is broken by his moral certitude. Valjean is saved by his sacrifices. He learns love by raising a daughter, and then the far reaches of love by giving her away. The ending is not particularly happy. Handing over his child to the future also leaves the protagonist broken. In the end, he has surrendered everything he possessed except God. But that is enough.

There is a reason the great stories persist in provoking our lacrimal system: the hope that life is a story, that all the suffering, vulgarity, pity, and sacrifice add up to something and lead somewhere.

So perhaps my sons will someday understand there is much to learn about being human from imagined lives. From Hugo and others, they may gain some skepticism about skepticism. They may even eventually discover why it is difficult for a father to contemplate giving up his children to the future, in the long, natural sacrifice of the best things about us. And I hope they will find, as Valjean does in the end, that "there is scarcely anything else in the world but that: to love one another." Which is worth a few tears.

# PART 4

# Heroes

# Frederick Buechner Was a Writer Tuned In to the Frequency of Grace

*The Washington Post*, August 22, 2022

WHEN THE LATE FREDERICK BUECHNER—novelist, preacher, Christian apologist—was asked to summarize the single essential insight of his prolific writing and speaking career, he would respond, "Listen to your life."

"If indeed there is a God," he explained, "which most of the time I believe there is, and if indeed he is concerned with the world, which the Christian faith is saying . . . one of the ways he speaks to us, and maybe one of the most powerful ways, is through what happens to us."

Life's temptation, of course, is to move from place to place on cruise control, which means, for me, focusing on failures in the past or worries about the future. So how, some questioners would persist with Buechner, do we start getting into the habit of fully inhabiting our experience? "Pay attention to moments," he said, when "unexpected tears come to your eyes and what may trigger them." He was talking about those sudden upwellings of emotion we get from the sublimity of nature or art, when we see a whale breaching, or are emotionally ambushed by a line in a film or poem. We are led toward truth and beauty by a lump in the throat.

I felt that kind of lump when I heard of Buechner's recent passing. It was not primarily the evidence of grief. How could anyone die better than at ninety-six, in his own bed, after a life filled with significance and heaped with honors? My unbidden tears were triggered by gratitude to the mentor I had never met. More than anyone else in recent literary history, he showed how a modern person, schooled in skepticism, pursued by appropriate doubts, could find the frequency of grace, as if he were tuning an old radio.

We were encouraged to listen to our lives because Buechner allowed us to listen in on his. His model of ministry was heroic vulnerability. All that took was for him to rip his own heart out and put it on display. This would be hard for anyone, but especially for someone with a reticence that was not just a protective bark, but found, ring by ring, all the way to his core. In his brilliant and moving memoirs, Buechner tells us about the ten-year-old boy, playing indoors with his brother, while his business-failure of a father kills himself with carbon monoxide in the garage. The sensitive child had perceived that "something had gone terribly wrong with his laughter." On the final page of the family copy of *Gone with the Wind*, his father had written a suicide note: "I adore and love you, and am no good."

Buechner tells of being a writer whose first novel is given rave reviews. "I had written a book," he wrote, "that was compared with Henry James and Marcel Proust and, headier still, was labeled decadent." After moving to New York with great expectations, he finds he can hardly write a word. Though from a secular background, he finds himself almost inexplicably drawn to the Presbyterian ministry. "In the midst of our freedom," he wrote, "we hear whispers from beyond time" and "sense something hiddenly at work in all our working." Someone asked him whether he had ever considered putting his talents to work for God, which he had not. And then his whispers organized themselves into a faith. "Something in me recoils from using such language," he said, "but here in the end I am left with no other way of saying it than that what I finally found was Christ. Or was found. It hardly seems to matter which."

Rather than arriving at faith along the sawdust trail of American evangelicalism, Buechner came via Princeton University and, eventually, Union Theological Seminary. And when he encountered evangelicals for the first time, the cultural contrast was obvious. He accepted modern levels of doubt about the historicity of scripture and understood the reasons for skepticism about organized religion. But over the decades, Buechner came to find his enduring popularity in evangelical circles. He taught at Wheaton College in Illinois in 1985, and his public papers now reside there.

Buechner's warm welcome among evangelicals points to a revealing fact. Their literary heroes tend to be decidedly non-evangelical. Neither C. S. Lewis (a traditional Anglican) nor G. K. Chesterton (after his conversion, a tireless Catholic apologist) nor J. R. R. Tolkien (a devout Catholic from boyhood) would be comfortable within the theological and aesthetic confines of conservative Protestantism. Which means those confines are too narrow. Evangelicals prove through appropriation that they are missing out on the power of myth, on the sacramental nature of reality, on what Graham Greene called "the appalling strangeness of the mercy of God."

Buechner fit this company. He understood that faith and doubt are not opposites but integral parts of the human journey. He knew that openness is ultimately a more important virtue than certainty. He presented, especially in his powerful novels, the mixture of sacred and profane at the heart of humanity, even at the heart of holiness.

Now he rests, if there is any justice in the world, in the grace that pursued him for so long.

# Why Anthony Fauci Is the Greatest Public Servant I Have Known

*The Washington Post*, October 10, 2022

AMERICAN POLITICAL DISAGREEMENTS HAVE OFTEN COME down to us in the form of vivid dyads. Alexander Hamilton vs. Thomas Jefferson. Stephen A. Douglas vs. Abraham Lincoln. Franklin D. Roosevelt vs. Arthur H. Vandenberg.

One such conflict over the past few years has been Senator Rand Paul (R-Ky.) vs. Anthony S. Fauci, the longtime head of the department of infectious diseases at the National Institutes of Health.

I am not referring here to any moral or intellectual equivalence between the figures. Their inequality, in fact, is a central part of the story. Paul's contempt for expertise, his spread of conspiracy theories, his use of oversight as ambush—all this indicates a performative approach to governing. Reality does not ultimately count; the play is the thing. And Paul has found an audience among ideologues who demonstrate their fidelity by taking some extra poison in their pudding.

The single most shocking fact to come out of the recent pandemic has been the unfair self-apportionment of pain and death. People in majority-Republican counties experienced 73 more deaths from Covid-19 per 100,000 people than those in majority-Democratic counties. There are a variety of explanations. One is certainly the use of high office to discourage the most basic means of self-preservation during a deadly disease outbreak. Imagine if it had been Democratic public authorities encouraging Republican self-victimization. But it was Republican officials who did it—and found it an effective method of self-publicization.

On the other side has stood Fauci. In more than fifty years at the NIH, Fauci has been accustomed to scientific debates in which disagreements emerge as the result of seeking different methods in the pursuit of the same goals. But Paul and his co-ideologues have left the assumption of shared objectives in tatters. And this has constituted an attack on the very idea of public service—the notion that true experts can make a career in seeking the common good.

For Fauci, it has been a professional and moral commitment that politics should stop at the human biome's edge. This does not imply that scientific experts are perfect. To the contrary, the purpose of the scientific method is to organize failure into deeper insight. But it does mean that scientific truth is not relative—or determined in the political realm.

In attempting to demonize Fauci, his critics gained a fundraising target. And that, by their own lights, is the definition of political success. But seldom has the choice of an attack been more of a self-indictment. Fauci is not only a symbol of public health orthodoxy; he has done as much as any scientist to turn medical innovation into humanitarian progress.

For generations, Fauci has applied a low-key excellence to fighting domestic AIDS, tropical infectious diseases, global AIDS, and Ebola. His role in the creation of the President's Emergency Plan for AIDS Relief has helped save tens of millions of lives and built medical infrastructure across the developing world. His focus and public investment have brought us to the verge of vaccines against malaria, one of the world's deadliest parasites.

Fauci is a symbol of sorts. He demonstrates what can happen when a nation at the height of its power employs the finest scientific minds of their generation in the pursuit of public health goals few believed were possible. The result has been a golden age of public health, motivated by an American belief in human dignity.

This is not the kind of reputation to be dented by political attacks or

Internet rumors. It is a legacy praised each day by the chorus of millions of breaths that would otherwise be silent. A vast chorus of the nearly lost.

As someone who worked for a few years with Fauci during George W. Bush's administration, I saw how he pushed for new ideas and new funding: by expressing his passion for the scientific project itself. He is the ultimate explainer. In briefings, he did not conspire to make himself seem smart. He made those he briefed feel they had spent a few minutes looking out on a vast landscape of innovation.

Fauci assumes that everyone is rational and thus persuadable. That is not quite true. But when he described to me the shifting shell of sugars that surround and protect the AIDS virus, or how mRNA vaccines work, it left a few impressions. First, how something that can kill you can be so fascinating. But also how much Fauci's friendship felt like mentorship. The greatness of his calling rubbed off a bit. And one was left with the infection of his mission.

Fauci's forthcoming retirement as director of the National Institute of Allergy and Infectious Diseases will cost Americans, and people around the world, far more than they realize. But he will ever remain the greatest public servant I have known.

# George H. W. Bush's Life Proves That, Sometimes, Things Go Gloriously Right

*The Washington Post*, December 3, 2018

Aʟʟ ᴛʜᴇ ᴛᴀʟᴋ ᴀʙᴏᴜᴛ ᴛʜᴇ ᴀᴛᴛʀɪʙᴜᴛᴇs of this generation or that generation is usually overblown. But there is an exception when a cohort of young Americans share a massive, overwhelming experience of economic depression or war. A certain view of their country is often formed and fixed.

This can be said of Lt. John F. Kennedy, the commanding officer of PT-109. And Lt. Cmdr. Richard M. Nixon, who ran the South Pacific Combat Air Transport Command. And navy aviator George H. W. Bush. Serving in the Pacific theater of World War II, these young men had few traits of temperament or character in common. But the war shaped their conception of the United States' global role and their view of the necessity and capability of government in general.

People who fought in World War II were marinated in the ideas that evil is real and that American power is an essential, irreplaceable force for good. They intuitively understood the moral narrative of Munich, Buchenwald, D-Day, Hiroshima, NATO, and the twilight struggle. And they generally shared the notion that the United States could do anything that power, wealth, will, and courage could accomplish.

This presented the temptation of overreach, as in Vietnam. Kennedy's inaugural pledge to "pay any price, bear any burden" should be taken seriously, but not literally. But the children of World War II really did believe that a torch was passing from Dwight Eisenhower's generation—the generation of their commanding officers—to a group of Americans who had rescued the world and fully intended to lead it. Given the other paths the United States might have taken, they did an extraordinary job. They twice saved humanity from well-armed, aggressive, totalitarian ideologies—first as soldiers, sailors, and airmen, and then as statesmen. The United States and the world owe them a great deal.

Being one of the youngest navy pilots in World War II, and blessed with longevity, George H. W. Bush was among the last of his cohort to leave us. As intelligence chief, diplomat, and president, he brought to his calling a set of values that might be called patrician. He was less New Frontier and more old school. He rose in government on the impulse of service. He lived by high standards of decency, fair play, humility, love of family, and love of country. He was relentlessly moderate in both temperament and political instinct.

This type of "establishment" code is easier to lampoon than replace. So much of what a graceless age dismisses as repression is actually politeness, compassion, and dignity.

And Bush's moral sensibilities turned out to be exactly what was needed at a decisive historical moment. As the Soviet Union collapsed under the weight of its economic and moral failure, what was needed from the United States was patience, wisdom, steady purpose, and the generosity of true power. In presiding over the breaking of nations, an excess of vision or ambition might have been dangerously disruptive. Crowing would have led to bitterness and unpredictable anger. And Bush was incapable of crowing.

On closer exposure to Bush, there was something more at work than a moral code. I generally saw the elder Bush through the eyes of his son, former president George W. Bush, for whom I worked. And he could hardly mention his father's name without welling up with tears of affection. During the younger Bush's first Republican National Convention speech, we had to cut short the section praising his father, because he could not get through the words without breaking down. There was a sweetness to their relationship that is a tribute to both men. George H. W. Bush loved deeply, and was deeply loved. He was sentimental without being fragile. And those who saw weakness in his manner know nothing about true strength—the victory over ego, over impulse, over hatred.

Dying can be cruel and unfair. But there was a profound and encouraging sense of rightness, of fittingness, at Bush's death. He left few things unaccomplished, and none that mattered. He was only briefly parted from the love of his life. His strength failed before his spirit. Bush died as well as a man could manage—full of years, full of honors, surrounded by affection, confident in his faith, knowing that his work on earth was done.

Bush's life provides assurance that sometimes things go gloriously right. Sometimes Americans vote for a decent and honest leader. Sometimes a president finds his calling and his moment. Sometimes a good man meets a good end.

And still. It is a sad and solemn task to dig the graves of giants.

# Billy Graham Was Consumed by Grace

*The Washington Post*, February 21, 2018

BILLY GRAHAM WAS EASILY THE MOST influential evangelical Christian of the twentieth century—a man at home in the historical company of George Whitefield and John Wesley.

But this would be hard to tell from reading his sermons, which even close associates described as ordinary. His books are hardly more memorable. So what was it that compelled hundreds of millions of people to attend and watch his evangelistic "crusades" and to find personal transformation in his words?

Graham's global ministry was the triumph of complete sincerity, expressed with a universally accessible simplicity. "There is no magic, no manipulation," said publicist Gavin Reid. "The man just obviously believes what he says." Graham could display charisma in meetings with presidents and queens. In the pulpit—the place of his calling from an early age—he was nearly transparent, allowing a light behind him to shine through him. He had the power of a man utterly confident in some other, greater power.

American fundamentalism from the Scopes monkey trial to the 1950s was traumatized, marginalized, and inward-looking. Graham's achievement was to turn the face of fundamentalism outward toward the world—shaping, in the process, a distinct religious movement. His evangelicalism was more open and appealing, more intellectually and culturally engaged. Graham took his fellow evangelicals from the margins to the center—from the sawdust trail to the White House. He managed to be winsome without being compromised. And evangelical Christians felt grateful to have a public representative who—through his integrity and consistency—brought credit to their faith.

There was initial resistance to Graham's work among mainline Protestants. As Graham announced more and more crusades, theologian Reinhold Niebuhr was not amused. Graham, Niebuhr warned, would "accentuate every prejudice which the modern, 'enlightened' but morally sensitive man may have against religion." Graham responded: "I have read nearly everything Mr. Niebuhr has written and I feel inadequate before his brilliant mind and learning. Occasionally I get a glimmer of what he is talking about . . . [but] if I tried to preach as he writes, people would be so bewildered they would walk out."

More than 2 million people walked into Graham's sixteen-week New York crusade in 1957. And Graham was joined one night at Madison Square Garden by the Reverend Martin Luther King Jr.

There was also resistance among some fundamentalists.

I grew up in a theologically conservative Calvinist church in which the Reformation was refought on a weekly basis. The man who would become my father-in-law—blessed with a fine voice—decided to sing in the choir at a Graham crusade that came into town. Afterward, he was hauled in front of the elders of the church to be questioned. They were upset at this participation because Graham—when people would come forward during the altar call—would refer them back to their home churches, including Catholic churches.

In fact, the tone of Graham's public voice changed over the years, becoming more ecumenical, less harsh and nationalistic. Some of this he credited to broader exposure to the world. "I think now when I say something, 'How is this going to sound in India? How is it going to sound to my friends in Hungary or Poland?'" But this also involved a theological shift. "I used to believe that pagans in far countries were lost if they did not have the gospel of Christ preached to them," he reflected in 1978. "I no longer believe that."

His faith in the essentials of the Christian gospel, however, never changed. And it made him into a busy builder of institutions that still carry the Christian message. Graham was instrumental in the founding of *Christianity Today*, the Billy Graham Center at Wheaton College, and Gordon-Conwell Theological Seminary. He was a major supporter of the National Association of Evangelicals and Fuller Theological Seminary.

As in any long, public life, there were low moments, particularly when Graham came into contact with political figures such as Lyndon B. Johnson and Richard Nixon. But he also had a powerful, positive influence in the life of the young George W. Bush and countless others. And this much is clear. For Graham, faith was not the instrument to some other end; it was the prize itself. He had no ulterior motives. No trace of cynicism. He was consumed by grace and spoke in gratitude.

For a Christian, it is not a small thing for a man to talk about Jesus Christ, face-to-face, to more people than anyone has ever done. Or to see how remarkably God used his servant Billy, just as he was.

# Nelson Mandela Steered South Africa from the Abyss

*The Washington Post*, August 2, 2013

THE CELEBRATION OF NELSON MANDELA'S ninety-fifth birthday and the realization that he nearly did not reach it have occasioned a torrent of tributes, all deserved but some misdirected.

Mandela spent twenty-seven years in prison, much of it in a seven-by eight-foot cell with a bedroll and a bucket, embodying the wall-less captivity of a majority of his compatriots. But his historical place was secured during the four troubled years between his release in February 1990 and his inauguration as president in May 1994.

In this period, South Africa stared into an abyss. Violence among various white and black factions threatened to overwhelm constitutional negotiations. Mandela accused security forces of ignoring or inciting the bloody feud between the African National Congress (ANC) and its Inkatha rival. Political talks with the government eventually broke down. At ANC rallies, signs appeared reading, "Mandela, give us guns" and "Victory through battle not talk."

Then in April 1993, Mandela's friend and possible successor as ANC president, Chris Hani, was assassinated in front of his home by a white supremacist. The nation, Mandela later recalled, was on the verge of a "race war."

Seldom has the contingent nature of history, or the decisive role of a leader within it, been more evident. The wrong word would have set spark to tinder. Instead, Mandela urged his followers to be a "disciplined force for peace."

"Tonight," he said, "I am reaching out to every single South African, black and white, from the very depths of my being.... Now is the time for all South Africans to stand together against those who, from any quarter, wish to destroy what Chris Hani gave his life for—the freedom of all of us."

The old South Africa, founded on bigotry and oppression, offered plenty of excuses for retribution. Because of Mandela, a new South Africa was conceived in magnanimity.

Mandela is sometimes compared to Mahatma Gandhi or Martin Luther King Jr. Such well-meaning praise encourages a misunderstanding of Mandela's accomplishment. After employing nonviolent tactics in the 1950s, he became an early ANC advocate of "armed struggle" and was the first commander of its military wing, Umkhonto we Sizwe, the Spear of the Nation. (He received guerrilla training in Morocco from Algerian fighters.)

At the time of his greatest influence in the 1990s, Mandela was not a holy man pleading for peace. He was a warrior calling for reconciliation. Having resisted his oppressors, he had the standing to engage them. It was a role that invites comparison to Anwar Sadat or Menachem Begin, or to Abraham Lincoln. He was also, of course, modern South Africa's George Washington, its first citizen. Postcolonial nations are blessed or cursed by their founding presidents. Across the border in Zimbabwe, that nation's Washington turned out to be a petty, corrupt, vengeful despot. Mandela, in contrast, honored constitutional procedures, respected minority rights, and instilled democratic habits.

And while not a religious leader, he exercised a form of spiritual leadership. He took a leap of faith to trust the representatives of a police state. He displayed the grace that was necessary to break a chain of violence. And he understood the enormous power of a blow unstruck.

Historians have excavated the biographical layers that produced such leadership. From the tribal court—his father was the counselor to a Thembu chief—Mandela gained a dignity and self-confidence that can only be called aristocratic. From missionary schools, he seemed to absorb Victorian lessons of fair play and respect for law. One Mandela biographer, Tom Lodge, argues that this background produced "a politics of grace and honor that, notwithstanding its conservatism, was probably the only politics that could have enabled South Africa's relatively peaceful transition to democracy."

As a young man, Mandela embraced militant ideology. On the far side of prison—against the predictions of many—he was a political pragmatist. He could see and accommodate the interests of his former oppressors. He did not want to rule over a ruin. But there was also a core beyond compromise. From prison, he smuggled out a note reading: "Any man or institution that tries to rob me of my dignity will lose." And they did.

Given its history, South Africa is never far from the abyss, and Mandela's successors have been smaller leaders. The country, in some ways, has regressed toward division—racial resentment, persistent inequality, and abuses by party elites. But South Africa will always have one advantage, and one thing in common with America: At every point of decision, it is improved by honoring the example of its first citizen.

# Charles Colson Found Freedom in Prison

*The Washington Post*, April 22, 2012

CHARLES W. COLSON—WHO SPENT SEVEN MONTHS in prison for Watergate-era offenses and became one of the most influential social reformers of the twentieth century—was the most thoroughly converted person I've ever known.

Following Chuck's recent death, the news media—with short attention spans but long memories—have focused on the Watergate portion of his career. They preserve the image of a public figure at the moment when the public glare was harshest—a picture taken when the flashbulbs popped in 1974.

But I first met Chuck more than a decade after he left the gates of Alabama's Maxwell prison. I was a job-seeking college senior, in whom Chuck detected some well-hidden potential as a research assistant. In him, I found my greatest example of the transforming power of grace. I had read many of the Watergate books, in which Chuck appears as a character with few virtues apart from loyalty. I knew a different man. The surface was recognizable—the Marine's intensity, the lawyer's restless intellect. The essence, however, had changed. He was a patient and generous mentor. And he was consumed—utterly consumed—by his calling to serve prisoners, ex-prisoners, and their families.

Many wondered at Chuck's sudden conversion to Christianity. He seemed to wonder at it himself. He spent each day that followed, for nearly forty years, dazzled by his own implausible redemption. It is the reason he never hedged or hesitated in describing his relationship with Jesus Christ. Chuck was possessed, not by some cause, but by someone.

He stood in a long line of celebrated converts, beginning with the Apostle Paul on the Damascus road, and including figures such as John Newton, G. K. Chesterton, and Malcolm Muggeridge. They were often received with skepticism, even contempt. Conversion is a form of confession—a public admission of sin, failure, and weakness. It brings out the scoffers. This means little to the converted, who have experienced something more powerful than derision. In his poem "The Convert," Chesterton concludes: "And all these things are less than dust to me / Because my name is Lazarus and I live."

Prison often figures large in conversion stories. Pride is the enemy of grace, and prison is the enemy of pride. "How else but through a broken heart," wrote Oscar Wilde after leaving Reading Gaol, "may Lord Christ enter in?" It is the central paradox of Christianity that fulfillment starts in emptiness, that streams emerge in the desert, that freedom can be found in a prison cell. Chuck's swift journey from the White House to a penitentiary ended a life of accomplishment—only to begin a life of significance. The two are not always the same. The destruction of Chuck's career freed up his skills for a calling he would not have chosen, providing fulfillment beyond his ambitions. I often heard him quote Alexander Solzhenitsyn, and mean it: "Bless you, prison, for having been in my life."

Chuck was a powerful preacher, an influential cultural critic, and a pioneer of the dialogue between evangelicals and Catholics. But he was always drawn back to the scene of his disgrace and his deliverance. The ministry he founded, Prison Fellowship, is the largest compassionate outreach to prisoners and their families in the world, with activities in more than one hundred countries. It also plays a morally clarifying role. It is easier to serve the sympathetic. Prisoners call the bluff of our belief in human dignity. If everyone matters and counts, then criminals do as well. Chuck led a movement of volunteers attempting to love some of their least lovable neighbors. This inversion of social priorities—putting the last first—is the best evidence of a faith that is more than crutch, opiate, or self-help program. It is the hallmark of authentic religion—and it is the vast, humane contribution of Chuck Colson.

It is a strange feeling to lose a mentor—a sensation of being old and small and exposed outside his shade. Chuck's irrational confidence in my twenty-one-year-old self felt a little like grace itself. The scale of his life—a broad arc from politics to prison to humanitarian achievement— is also the scale of his absence. But no one was better prepared for death. No one more confident in the resurrection—having experienced it once already. So my grief at Chuck's passing comes tempered—because he was Lazarus, and he lives.

# Still Hope for the U.N.

*The Wheaton Record*, November 22, 1985

IN CASE YOU SOMEHOW MISSED the festivities, the United Nations celebrated its fortieth anniversary last month. The birthday was commemorated with a number of addresses by international leaders as well as the greatest New York traffic jams in recent memory. Few could determine which was more frustrating, the speeches or the traffic.

The world has long grown accustomed to the bluster and bombast of the United Nations. Most spectators expected very little from the solemn posturing and interminable diatribes that normally characterize such proceedings. For the most part, they were not disappointed.

Ronald Reagan was there to outline his five-point regional peace plan. In essence, he simply asked the Soviet Union to forsake its meddling in Ethiopia, Afghanistan, Nicaragua, and elsewhere. To put it mildly, the Soviets were not receptive to this rather unrealistic proposal.

Soviet foreign minister Eduard Shevardnadze gave a rather limp defense of his nation's lopsided arms control proposals.

President Daniel Ortega of Nicaragua posed for photographers at Macy's and jogged in Central Park. He predictably blamed the United States for the fact that he has dramatically stepped up his repression of human rights in Nicaragua. Apparently there is no end to the gall of these petty Marxist dictators.

Prime Minister Nakasone of Japan waxed philosophical and proclaimed with great gravity, "All living things—humans, animals, trees, grasses—are essentially brothers and sisters." I can understand the brotherhood of man, possibly animals, maybe even trees, but grasses?

In short, the United Nations was just being its futile, humorous, disturbing self. There was, however, one overwhelming exception to the general rule of deception and pomposity. One speech stung the conscience of the world with its convicting purity.

Before the assembly of diplomats and dignitaries came an elderly nun in sandals and sari to speak of love and justice. This frail and saintly woman was Mother Teresa.

Her message was first one of reconciliation. Asserting that "we are all children of God," she prayed that "no color, no religion, no nationality should come between us." She went on to remind the world of its responsibility to the starving and diseased.

In an act of compassion that evangelicals could learn much from, she announced her plan to build a shelter for AIDS victims in New York.

Yet her words were also ones of confrontation. She said, "We are frightened of nuclear war, we are frightened of this new disease [AIDS], but we are not frightened to kill a little child. When we destroy the unborn child we destroy God."

This exceptional woman, who has seen the worst of war, poverty, and disaster proclaimed, "Abortion has become the greatest destroyer of peace."

Christians are told they can uphold Christ before the kings of the earth and not be ashamed. Mother Teresa came from the slums of Calcutta to the halls of the United Nations to do exactly that.

Speaking on behalf of the diseased, the poor, and the helpless unborn, she became Christ to a desperate world. If such a thing can happen at the United Nations, perhaps there is hope for it after all.

# PART 5

# The Arena

# How the Gay Rights Movement Found Such Stunning Success

*The Washington Post*, June 13, 2022

I<small>N</small> D.C.—AND EVERYWHERE ELSE, I SUSPECT, with a Bohemian pulse—Pride celebrations are in full swing. Some people who are gay have come to resent the relentlessly commercial aspects of the season, reflected in Pride bocce ball sets from Target and Pride dog bandanas from Walmart. But nothing important in America is not monetized. And gay rights are easily the most dramatically successful social movement of the past few decades.

This is not to say gay life in America is all rainbows. Many LGBTQ youths still face homelessness and are drawn to the false, cruel consolation of suicide. In redder parts of the country, school libraries are targeted for carrying LGBTQ literature. And middle America seems largely unreconciled to conceptions of gender that involve prepubescent medical intervention.

Yet most people now regard the equal treatment of gay people as a minimal commitment of a just society. In 1996, only 27 percent of Americans supported same-sex marriage. But this has changed in group after group. In 2016, for the first time, a majority of adults sixty-five and older said they supported same-sex marriage. The same became true of a majority of Protestants in 2017 and of Republicans in 2021. Weekly church attenders remain the most resistant category. But even among this group,

40 percent approve of gay marriage. Overall support among Americans now exceeds 70 percent.

This is a battle in the culture war that was never fully joined. After the Supreme Court's *Obergefell v. Hodges* decision in 2015 legalizing same-sex marriage nationwide, few politicians—including social conservatives— seemed eager to revisit the issue. And it is hard to imagine that even a conservative Supreme Court majority would want to challenge such a decisive U.S. majority.

Consider the contrast to abortion politics, where a Supreme Court decision in 1973 set off one of the most durable struggles in American public life. Why have these two examples of social controversy worked out so differently?

Perhaps the strongest reason is the simplest. The argument over abortion involves conflicting perspectives on human rights—one that emphasizes the autonomy of women, the other that emphasizes the value of nascent human life. It is a fundamental clash of visions that often ends in bitterness and the questioning of motives.

In the conflict over gay rights, supporters have asserted a compelling view of human dignity, while opponents have struggled to explain how broadening rights harms others. The advance of same-sex marriage, it seems, has generally ended in cake and dancing.

Some conservatives claimed that gay marriage would somehow weaken the institution of straight marriage. But the evidence that same-sex marriage increases rates of divorce, child poverty, or children living in single-parent homes appears nonexistent. (A decline in family stability in the United States has caused harm to children, but its roots long predate same-sex marriage.)

A second reason for gay rights' rapid solidification as a core American value is an implication of genetics. Though there seems to be no single "gay gene," scientists in the field generally affirm a role for genetics in the determination of sexual orientation. And imposing social or legal disadvantages on individuals for an unchosen disposition seems a violation of basic fairness.

The claim by some social conservatives that a genetic tendency toward homosexuality doesn't make it moral—any more than a genetic tendency toward violence or crime makes them permissible—strikes me as tendentious. There is a wide ethical difference between the felonious theft of life or property and the sexual activities of LGBTQ people that are roughly equivalent to those of their heterosexual counterparts. We ask everyone to refrain from assault and robbery; opponents of homosexuality would have only one group refrain from sex.

Third, opposition to same-sex marriage seems less religious than generational. Half a century ago, leaders could simply count on a general social uneasiness about people who are gay. Such discomfort now cannot be assumed, particularly among the young. Opponents of gay rights are forced to argue directly for their views—which must feel intolerant while emerging from their mouths.

Among religious young people, certain questions are growing more insistent: Why should we assess homosexuality according to Old Testament law that also advocates the stoning of children who disobey their parents? Isn't it possible that the Apostle Paul's views on homosexuality reflected the standards of his own time, rather than the views of Jesus, who never mentioned the topic? There is little wonder that, according to a Pew Research Center poll, over half of white evangelicals fifty and older oppose gay marriage while over half of those under fifty years old in the same group support gay marriage.

It is still possible for the gay rights movement to destructively overreach—as in denying the right of religious schools and charities to shape their own institutional standards. But in the meantime, I'm up for some Pride bocce.

# Abortion Deserves a Sober Debate. Instead, It Gets a War of Unreason.

*The Washington Post*, July 27, 2022

THIS IS A DIFFICULT MOMENT FOR *Roe v. Wade* to have fallen.

A complicated debate about life and death—involving science, law, and moral philosophy—has been thrown into the middle of an escalating culture war. And intemperance is the order of the day.

Decades ago there were more pro-choice Republicans and pro-life Democrats to help blunt the partisan edge of the debate. Now, views on the topic have sorted by party and geography. The GOP has become captive to an ideology of power that often (on issues such as immigration, refugees, and poverty) belies its pro-life pretenses. And many Republican state legislatures—where post-*Roe* legal changes will mostly play out— have become laboratories of radicalism.

The question naturally arises: Are governors and state legislators who opposed lifesaving vaccination in the middle of a pandemic really equal to Solomonic choices about the reach of human autonomy and worth of nascent life?

Yet some ill-timed events are also inevitable. *Roe* has always been vulnerable because it was so poorly argued. Its medical line-drawing was fundamentally arbitrary. Its legal reasoning was uncompelling, even to many liberals. "The failure to confront the issue in principled terms," said Archibald Cox, President John F. Kennedy's solicitor general, "leaves the opinion to read like a set of hospital rules and regulations. . . . Neither historian, nor layman, nor lawyer will be persuaded that all the prescriptions of Justice [Harry] Blackmun are part of the Constitution."

The breathtaking overreach of *Roe* has been cited as the cause for an enduring political backlash. And one legal mind who famously did the citing was Justice Ruth Bader Ginsburg, a strong supporter of abortion rights. Speaking at the University of Chicago Law School in 2013, Ginsburg faulted *Roe* as being too sweeping, giving the pro-life movement "a target to aim at relentlessly." Abortion rights, she argued, would have been more deeply rooted had they been secured more gradually, in a process including state legislatures—which in the early seventies were moving toward liberalized abortion laws. "My criticism of *Roe*," she said, "is that it seemed to have stopped the momentum that was on the side of change."

*Roe* has been one of the first and largest sources of ideological polarization. Tens of millions of Americans believe abortion is a fundamental right. Tens of millions believe developing human life has moral worth and should have legal protection.

In 1973, the Supreme Court came down heavily on one side, essentially telling pro-life citizens they could never politically win because the Constitution wouldn't allow it. They naturally felt disenfranchised. If in 1973 the court had held that fetal life deserved all the protections of the 14th Amendment, I imagine pro-choice citizens would have felt disenfranchised as well.

This is the problem of seeking monumental social change by convincing a Supreme Court majority rather than working toward a social and political consensus. In the United States, lasting legitimacy is the product of democratic consent. Rule by court diktat is written in sand, even if the tide rises only once in a half century.

It's disappointing to watch elements of the left react to the democratization of the abortion issue by attacking democracy itself. The argument goes: The electoral college gives Republicans—who have lost the popular vote in five of the last six elections—an advantage in winning the presidency and appointing Supreme Court justices. And the

gerrymandering of state legislative districts has resulted in a GOP stran-
glehold on many state legislatures. Thus, the institutions where the left
loses are rigged and illegitimate. That sounds much like the attitude it
has been criticizing and fighting on the Trump right.

A universal principle of politics is that whinging is not an effective substitute for organization. Neither is vituperation. I accept that
pro-choice advocates believe they are seeking the welfare of women. But
when they accuse pro-life people of intentional cruelty, or seeking to
turn back the clock on civil rights, or advocating "a crime against humanity" (as Rep. Alexandria Ocasio-Cortez [D-N.Y.] has charged), they
poison our politics with venomous libel. Almost uniformly in my experience, pro-life advocates believe they are serving the most vulnerable
members of the human family by expanding the circle of legal inclusion
and protection.

I'm more comfortable with the gradualism recommended in Chief
Justice John G. Roberts Jr.'s prickly concurrence to *Dobbs*. He criticized
the stridency and "relentless freedom from doubt" in Justice Samuel A.
Alito Jr.'s ruling opinion. Roberts's temperamental conservatism might
have reached a similar conclusion over the course of a few more cases and
lowered the initial shock to the body politic.

For the foreseeable future, the abortion debate—with all its tragic
complexities—has been returned to the realm of democracy. And there is
little evidence our democracy is prepared for it.

# "Gaffes" Aside, I Once Assumed GOP Goodwill on Race. I Was Wrong.

*The Washington Post*, October 20, 2022

WHAT DOES THE RETURN OF UNVARNISHED RACISM to the center of our political culture mean?

The problem I'm highlighting is greater than former Los Angeles city councilwoman Nury Martinez's racist comments against the city's black and Oaxacan communities—though they were bad enough. The tapes were leaked to hurt Martinez, not chosen by her as a political stratagem.

For decades, the Martinez model of scandal has been the (more or less) typical response to gaffe-revealed racism in both parties. Remember the case of minority leader Trent Lott (R-Miss.) in late 2002, when he essentially endorsed Senator Strom Thurmond's (R-S.C.) 1948 Dixiecrat presidential campaign as a GOP ideal? Later, Lott dismissed his statement as an attempt to be "lighthearted." Few got the joke. And Lott soon resigned his Senate leadership office.

Though I supported Lott's resignation at the time, when I was a White House staffer I assumed that many such statements by Republicans were blunders, rooted in ignorance. Many GOP officials took a view of history that praised the Emancipation Proclamation and affirmed the Civil Rights Act of 1964, while essentially skipping over white supremacists' Redemption policy, lynching, routine police brutality, and the injustice of over-incarceration. Republicans sometimes committed career-ending acts by falling into a historical memory hole. But the general goodwill of the GOP on racial issues could still be broadly assumed.

This is among the worst errors of moral judgment I have made as a columnist. I tended to view bigotry as one of America's defects or failures. The historical works I read often tried to defend the best elements of the American ideal as dramatically outweighing the worst moments of its application.

But no: The country was soiled by the sin of slavery from its birth. Many white people became wealthy by systematically stealing the wages and wealth of their black neighbors. White Americans established a social and religious system designed to grant themselves dominance, often while trying to convince African Americans of God's lower regard for their souls. Such systemic abuse could be found in North and South (though it was more heavy-handed in the South). Slaves were raped with impunity and murdered without consequence. And if someone in the North promulgated abolitionist ideas with too much effect, they could be targeted for bounties, beaten in the street, or killed.

The conflict over constitutional protection for people with a different amount of melanin in their skin was the foundational test of American ideals. Many of the founders who supported slavery were the functional equivalent of terrorists: Maintain white superiority, they said, or we will blow up the whole system. Which they tried to do. An argument over political philosophy was settled only by a torrent of blood.

Yet it is still not fully resolved. Many in the South launched a successful campaign to secure white supremacy through states' rights and Klannish violence. And many in the North were content with the appearance of equality as long as it did not include actual social equality. This consensus of white people in support of fallacious freedom was challenged by the civil rights movement, which asserted a comprehensive legal, political, social, educational, and spiritual equality. The words of that movement—"Now is the time to lift our nation from the quicksands of racial injustice to the solid rock of brotherhood"—still echo. But the goals of that movement remain only partially fulfilled.

This is the environment into which the MAGA movement is pumping a toxic discharge of bigotry. Former president Donald Trump recently employed his own (supposedly) lighthearted treatment of racism's cruelest epithet. "The n-word!" he told a campaign rally. "Do you know what the n-word is?" The crowd certainly did, when given permission to use it by Trump. "It's—no, no, no. It's the 'nuclear' word." This was not a dog whistle; it was a Confederate trumpet.

During his last campaign, Trump warned suburban white women that "low-income housing would invade" their neighborhoods. Now he teases that he might run in 2024 "to take back that beautiful, beautiful house that happens to be white." Even using the language and argumentation of the playground, Trump does his damage. He implies that the institutions of American government are and should be white dominated. He directly defends the segregation of housing. He encourages the idea that minorities are aggressors against whites.

And Trump effectively gives permission to other MAGA fools. "They want crime," Senator Tommy Tuberville (R-Ala.) said about Democrats at a recent Trump rally. "They want crime because they want to take over what you got. They want to control what you have. They want reparations because they think the people that do the crime are owed that."

In MAGA world, the incitement of white grievance *is* the strategy. Such appeals are inseparable from racism. And they reopen a wound that nearly killed the patient before. It is politics at its most pernicious.

# The Real Religious-Liberty Issue Is About Identity, Not Discrimination

*The Washington Post*, June 7, 2018

SOMETIMES A MOVEMENT CAN BE SABOTAGED by its victories.

Such is the case with the Supreme Court's *Masterpiece Cakeshop* ruling. The decision properly smacked down the anti-religious bigotry of the Colorado Civil Rights Commission, which wanted not only to compel baker Jack Phillips to provide a cake for a same-sex wedding but also to sneer at him in the process. The broader question—could Phillips be compelled by a non-bigoted state authority?—was left for another day. The substance of the concurrence by Justices Elena Kagan and Stephen G. Breyer indicates that a ruling on the underlying issue—given the current composition of the court—would be 5 to 4 either way, with Justice Anthony M. Kennedy the deciding vote.

But a focus on commercial services is ultimately unhelpful for advocates of religious liberty. This is a debate over a vanishingly small exception—the denial of artistic expression (such as cakemaking or singing) for a ceremony that an artist finds religiously objectionable. In the case of Phillips, it did not matter who actually purchased the cake. If the straight friend of a gay couple being married had paid for the cake, Phillips would still have objected. And if a gay person had bought a wedding cake for a straight couple, Phillips would have done his work.

Even if you side with Phillips, the general rule in commercial settings is clear: It is unjust (and, in any serious version of Christian ethics,

immoral) to refuse the sale of goods and services to anyone simply because they are gay. And, in fact, it seldom happens. Violence directed at
gay people and the tragedy of suicide by gay teens are far more urgent
problems than being refused service at the local Wendy's.

No, the real religious-liberty issue is not discrimination in commercial settings. It is the right of religious institutions to maintain their
identity—including their views on sexuality—when they interact with
the public realm. Can students receive Pell Grants when they attend a
religious college that regards homosexual sex as immoral? Can the government work with a religious adoption agency that places children only
with a mother and father?

Here the issue is not whether you agree with such views. Rather:
Does the constitutional order make a place—within limits—for institutions that don't share the broader social consensus?

According to one form of liberalism, the answer is "no." In this view,
only individuals and the government have real, public, legal standing.
Other institutions—particularly hierarchical institutions—are sources of
oppression from which individuals need to be protected by the state.
Religion, therefore, should be privatized as much as possible.

The alternative is a principled pluralism—which often is embraced
in conservatism and in a different school of American liberalism. In this
view, freedom of religion implies and requires freedom of association.
People can effectively pursue their beliefs only in a community of fellow believers. And such communities—to maintain their identities—will
have different standards than those of the public order. Religious institutions (including not only houses of worship but also colleges, hospitals,
and charities) may hold to traditional sexual norms, or refuse to perform
abortions, or forbid female priests, or deny the Eucharist to unbelievers.
In a pluralistic society, the state does not endorse such views. But it does
not punish them. And more than that, it affirms that a genuinely pluralistic society is ultimately more free, virtuous, and purposeful, because
it is in the context of religious institutions that many people pursue the
meaning that gives direction to their freedom.

Some conservatives are too pessimistic about the future of pluralism; they think all of America is on the verge of having the enforced political correctness of Evergreen State College. This is simply false. Conservatives, however, are correct about one thing. Liberals of the first, more overbearing sort may view themselves as neutral arbiters of law, but they seek to impose a set of beliefs that is no less sectarian for being secular. In some ways, they play the role of an established church, requiring people such as Phillips to take part in its rites.

Particularly on the issue of gay rights, this is unnecessary. The social consensus—not least among younger religious believers—is shifting rapidly in favor of inclusion. We are headed toward an accommodation in which the majority culture accepts homosexuality but some small communities stay out of that consensus. Attempting to pressure and compel those communities is the one thing that could make an accommodation more difficult and bitter.

# Republicans in the Immigration Minefield

*The Washington Post*, January 26, 2015

Any REPUBLICAN EVENT CONVENED BY Rep. Steve King—he of "calves the size of cantaloupes" fame—could easily have degenerated into a festival of immigrant-bashing. It is to the credit of the serious GOP presidential prospects in attendance that the Iowa Freedom Summit generally did not.

Yes, Donald Trump emerged from his stretch clown car to say that "half of them are criminals." And King declared that protesting Dream Act supporters were from "the other planet." But the Republican script in Iowa was mainly focused on criticizing President Obama's immigration executive actions rather than negatively characterizing illegal immigrants themselves. Avoiding offensive language is admittedly a low bar. But it is progress for Republicans to realize that they are walking in a minefield instead of a meadow.

The greatest hazard to Republican prospects with rising demographic groups came in the form of an argument rather than an epithet. Former senator Rick Santorum made the case that the GOP should be "the party of the worker." Which is better than being the party of disdain for "takers" and the "47 percent." But Santorum went on to claim that immigration has depressed the earnings of native-born Americans. "We need to stand for an immigration policy," he said, "that puts Americans and American workers first."

The campaign slogan "America first," it turns out, is already taken. But Santorum is proposing a serious response to the GOP's national electoral challenge. Republicans, in this view, need to shift their focus away from high earners to struggling middle- and working-class families; and they also need to choose between courting the working class and courting Hispanic voters, because immigrants take jobs and depress wages at the low end. The party of the worker, therefore, must be the party of immigration restrictionism.

Santorum is often thoughtful; in this case, he is thoughtfully wrong. His economic case is overblown. Economists sift and dispute the evidence. But the long-term impact of immigration on native wages seems to be slight—slightly positive for those with a high school and some college education, slightly negative for those who don't graduate from high school. These effects, however, are overwhelmed by other economic trends, such as the advance of technology and globalized labor markets. The white working class does have many problems, but competition from low-skilled immigrants is not among the biggest ones.

Effectively focusing on the white working class also buys into the notion that Republicans can win the presidency by running up the white vote. This might, for all I know, work in the next presidential election. If (a significant "if") Hillary Clinton is the Democratic nominee and gets 80 percent of the minority vote, Republicans would probably need (in an estimate by *National Journal*'s Ron Brownstein) about 63 percent of white voters. (The highest percentage Republicans have ever gotten was Ronald Reagan's 64 percent in 1984.)

This is not impossible, with the right conditions and candidate. But because the electorate is growing less white over time—by about 2 percentage points every four years—this strategy becomes harder and harder to implement. Mitt Romney won the white vote in a landslide—59 percent—and lost his election handily. Republicans, in other words, need the appeal of Reagan at his height to narrowly win the presidency in the current electorate. Eventually, even that will not be enough.

Any strategy that pits the white working class against immigrants should also attract heightened moral scrutiny. It is one thing for a political analyst to recommend a get-out-the-whites strategy. But when this thought is consciously entertained by a politician, something disturbing has happened. We have too much tragic history with political lines drawn along ethnic and racial faults.

The issue of immigration has a way of clarifying some of the deepest beliefs of a political movement. Does it regard outsiders as potential threats or potential allies? Does it empathize or dehumanize? The public character of a political figure is often judged by voters—especially immigrant voters—intuitively, by signals and symbols. When arriving at a party, you generally know immediately if you are welcome or not.

No effective reconstitution of the Republican Party's appeal can begin with pessimism about the drawing power of Republican ideals. A party that has lost the ambition to convince is a party in decline.

# Americans' Aversion to Science Carries a High Price

*The Washington Post*, May 12, 2014

AMERICANS HAVE SOMETHING OF A SCIENCE PROBLEM. They swallow, for example, about $28 billion worth of vitamins each year, even though the *Annals of Internal Medicine* recently concluded that "most supplements do not prevent chronic disease or death, their use is not justified, and they should be avoided." Americans often fear swallowing genetically modified plants (and Vermont recently required labeling of food containing genetically modified organisms, known as GMOs), though GMOs have "been consumed by hundreds of millions of people across the world for more than 15 years, with no reported ill effects," according to the *Journal of the Royal Society of Medicine*.

Other opinions are closer to astrology than science. Some deny a link between HIV and AIDS or confidently assert a connection between cell phone usage and cancer. Rep. Michele Bachmann (R-Minn.), during the last presidential campaign, contended that the HPV vaccine causes "mental retardation." (And, yes, about a quarter of Americans believe in astrology.)

Science has its own explanation for why people are resistant to scientific beliefs. In evolutionary theory (assuming you believe such a thing), our intuitions about the physical world are generally accurate on a human scale—calculating the proper force and trajectory to hit a mammoth with a spear. But on matters that are not immediately related to our survival—say, on quantum motion, or the nature of black holes, or the effect of radio-frequency energy on the DNA in cells—our intuitions are pretty much useless. Science has often advanced in an uphill fight against common intuitions.

These intuitions can be shaped by a variety of factors: ideology, religion, philosophy, or culture. Resistance to vaccination or GMOs is sometimes rooted in a nearly religious belief that natural things are better—including, apparently, disease outbreaks and plants that die easily in droughts. A decade ago, I met a South African health official who argued that AIDS could be treated with garlic because she believed that pharmaceutical treatment was a neocolonial plot. Resistance in the United States to evolution is often associated with conservative religion. And skepticism about climate change is correlated with libertarian and free-market beliefs.

Merely raising climate disruption in this context will cause many to bristle. Skeptics employ this issue as a prime example of motivated reasoning—politicians motivated by the prospect of confiscation, scientists motivated by securing acclaim and government contracts. In its simplest, cable-television version, this charge, at least against scientists, is outrageous. The assumption that the vast majority in a scientific field is engaged in fraud or corruption is frankly conspiratorial. In this case, the conspiracy would need to encompass the national academies of more than two dozen countries, including the United States.

Other, more measured criticisms ring truer. Some scientists have displayed an artificial certainty on some matters that seems to cross into advocacy. Others assume that the only way to deal with greenhouse gas emissions is a strict, global regulatory regime—an economic and political judgment that has nothing to do with their actual expertise.

But none of these objections relates to the scientific question: Is a 40 percent increase in the atmospheric concentration of carbon dioxide since the Industrial Revolution driving disruptive warming? And further: Can this process be slowed, allowing societies and ecosystems more time to adapt?

Our intuitions are useless here. The only possible answers come from science. And for non-scientists, this requires a modicum of trust in the scientific enterprise. Even adjusting for the possibility of untoward advocacy, it seems clear that higher concentrations of carbon dioxide in the atmosphere have produced a modest amount of warming and are likely to produce more. This, in turn, is likely to produce higher sea levels, coastal flooding, shifting fisheries, ocean acidification, water shortages, lower crop yields, and vanishing ecosystems. The consequences will vary by region but are likely to be more severe in poorer nations. New York City can adapt to a rising ocean better than Bangladesh.

This scientific consensus raises difficult political questions. Is some grand global bargain on carbon-dioxide emissions, including China and India, even a possibility? Might it be more practical to make polluters pay—perhaps with a revenue-neutral carbon tax, fully rebated to taxpayers—thereby encouraging the development of new technologies that limit future carbon emissions? And I'd add: How can you oppose GMOs that resist pests and drought while pretending to help poor nations cope with climate disruption?

But perhaps the most difficult question is this: How can you make serious political decisions based on scientific likelihoods when politics thrives on the feeding of ideological certainties?

# PART 6

# Life and Death

# Too Many Americans Are Still in Covid Denial

*The Washington Post*, May 19, 2022

W HEN JOHNS HOPKINS UNIVERSITY ANNOUNCED THAT the United States had surpassed 1 million deaths from Covid-19, I was recovering from my first (and hopefully last) bout of the disease. I had prepared as much as I could—shout-out to Pfizer—so the infection passed like a nasty flu. Earlier in the crisis, an immunocompromised man in his late fifties, as I am, might have ended up in the hospital, on a ventilator, a coin flip away from eternity.

In a way, I now feel more connected with people whose lives have been touched by Covid. But of course, many lives have not been just touched but crushed by the disease. The cost of 1 million friends and relatives lost during the past twenty-seven months resists summary and comparison. There is no adequate scale on which to measure this mass of grief.

Yet trying is better than living in denial—pretending that the hurricane never passed or the earthquake never happened. At its worst, Covid-19 became the third leading cause of death in the United States, behind heart disease and cancer. The country saw its largest drop in life expectancy since World War II. More than two hundred thousand children have lost a parent or caregiver.

People try to grapple with this experience in different ways. My interpretive construct is global health in other countries. The United States is quite good at saving people from infectious diseases in other places. The President's Emergency Plan for AIDS Relief has saved more than 20 million lives since 2003. The President's Malaria Initiative has reduced malaria death rates by about 50 percent in the countries where it operates. In the process, it has saved the lives of roughly 2 million children.

When I have visited these programs abroad, I have seen how health technology plays an important role—things such as antiretroviral drugs and long-lasting, insecticide-treated bed nets. But the progress made depends on the human factor of adherence: taking the pills every day, even when you don't feel sick, and putting up the bed net every night without fail. Adherence to AIDS medicines was spotty at first because Africans sometimes distrusted Western medicine and turned to traditional healers. But over time, people saw the immediate, nearly miraculous healing power of the AIDS drugs in their friends and neighbors. Soon stigma was reduced, and AIDS patients in most places were achieving Western levels of adherence.

Now imagine yourself part of a country seeking to help the United States with its Covid-19 crisis. You are trying to deliver a miraculous vaccine that deters most infection and nearly guarantees freedom from severe disease. The key, as always, is adherence. But there is a powerful Red Faction—dominant in much of the country—that is partial to quack treatments, distrustful of modern medicine, and resistant to vaccines (and mask-wearing) as a point of political pride.

Surely, over time, the Red Faction would witness the health benefits of three or four jabs of a needle. Surely it would refuse to take health advice from wacko politicians and unreliable community healers. Surely the stigma would fade as the vaccine proved safe and effective.

But no. After more than two years, California reached more than 70 percent with full vaccine coverage. But a large number of states—including Missouri, Georgia, Arkansas, Alabama, Wyoming, Indiana—have barely reached 50 percent. While about half of residents are well protected in these states, little has been accomplished in building the kind of herd immunity that protects a whole community.

In any normal vaccination campaign—with the goal of 80 to 90 percent uptake—this would be judged a failure. A donor country would be forced to reconsider its methods. And questions would naturally arise: Why would a country with a relatively advanced health system have the highest number of Covid deaths in the world? Why were health outcomes so dramatically influenced by class and race? Why didn't efficacy eventually override stigma? Does this Red Faction have contempt for its elders, as indicated by who has taken the brunt of the casualties? Is this country prepared for any crisis requiring communal action?

There is another question that seems the most unexpected, at least to me. Since death rates for vaccinated people are fully twenty times lower than for the unvaccinated, what force, what faith, what ideology has led a large portion of the country to live so recklessly? We are dealing with a form of polarization that is stronger than self-preservation—a kind of populism that causes populists to die.

Yet most Americans still float down Covid River, living in denial of the rocks ahead: new variants, long Covid, continuing deaths. Who would have predicted that so many people's response to an existential crisis should be folk cures and complacency?

# George W. Bush's Words in State of Union Saved Millions of People

*The Washington Post*, February 11, 2013

EVEN AMONG THE FEW, ODD, NERDY CHILDREN who want to be speechwriters when they grow up (I was one), none dream of writing a State of the Union address. These tend to be long and shapeless affairs, lumpy with random policy, carried along by strained applause lines, dated before they are transcribed.

There are a few exceptions: Lyndon Johnson announcing a War on Poverty; Bill Clinton, as a scandal unfolded, undismayed in the lion's den. And then there were these sentences in the 2003 address ten years ago: "Tonight I propose the Emergency Plan for AIDS Relief," said President George W. Bush, "a work of mercy beyond all current international efforts to help the people of Africa. This comprehensive plan will prevent 7 million new AIDS infections, treat at least 2 million people with life-extending drugs, and provide humane care for millions of people suffering from AIDS and for children orphaned by AIDS."

In retrospect, the words were not particularly memorable. But the moment was remarkable. An initiative of this scale and ambition—the largest effort to fight a single disease in history—was utterly unexpected. Bush's strongest political supporters had not demanded it. His strongest critics, at least for a time, remained suspicious. The President's Emergency Plan for AIDS Relief (PEPFAR) existed entirely because of a willing leader, a creative policy team, a smattering of activists, and a vast, bleeding need.

I remember my first visits to sub-Saharan Africa as a policy adviser to President Bush soon after the announcement. Of about 30 million people with HIV, perhaps fifty thousand were receiving treatment. The pandemic had already produced 14 million orphans. Child-headed households were common; child-headed villages were not unknown. Walking through South African shantytowns, you mainly met grandparents and their grandchildren. The intervening generation had been nearly erased. Millions were dying at the same time and yet in total isolation, surrounded by the barbed wire of stigma. In the worst-affected countries, life expectancy had fallen by twenty years.

PEPFAR gathered the support of an odd coalition. Its congressional sponsors included Rep. Henry Hyde (R-Ill.), a pro-life leader, and Rep. Barbara Lee (D-Calif.); Senate Republican leader Bill Frist of Tennessee and Senator John Kerry (D-Mass.). Religious conservatives joined with traditionally liberal health organizations to push for the measure. It was signed into law four months after it was announced.

Implementation was swift, under a theory that PEPFAR's first administrator, Ambassador Randall Tobias, described as "Ready, fire, aim." By late 2005—with the help of PEPFAR and the Global Fund to Fight AIDS, Tuberculosis and Malaria—there were about eight hundred thousand people on treatment. That number today is more than 5 million.

On the tenth anniversary of PEPFAR, what lessons does it offer? Some of them relate narrowly to development. Scale and boldness matter. A collection of pilot projects is invariably run from the outside. National scale-ups require the creation of supply and management systems and encourage the sort of professionalism that can permeate a health system and beyond.

PEPFAR offers some political philosophic lessons. Liberals had to get accustomed to measured outcomes and accountability. Conservatives had to abandon an indiscriminate cynicism about the capabilities of the state. I remember once citing PEPFAR's achievements to a conservative leader as one example of successful governmental action. He responded dismissively, "But other than that?" Other than saving a few million lives on a distant continent from a cold start in less than a decade?

There is also a potent lesson here about America. My first professor of international relations assured me that altruism is always a ruse in the affairs of nations—nothing more than the pursuit of interest in the camouflage of morality. I now know—personally know—this is untrue. The Irish historian William Lecky once claimed, "The unwearied, unostentatious and inglorious crusade of England against slavery may probably be regarded as among the three or four perfectly virtuous pages comprised in the history of nations." Nothing human is "perfectly virtuous," but PEPFAR is an addition to his list.

America is a flawed and fallible nation. It is also the nation that does things such as this. During the twentieth century, in government meetings, in Berlin, Beijing, and Moscow, leaders made decisions that resulted in the deaths of millions of innocent people. I watched a leader make the decision to save the lives of millions of innocent people. Ten years later, it is still the noblest thing I have ever seen.

# The Found Generation of the HIV/AIDS Epidemic in Africa

*The Washington Post*, July 22, 2012

> *Everybody knows that pestilences have a way of recurring in the world; yet somehow we find it hard to believe in ones that crash down on our heads from a blue sky.*
>
> —Albert Camus, *The Plague*

A MEMORY FROM THE AIDS CRISIS. It was 2005, the year that global AIDS deaths peaked at 2.3 million. At the end of a dirt road in Kericho, Kenya, I visited Sister Placida, an energetic nun caring for a few dozen equally energetic AIDS orphans. She showed me several "memory boxes" that dying mothers had prepared for their children, holding photos, letters, a few mementos. The exercise struck me as forlorn—a short life poured into a shoebox—but also as defiant. Facing an absurd death sentence, these women wanted to be recalled not as victims but as humans. They wanted to leave a mark, to make a statement: Once there was such a life as mine.

As the International AIDS Conference meets in Washington, D.C., the news on HIV/AIDS is not all encouraging. About 44 percent of people needing treatment still lack it. AIDS remains the world's leading cause of death for women of reproductive age.

And yet: 8 million people in lower-income countries are now on AIDS medication. This includes 6.2 million in sub-Saharan Africa—more than a hundredfold increase in less than a decade.

How to comprehend such figures? An economist might calculate the productivity contained in more than 10 million cumulative life-years saved in the developing world by antiretroviral drugs since 1996. Not being an economist, I imagine millions of unfilled memory boxes. A lost generation, unexpectedly returned. A found generation.

In America, it is common to distrust institutions—to express a lack of confidence in Congress, the federal government, and major companies. The response to AIDS weighs on the other side of the balance.

It has brought great credit to the scientific enterprise, which first helped allay unreasoned fears, then guided evidence-based treatment and prevention. It has illustrated the power of government to do good in ways denied to individuals and private groups. Public agencies—particularly the President's Emergency Plan for AIDS Relief (PEPFAR)—met ambitious treatment goals, and on budget. The response to HIV/AIDS has been a reminder: The quest of politics is not big government or small government but effective government on the necessary scale.

The entities and individuals deserving a share of credit in the AIDS movement are marvelously diverse. Gay men in New York and San Francisco who refused to pass away in silence. Pharmaceutical companies that developed tests and antiretroviral drugs. Members of Congress from both parties who appropriated money to save lives outside their districts, outside their experience, outside their country. Taxpayers who paid the bills. Billionaire philanthropists, irritatingly persistent rock stars, nuns in Kericho. What other social movement, in its hall of fame, would need to reserve places for Gay Men's Health Crisis and for George W. Bush, the author of PEPFAR?

And for Africans as well, who saw the world crash down on their heads from a blue sky. Heads of state who pulled together national plans. Families who routinely took in the children of the dead. A man named Moses, in a shack in Kampala, who proudly showed me his pink adherence book, with its careful checks each day for the pills he took.

There are criticisms to be made in the global response to AIDS—failures of empathy, policy, and urgency—but the sum is an anecdote to cynicism. And it has brought the world to the verge of a previously unimaginable prospect. The next generation of AIDS prevention—including male circumcision, early treatment to reduce infectiousness, and drugs to stop mother-to-child transmission—holds the promise of dramatically reducing new infections.

Turning efficacy in medical trials into effectiveness in the field is the hardest part of public health, because the only thing more complicated than the structure of the AIDS virus is human behavior. Bending the curve of new infections downward will require sustained political will and serious resources. But such a struggle is no longer inconceivable. There is now a precedent of defiance, idealism, and success.

"What's true of all the evils in the world," wrote Camus, "is true of the plague as well. It helps men to rise above themselves. All the same, when you see the misery it brings, you'd need to be a madman, or a coward, or stone blind, to give in tamely to the plague."

We didn't and we won't.

# It Takes More Than a Village to Fight Malaria in Zambia

*The Washington Post*, April 5, 2012

IN A GLOBAL ANTI-MALARIA MOVEMENT I saw begin in Oval Office meetings and international summits, Mongu is at the end of a very long road. Located in western Zambia, about seventy-five miles from the Angolan border, the town is not close to anywhere. The rivers of the region are more like swamps filling a floodplain, their courses hidden by tall grasses—from the air, wide, serpentine bands of lime green. If rivers are like arteries, these are clogged.

Standing water breeds mosquitoes, which carry the malaria parasite, which takes the lives of children in seasonal waves. In this part of the world, some parents don't officially name their children until the age of five, since so many don't survive the killing fields of childhood.

Zambia has been the main test case for anti-malaria efforts during the last several years—a focus of funding by the U.S. government, the Gates Foundation, and the Global Fund to Fight AIDS, Tuberculosis and Malaria. Now the Anglican Church, international aid groups, and philanthropists such as Neville Isdell and Chris Flowers are attempting to fill remaining gaps in bed-net coverage in remote border areas, including Mongu.

The work isn't easy. About nineteen thousand nets are currently distributed in an area needing two hundred thousand. Their proper use requires education. At a ceremony I attended launching a local anti-malaria campaign, a Zambian government official threatened to confiscate bed nets employed as fishing nets or sewn into wedding dresses.

Despite such obstacles, anti-malaria efforts in Zambia have a history of success. From 2001 to 2008, Zambia saw more than a 60 percent reduction in inpatient malaria cases and deaths. The methods of fighting malaria are reliable and relatively noncontroversial: long-lasting insecticide-treated bed nets, indoor residual spraying of insecticides, and treatment with effective new drugs.

Successful anti-malaria efforts are an odd hybrid—part military operation and part church meeting.

The logistics of distributing nets and spraying insecticides require martial scale and organization. Gains against other diseases come arithmetically, dose by dose. Gains against malaria come exponentially, as chunks of geography are secured.

But bed nets can't simply be thrown off trucks. Their employment depends on human behavior. And behavior is influenced only by trusted institutions. So the Anglican Church in Zambia organizes volunteer malaria control agents, each charged with overseeing perhaps fifteen households—making sure the nets are properly installed and not used for fishing and weddings. The success of a vast anti-malaria campaign ultimately depends on a group of compassionate, slightly nosey church ladies.

The whole effort is only sustainable if local governments take leadership and gradually assume greater burdens. Here, Zambia is fortunate. Its new president, Michael Sata, is a former health minister. Zambia's first lady is a former ob-gyn. Zambia's current health minister worked at the World Health Organization for twenty years. The government's first budget increased health spending by 45 percent in a single year—a commitment permitted by sustained economic growth and the rising price of copper in Zambian mines.

But much of the progress against malaria here has been made possible by the United States, particularly through the President's Malaria Initiative (PMI)—which has provided millions of nets in Zambia,

including those distributed by private groups in Mongu. It is an unexpected intervention for a superpower. China, for example, has taken a
different approach in Zambia—providing foreign assistance in exchange
for resource concessions. And China out-invests America in Zambia by
more than ten-to-one. China's influence is everywhere—and resolutely
self-interested.

The American Embassy, in contrast, is mainly a health-care provider.
Of the $400 million the United States spends each year on foreign assis-
tance to Zambia, about $370 million goes to fighting AIDS and malaria.

Zambia has issued a recent judgment on the merits of China's trans-
actional, extractive foreign policy. President Sata ran and won on a platform opposed to outsize Chinese influence. Upon taking office, his first
diplomatic meeting was with the Chinese ambassador—whom he publicly excoriated for bad Chinese labor practices. Sata's first public reception honored the Peace Corps and USAID—America's aid agency.

In much of sub-Saharan Africa, the American image is now defined
by the Peace Corps, by PMI, and by PEPFAR, the American AIDS relief
plan. It is a form of influence that is hard to measure or weigh. But people
remember when you help to save their children.

# PART 7

# Presidents

# Trump Is an Authoritarian Wannabe. He Must Never Hold Power Again.

*The Washington Post*, December 21, 2020

LOOKING ON THE BRIGHT SIDE OF a humiliating national disaster, the manner of President Trump's departure from power has clarified why he must never hold power again.

In leaks to a variety of news organizations, senior Trump administration officials reported: (1) Rudolph W. Giuliani urging the federal government to illegally seize Dominion voting machines; (2) presidential consideration of deranged conspiracy-monger Sidney Powell as a special counsel investigating nonexistent election fraud; and (3) a White House meeting involving disgraced former national security adviser Michael Flynn at which Trump discussed the imposition of martial law.

These accounts indicate the emergence of two distinct factions within Trump's inner circle. On one side are the lunatics—among them Giuliani, Powell, and Flynn—who want Trump to violate laws and assume authoritarian powers. On the other side are sycophants who supported Trump's spurious legal challenges to the election result but apparently draw the line at treason. By most accounts, Trump's sympathies lie with the lunatics.

Some respond, as usual, by suggesting that these provocations are merely the sad, silly reactions of a cornered narcissist. And it is indeed ludicrous to believe that the military would ever consider torching the Constitution, particularly in service to a draft-dodging coward who views their honored dead as "suckers." Even on the rumor of a coup, Army Secretary Ryan D. McCarthy and Gen. James McConville, the army chief of staff, issued a joint statement saying there "is no role for the US military in determining the outcome of an American election."

But the code-red level of worry within Trump's staff does seem unprecedented. "People who are concerned and nervous aren't the weak-kneed bureaucrats that we loathe," said a senior administration official to Axios. "These are people who have endured arguably more insanity and mayhem than any administration officials in history." At the very least, these freely leaking White House staffers are determined to distance themselves from outright subversion. It is nice to find there are still some limits to White House chief of staff Mark Meadows's servility.

It is most important to consider these events not in the context of an unlikely 2020 coup, but in light of the inevitable 2024 election. The front-runner for the Republican presidential nomination is clearly not committed to democratic self-government. He is willing, even eager, to overturn the constitutional process if it serves his interests. No ethical second thoughts restrain him. Selfishness is not the violation of his standards; it is the fulfillment of his creed. For Trump, self-sacrifice is the true sin.

This time around, Trump's lawless ambitions have been limited by unamused courts, by courageous state and local officials, by a vigilant mainstream press, by a Democratic House, by his own buffoonish leadership, and by an ideologically moderate Democratic candidate who won a reasonably large electoral victory. Only the Republican Party utterly failed in checking Trump's incipient authoritarianism.

But these conditions are hardly permanent. Could Trump win reelection in 2024 against a more ideologically extreme Democratic candidate? Of course he could. Would any Republican official, at any level of government, stand up against a vengeful authoritarian with electoral mandate? It is not likely. Would Trump expand executive power at every turn? He would, particularly if both the House and Senate are controlled by Republicans. Would Trump openly intimidate journalists and

political opponents with willing, armed militias? I don't doubt it. Would
he simply ignore court rulings that limit him? I bet he would try. Would
he try to manufacture a crisis to justify remaining in power past his term?
No scruple would prevent it.

This is not some exaggerated dystopian vision. These hypotheticals
are extensions of Trump's existing views and tendencies. He would do
these things, if he could. And how do we know this? Because Trump is
the leader of Trumpism's lunatic fringe. He is in fundamental sympathy
with Giuliani, Powell, and Flynn. Even out of power, he will remain the
main threat to American democracy. If he wins again, the constitutional
order may never be the same.

In the Trump presidency, the worst days are always the most authentic days. And each day now seems more revealing than the last. Desperation has shown Trump's instincts and nature as never before. He is an
authoritarian wannabe. Those who love our system of government must
now share one overriding goal: to ensure that Mar-a-Lago is Trump's
Saint Helena, not his Elba.

# One Final Election Plea, on the Behalf of U.S. Ideals

*The Washington Post*, November 3, 2016

SIXTEEN YEARS AGO I AWAITED the arrival of Election Day, anxious but hopeful. I was a part of a presidential campaign that had challenged the stereotype of Republicanism with a series of policy proposals on education, addiction treatment, and other elements of social welfare. Suspend, for a moment, your views on the efficacy of No Child Left Behind and the faith-based initiative. Accept that we viewed the coming election—if we won—as the mandate for a certain model of governance.

I was deeply and personally invested in the outcome of the 2000 election. I believed that the reform of Republican ideology would serve the whole country, the common good. When I walked into the West Wing for the first time, and entered the Roosevelt Room just as the picture above the fireplace was being switched from Franklin to Teddy, I felt the continuity and burden of a noble experiment in self-government.

In his first inaugural address (a document I helped produce), President George W. Bush expressed the goal of his administration this way: "Sometimes our differences run so deep, it seems we share a continent but not a country. We do not accept this, and we will not allow it. Our unity, our union, is the serious work of leaders and citizens in every generation. And this is my solemn pledge: I will work to build a single nation of justice and opportunity."

We were not, of course, unique in this idealism. This was the commitment of Barack Obama's administration when it entered the White House. And Bill Clinton's administration. And nearly all that preceded them.

I own up to being even more emotionally entangled in the result of the 2016 election—not because of any change in policy or ideology, but because of Donald Trump's proposed shift in the very purpose of the presidency. His political theory, such as it is, is "us" vs. "them." The "them" may be Republican elites, or liberal elites, or migrants or Mexicans or Muslims. Trump would be elected on the promise of fighting, rounding up, jailing, or humbling any number of personal and political opponents. Take away this appeal, and there is nothing left but grasping, pathetic vanity.

The undercurrents of economic anxiety and cultural disorientation that Trump exploits are real, deserving both attention and sympathy. But Trump has organized these resentments with an unprecedented message: The United States is weak and broken, a hell of crime, terrorism, and expanding misery, beset from within and without, and now in need of a strong hand—his strong hand—to turn things around.

The single most frightening, anti-democratic phrase of modern presidential history came in Trump's convention speech: "I alone can fix it." A Trump victory would be a mandate for authoritarian politics. Trump's ambitions would be bounded by strong legislative and legal institutions and by his own risible ignorance of real leadership. But a Trump administration would be a concession to the idea that America needs a little more China, a little more Russia, a little more "so let it be written, so let it be done" in its executive branch.

I never imagined that Republican leaders—many of whom I know and have respected—would fall in line with such dangerous delusions, on the theory that anything is better than Hillary Clinton. Most options are better than Clinton. But not all. And not this. The GOP has largely accommodated itself to a candidate with no respect for, or knowledge of, the constitutional order. Every constitutional conservative should be revolted. Those who are complicit have adopted a particularly dangerous form of power-loving hypocrisy.

But now, with polls tightening, it may not only be Republicans who abandon central tenets of their democratic faith. It is almost beyond belief that Americans should bless and normalize Trump's appeal. Normalize vindictiveness and prejudice. Normalize bragging about sexual assault and the objectification of women. Normalize conspiracy theories and the abandonment of reason. Normalize contempt for the vulnerable, including disabled people and refugees fleeing oppression. Normalize a political tone that dehumanizes opponents and excuses violence. Normalize an appeal to white identity in a nation where racial discord and conflict are always close to the surface. Normalize every shouted epithet, every cruel ethnic and religious stereotype, every act of bullying in the cause of American "greatness."

In the end, a Trump victory would normalize the belief that the structures of self-government are unequal to the crisis of our time. And this would not merely replace the presidential portrait above the fireplace. It would deface it.

# Our Complex President

*The Washington Post*, January 23, 2014

THERE HAVE ALWAYS BEEN TWO NOT entirely consistent elements of Barack Obama's powerful political appeal: his aspirational ambition and his personal sense of complexity and limits.

The aspirational—the promise of transcending our national divisions, resetting our relations with Russia and the Muslim world, slowing the rise of the oceans, and healing the planet—is behind us. In a recent, remarkable interview with David Remnick of the *New Yorker*, Obama admits as much. Assuming the role of political commentator, the president talks of being overexposed "after six, seven years of me being on the national stage" and asks, "Is there somebody else out there who can give [people] that spark of inspiration or excitement?" Perhaps someone else is the change we have been waiting for.

But it is exactly this objectivity—this ability to emotionally distance himself from, well, himself—that impresses many journalists and commentators. Remnick calls it the "archetypal Obama habit of mind and politics, the calm, professorial immersion in complexity." Like many before him, Remnick is impressed with Obama's "philosophical ambivalences" and his ability to "nimbly" argue the other side of debates.

Obama seems impressed with these traits as well. In the course of the interview, he states: "I'm not a purist." And: "I'm pretty pragmatic." And: "I'm not a particularly ideological person." And: "I do think one of my strengths is temperament. I am comfortable with complexity." On marijuana legalization, Obama convincingly argues for every possible side of the issue. On parenting, he favors both open-mindedness and structure. On federalism, he sees virtues and drawbacks. On pro football, he is a big fan but would not allow his son to play. Every question is an opportunity for a seminar.

I have to admit—like many people in the business of producing and distributing symbolic knowledge—that I love seminars. Writers, commentators, journalists, and historians have often chosen their profession because they never wanted their late-night dorm room discussions to end. Those who write about politics have a natural affinity for Obama's mode of discourse. This is not so much an ideological bias—though that can play a part—as a kinship of intellectual approach and style. Just as Middle America found Richard Nixon to be "one of us," America's knowledge class knows that Obama is very much like them.

Remnick's portrait of Obama typically leaves out the less attractive side of the academic persona—the tendency to view opponents as rubes and knaves. Few presidents have more consistently or aggressively questioned the motives of their political rivals. None, to my knowledge, used an inaugural address the way Obama used his second—to accuse his opponents of mistaking "absolutism for principle" and treating "name-calling as reasoned debate," and wanting the twilight years of seniors "spent in poverty" and ensuring that parents of disabled children have "nowhere to turn," and reserving freedom "for the lucky." Those outside the seminar aren't treated quite as well.

But even judged on the terms of Remnick's praise, Obama is in deep, second-term trouble. The president who embraces complexity is now besieged by complexity on every front. The U.S. health-care system has not responded as planned to the joystick manipulations of the Affordable Care Act. On the evidence of the article, Obama and his closest advisers are in denial about the structural failures of the program—the stingy coverage, narrow provider networks, high deductibles, and adverse-selection spirals already underway in several states.

And complexity is not a sufficient word to describe the chaos in the Middle East. Here Remnick raises questions about the utility of ambivalence in Obama's approach to Syria. In the article, the president recounts the careful, systematic study that preceded inaction, as more than one hundred thousand people died and U.S.-affiliated groups were crushed. "We have looked at this from every angle," he insists.

In fact, at the outset of the struggle, Obama declared that Syrian president Bashar al-Assad must go without having a plan to make him go. Then the Obama administration announced it would supply arms to the rebels, which never materialized on a serious scale. This is a case where disengagement has undermined national credibility and betrayed friends. Obama is likely to spend a portion of his post-presidency defending his studied inaction in the face of mass atrocities.

The largest question raised by the Remnick article goes unasked: Is the intellectual style that journalists find so amenable actually an effective governing strategy? The answer, it turns out, is complex.

# George W. Bush, a Principled President

*The Washington Post*, April 25, 2013

THE DEDICATION OF the George W. Bush Presidential Library and Museum here has been an occasion for both friends and critics of the former president to press their case. According to the polls, the number of critics has fallen over time. They make up for it with enthusiasm.

I fall into the friend category, having worked for President Bush for several years beginning early in the 2000 campaign. There are a number of reasons to join a presidential campaign, not least of which is the main-stage, high-wire excitement. But I can recall the day I decided that my guy was the guy. Bush, campaigning at a town hall meeting in Gaffney, South Carolina, got a question demanding to know how he would stop the flow of illegal immigrants. He took the opportunity to remind his rural, conservative audience that "family values don't stop at the Rio Grande" and that as long as "moms and dads" in Mexico couldn't feed their children at home, they would seek opportunity in America.

Not "illegals." Moms and dads and children. It was classic Bush: direct, decent, human.

Bush was born into a prominent political family, yet for much of his early life he didn't seem groomed for anything but trouble. On the morning after his fortieth birthday, he was a hungover, undisciplined dabbler. Under the influence of faith, hope, and Laura Bush, he was president by fifty-four.

He was not a political natural along the lines of Bill Clinton or Tony Blair, except for a potent likability in small groups. But while I was on the campaign, I saw Bush approach a series of ever-higher hurdles—weathering his first *Meet the Press* interview with Tim Russert, delivering a convention speech, debating the sitting vice president—and cross each with room to spare. As the stakes grew higher, he grew larger, which is the definition of a successful presidential candidate.

His two terms defy summary, just as a snapshot can't capture Niagara Falls during a lightning storm. I experienced the Bush presidency as a series of emergencies punctuated by holiday parties. I'll leave it to others to critique Bush's choices on Iraq and other issues, a task considerably easier than making them under pressure. I saw Bush's steadiness after 9/11, which steadied me and many others. His decision to pursue the troop surge in Iraq, after many of his generals had misplaced their judgment and nerve. His response to the financial crisis—extending FDIC protections, backing the Federal Reserve's increase in liquidity, passing the Troubled Assets Relief Program bill—which put guardrails along the economic abyss.

This record is Truman-like. Cheerful, right-track attitudes were rare during the Truman years, with China lost, the Soviet Union gaining the bomb, and Korea a bloody stalemate. But Truman was right on the Cold War, the Truman Doctrine, the Marshall Plan.

Historical judgments mature slowly, but they tend to reward being right on the large things. Bush was right in shaping the structures and doctrines of a serious war against terrorism—a vindication demonstrated by President Obama's imitation. Right in predicting a wave of change in the Middle East and North Africa and in urging autocrats to embrace reform or risk revolution. Right in pushing reluctant Republicans toward greater outreach, particularly to Hispanics and other rising minority groups. Right—if politically premature—in pressing Congress to act on entitlement and immigration reform.

Put this in the category of backhanded compliments: Many politicians who are eager to criticize the Bush legacy have managed to embrace the Bush agenda.

For years, I saw Bush through the small but revealing aperture of the

White House policy process. Someone would propose a sensitive meeting with a dissident, or a plan to save millions of lives from HIV/AIDS, or an initiative to help mentor the children of prisoners, or an effort to fight malaria in Africa. If such an idea ran the gantlet of lower-level objections and reached the president's desk, I knew how Bush would respond. He would be direct, decent, human.

Bush's frankly moral approach, on other issues, is precisely what enraged his critics. But more than most, he is a leader of undivided sentiments. The same man who regarded the authors of 9/11 as evil saw the fight against global AIDS as an ethical imperative. It was all one whole. And with the distance of years, it looks a lot like principle.

# *Acknowledgments*

I AM DEEPLY THANKFUL FOR MY TWO BOYS, who have been my rock and support during the past year. They made life bearable to keep moving forward. I love them from the bottom of my heart.

I cannot express my gratitude for the friendship of Pete Wehner and John Bridgeland during the most difficult days. Their example of kindness and generosity toward me and the boys will never be forgotten.

I also need to thank Priscilla Painton for the forethought of putting together this book to honor Michael's life. Priscilla has been kind and patient in helping me to construct the essays.

—DAWN GERSON

# Index